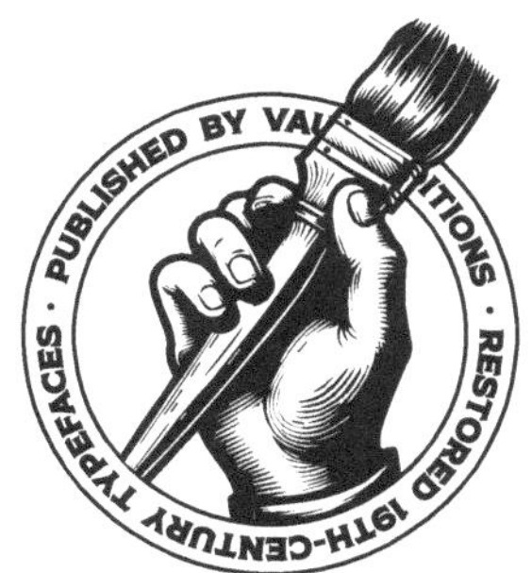

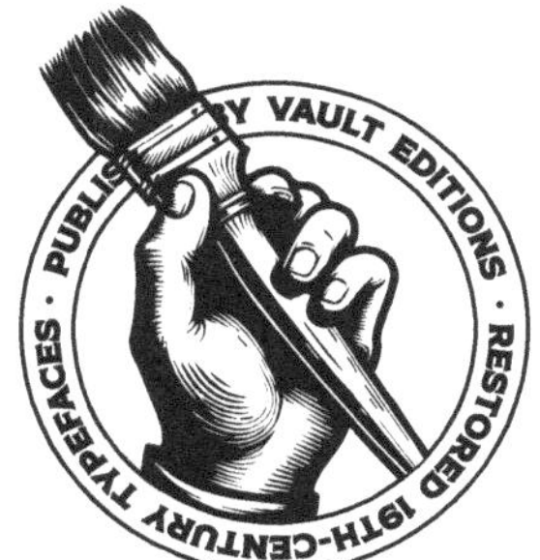

WITH EVERY STROKE. PERFECTION'S CHASE.
IN CRAFTSMEN'S GRIP. BEAUTY'S GRACE.

THE SIGN PAINTER AND

DOWNLOAD INCLUDED

LETTERING ARTIST'S

VINTAGE

DESIGNS

THIS → FEATURING 115 ALPHABETS ← THIS

REFERENCE BOOK
·OF ALPHABETS & ORNAMENTS·

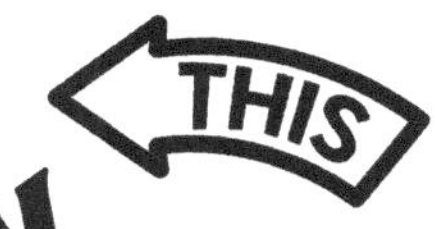

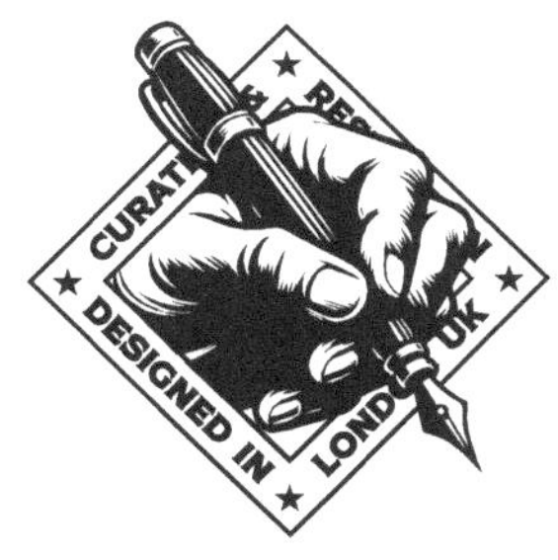

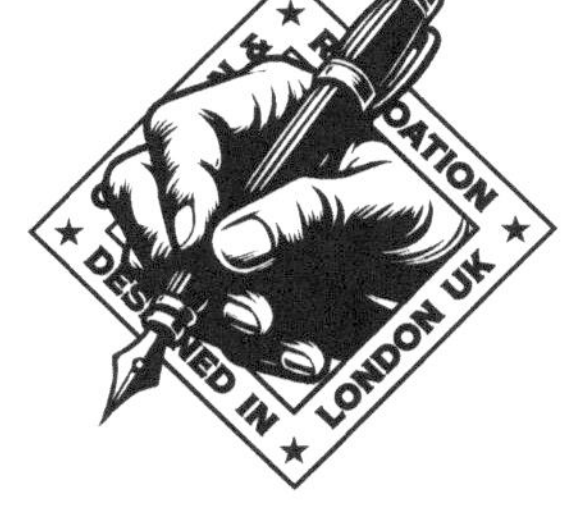

A CURATED COLLECTION OF 115 TYPEFACES
PLUS ORNAMENTS. AND SIGN DESIGN
ESSENTIALS FOR LETTERING ARTISTS. SIGN
PAINTERS AND TYPOGRAPHERS

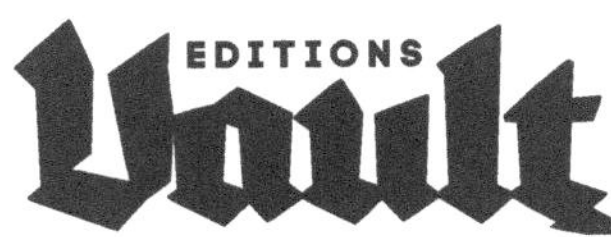

BIBLIOGRAPHICAL NOTE

This publication is a new work by Vault Editions Ltd.

AUTHOR

This publication was curated and authored by Kale James.

INTRODUCTION

PREFACE

By Kale James

In the world of typography and signwriting, the legacy of the 19th century stands unparalleled. It was an era marked by the flourishing of artistic expression and the evolution of letterforms. In this age, every brush and pen stroke carried the weight of aesthetic brilliance and functional necessity. Vault Editions' latest collection, a meticulously restored compilation of 115 alphabets from this golden epoch, is more than a mere assemblage of historical artefacts; it is a gateway to the past, a source of inspiration, and a testament to the timeless art and study of lettering and signwriting.

The 19th century, often hailed as the 'Golden Age of Signwriting,' witnessed an explosion in commercial signwriting fueled by the Industrial Revolution and urbanisation. Cities blossomed, and with them, the need for signs, be it for shop fronts, public houses, or the burgeoning world of advertising. This era saw signwriters emerge as respected artisans, their craft a blend of art and utility. They were the unheralded architects of the visual language of commerce and wayfinding for navigation.

This collection presents a rich tapestry of styles prevalent in the 19th century, from elegant Victorian scripts to bold, ornate block letters. These lettering sheets were not just tools of trade but were, in essence, the textbooks of the time for apprentices and masters alike. They served as a reference, a source of inspiration, and a guide to the diverse and evolving lettering styles.

Restoring these alphabets, Vault Editions embarked on a journey of reverence and discovery. Each sheet in this collection has been painstakingly brought back to its former glory, preserving

the integrity of the original while ensuring that it serves as a practical resource for contemporary artists. This restoration process involved meticulous digital enhancement and careful preservation of each character's unique attributes, ensuring that the charm and details of these 19th-century typefaces were not lost to time.

This collection is a bridge to the past for the modern lettering artist, signwriter, and typographer. It offers a glimpse into the historical context of their craft, providing a source of inspiration that is both aesthetically pleasing and historically significant. It is an invitation to explore the roots of typography and signwriting, to appreciate the evolution of letterforms, and to carry forward the legacy of this beautiful typographic art form.

In addition to the 115 alphabets, this collection includes an array of 19th-century ornaments and catchwords ranging from intricate floral-inspired designs to directional indexes, banners and catchwords to add interest and emphasis to typographic designs. Together, these elements showcase the decorative and creative spirit of 19th-century designers who sought to balance aesthetic appeal with communicative clarity.

As you turn each page, let these sheets guide you through a journey across time. May they inspire your work, inform your practice, and remind you of the rich history and enduring beauty of the art of lettering.

PUBLISHER	ISBN
Vault Editions Ltd vaulteditions.com	978-1-922966-26-1

TABLE OF CONTENTS

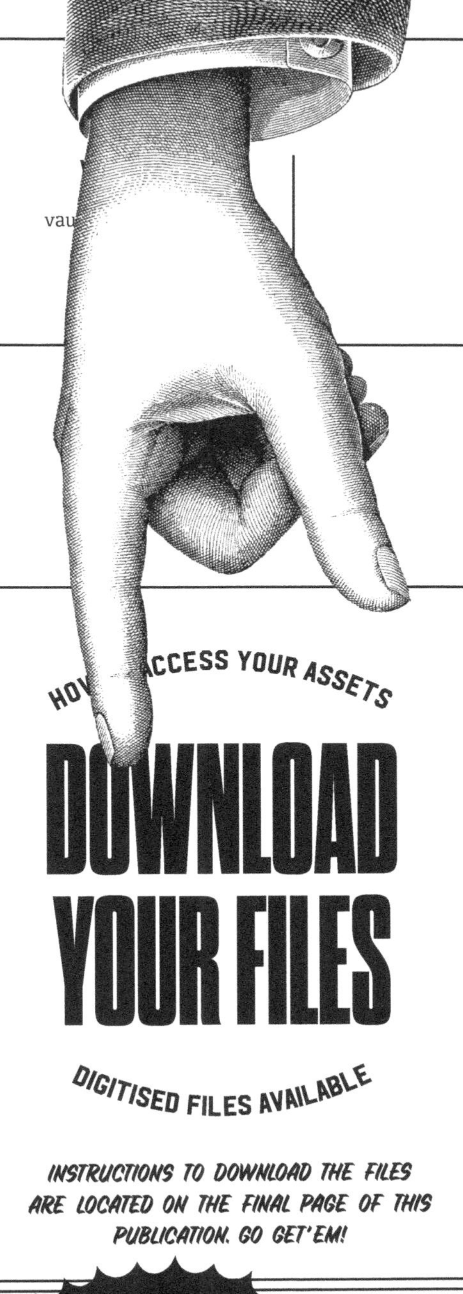

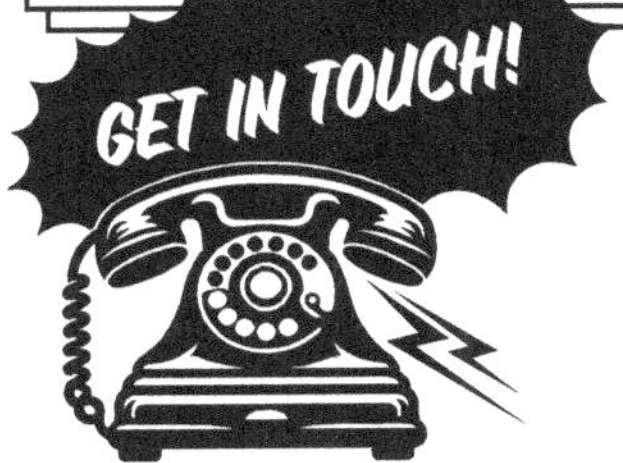

ACKNOWLEDGMENTS

As we stand in awe of the restored works within these pages, we must turn our gratitude to the giants upon whose shoulders we perch. This book is a tribute to the master typographers of the 19th century, whose skill and vision have left an indelible mark on the craft of lettering. It is their legacy that Vault Editions has had the honor of curating, and we are deeply humbled to be able to present their meticulous artistry to a new generation.

CONTACT

Do you need assistance accessing your files? Or do you have a questions about our products and services? If so, our team will be more than happy to help you. Please contact Vault Editions via: info@vaulteditions.com

300 DPI IND. STANDARD

DESIGNED IN LONDON

01

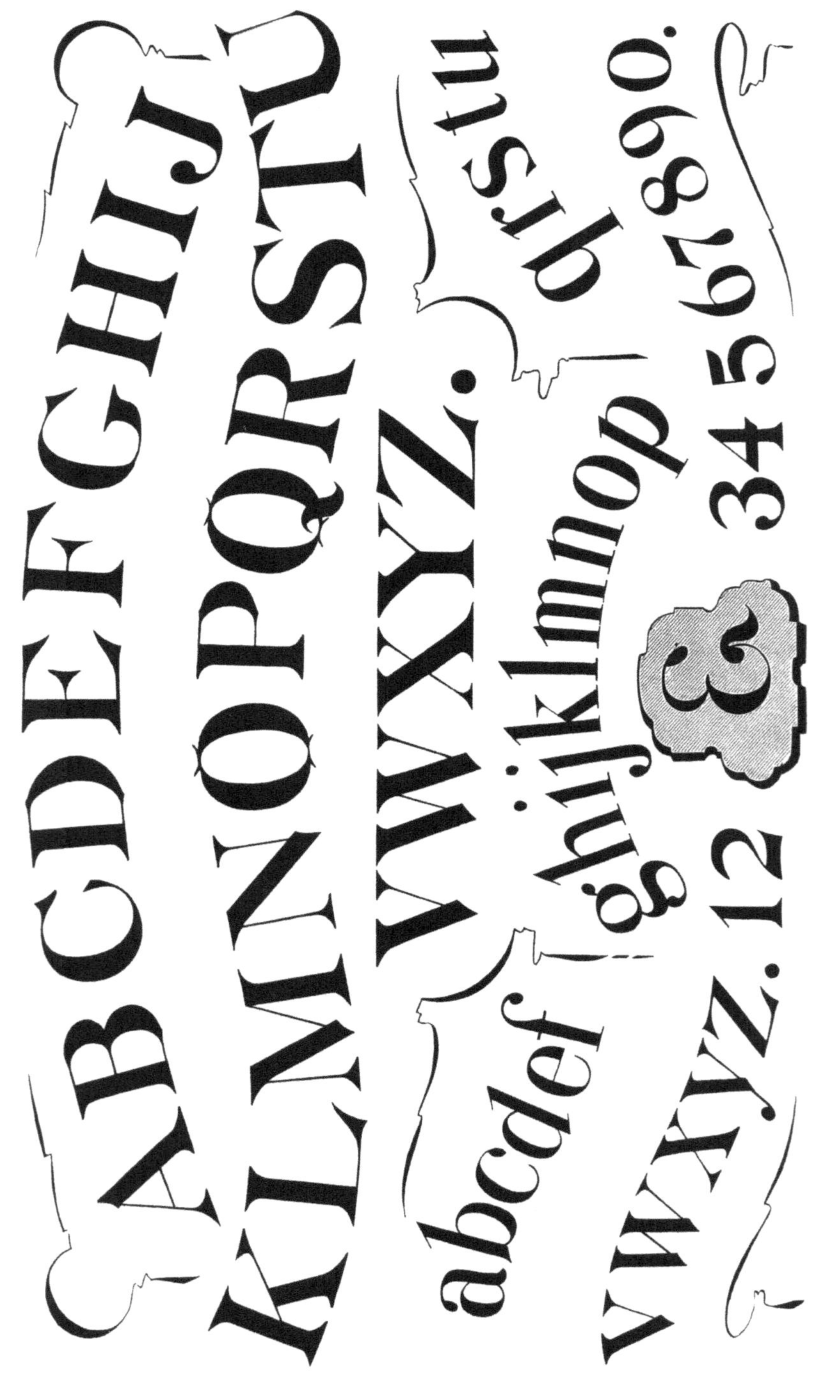

Vault Editions Ltd

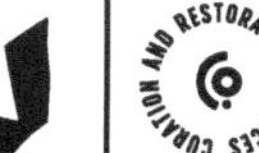

CURATION AND RESTORATION SERVICE

PRACTICE MAKES PERFECT

INDUSTRY STD

VAULTEDITIONS.COM

02

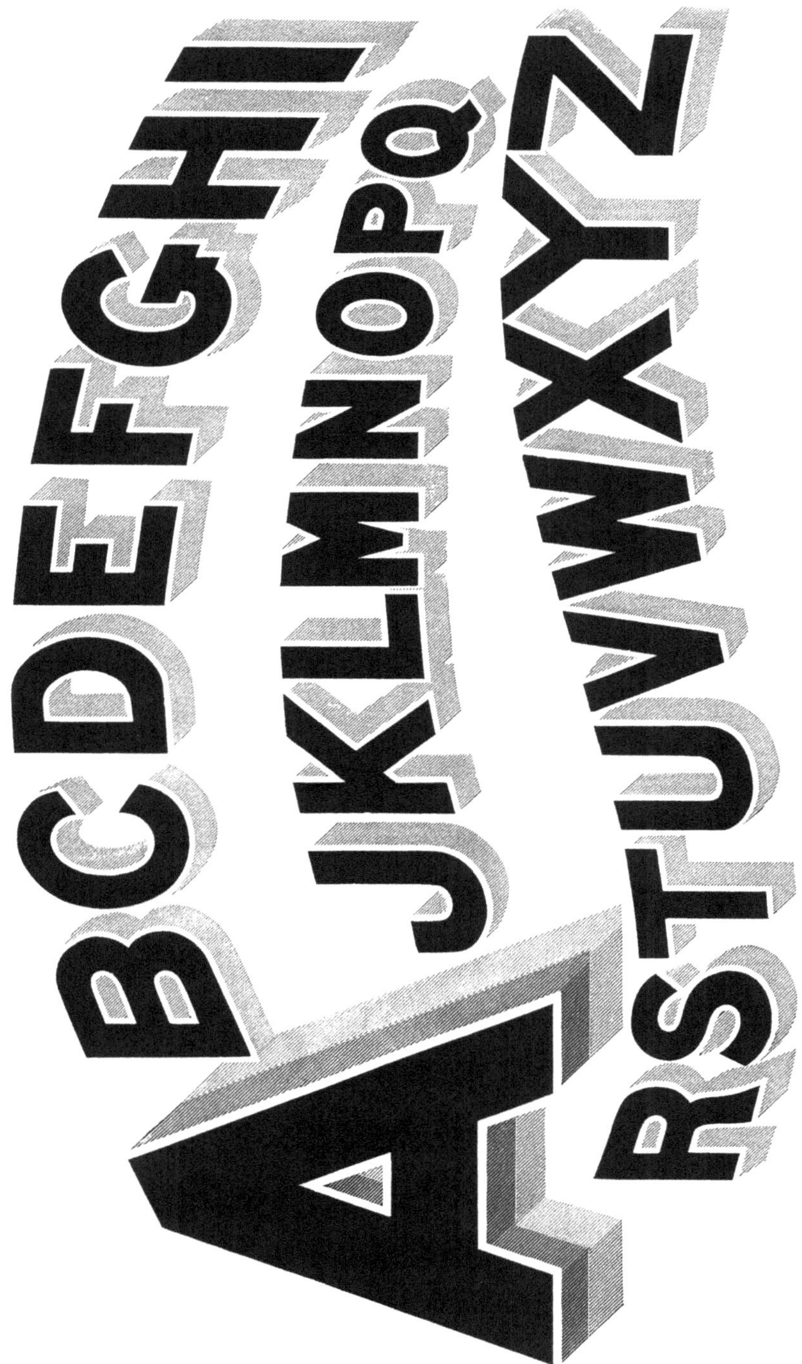

Vault Editions L^td

CURATION AND RESTORATION SERVICES

PRACTICE
MAKES
PERFECT
T·R·D M·R·K

INDUSTRY STD

VAULTEDITIONS.COM

03

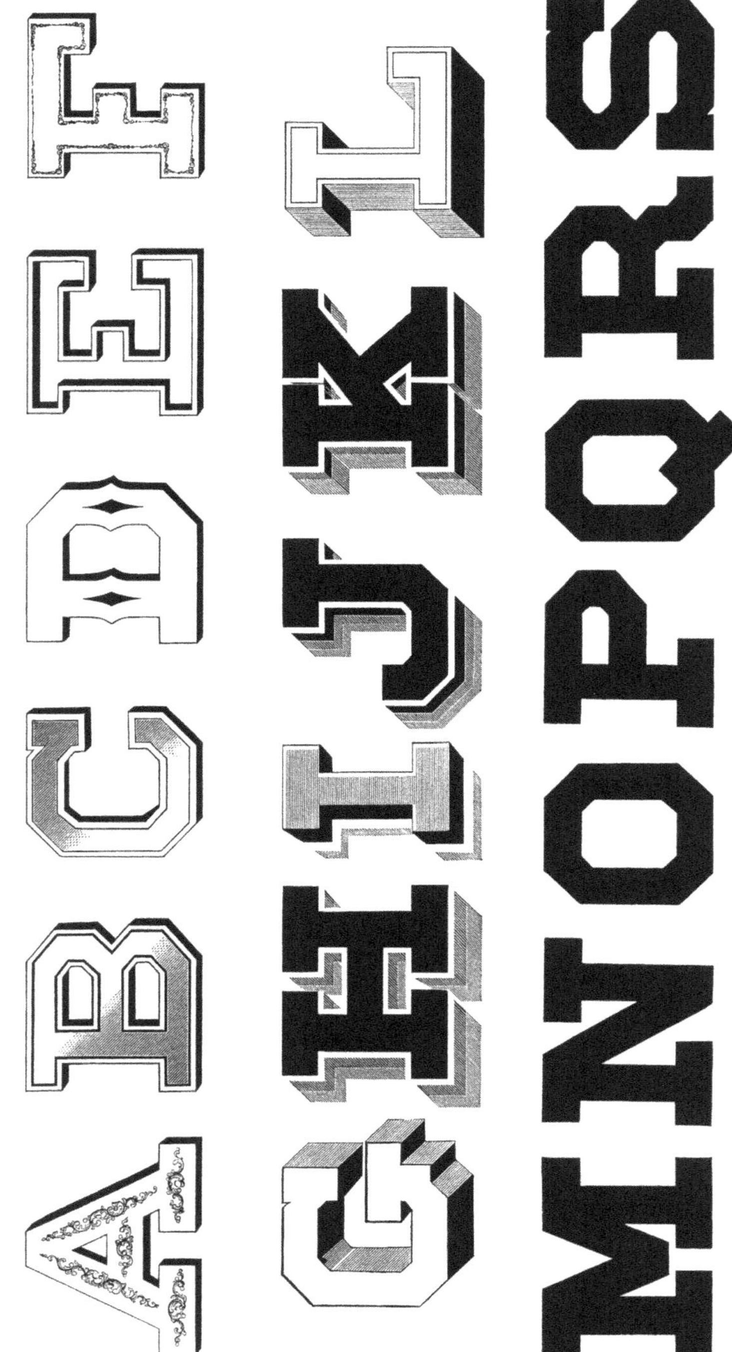

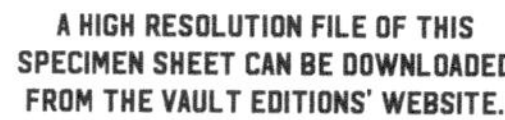

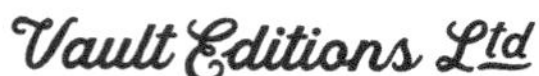

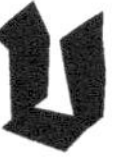

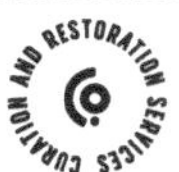

INDUSTRY STD

VAULTEDITIONS.COM

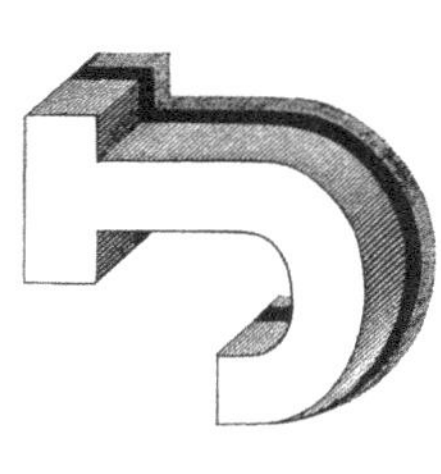

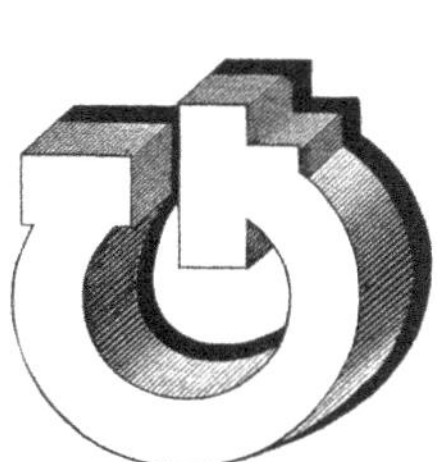

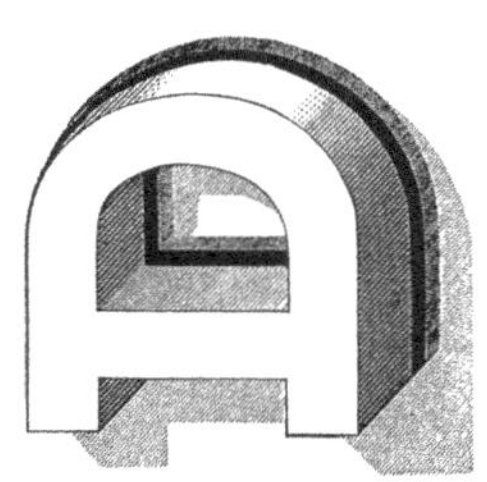

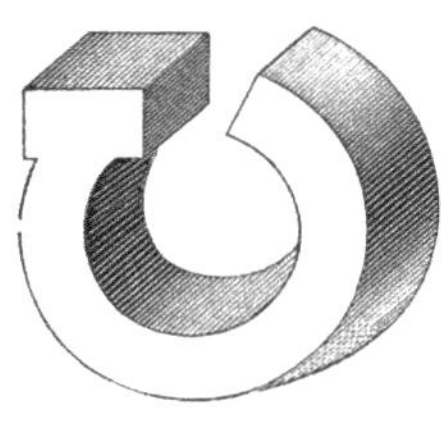

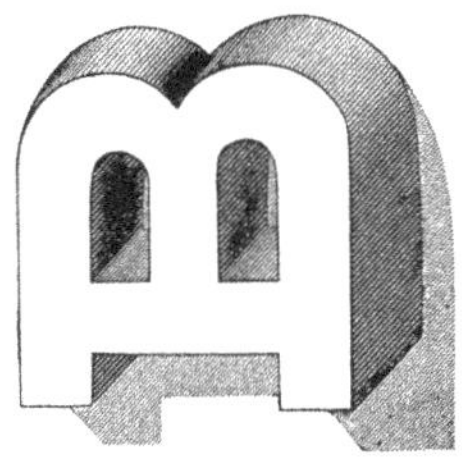

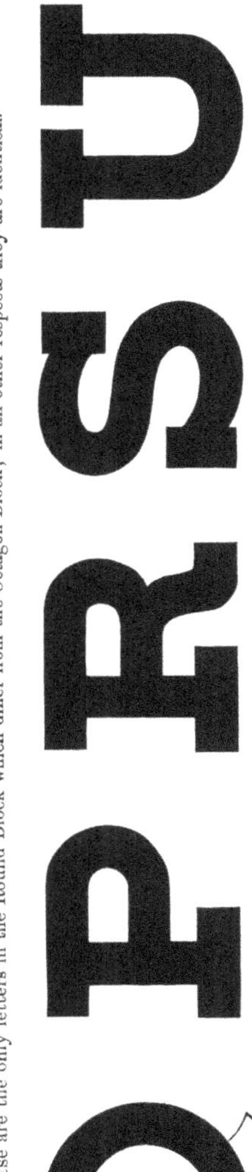

These are the only letters in the Round Block which differ from the Octagon Block; in all other respects they are identical.

05

ABCDEFGHI JKLMNOPQ RSTUVWXYZ

Vault Editions Ltd

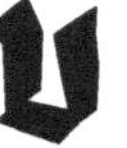

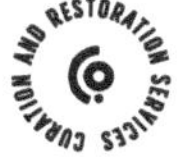

CURATION AND RESTORATION SERVICES

PRACTICE MAKES PERFECT ᵀᴿᴰ ᴹᴿᴷ

INDUSTRY STD

VAULTEDITIONS.COM

06

ABCDEF GHIJKL MNOPQR STUVW XYZ

Vault Editions Ltd

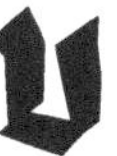
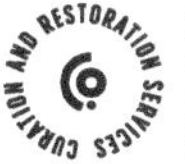
CURATION AND RESTORATION SERVICES

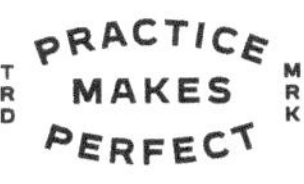

INDUSTRY STD

VAULTEDITIONS.COM

07

𝕬𝕭𝕮𝕯𝕰𝕱𝕲𝕳𝕴𝕵𝕶𝕷𝕸𝕹𝕺𝕻𝕼𝕽𝕾𝕿𝖀𝖁𝖂𝖃𝖄𝖅

𝖆𝖇𝖈𝖉𝖊𝖋𝖌𝖍𝖎𝖏𝖐𝖑𝖒𝖓𝖔𝖕𝖖𝖗𝖘𝖙𝖚𝖛𝖜𝖝𝖞𝖟

Vault Editions Ltd

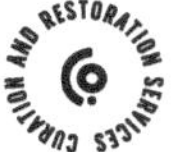

PRACTICE MAKES PERFECT
T R D   M R K

INDUSTRY STD

VAULTEDITIONS.COM

08

ABCDEFGHIJK
LMNOPQRSTU
VWXY
Z .
abcdefghijklmnopqrst
uvwxyz

Vault Editions Ltd

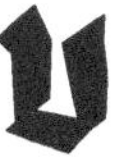

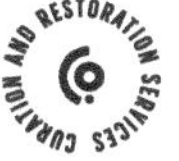

PRACTICE
MAKES
PERFECT
TRD   MRK

INDUSTRY STD

VAULTEDITIONS.COM

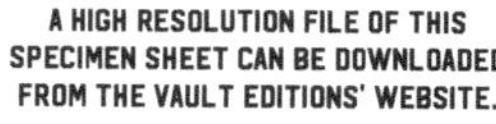

Vault Editions Ltd

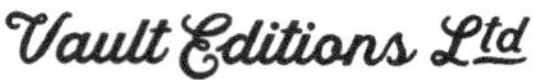

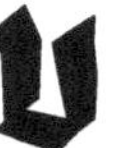

CURATION AND RESTORATION SERVICES

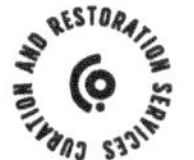

PRACTICE MAKES PERFECT
T R D   M R K

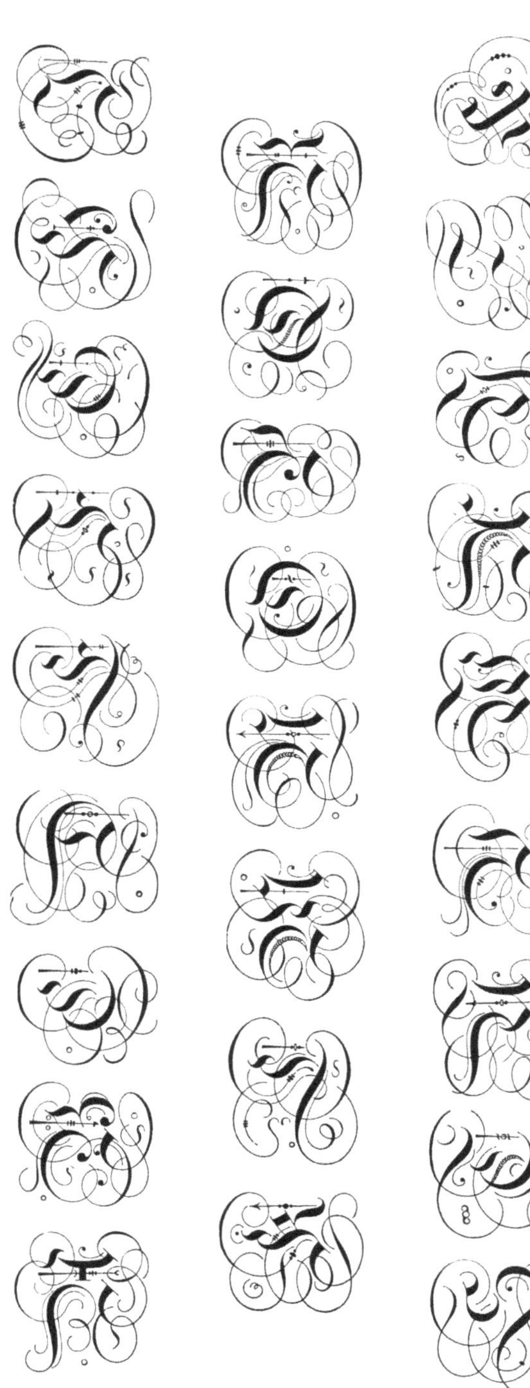

Vault Editions Ltd

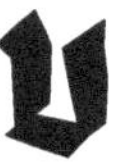

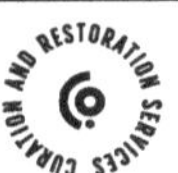

11

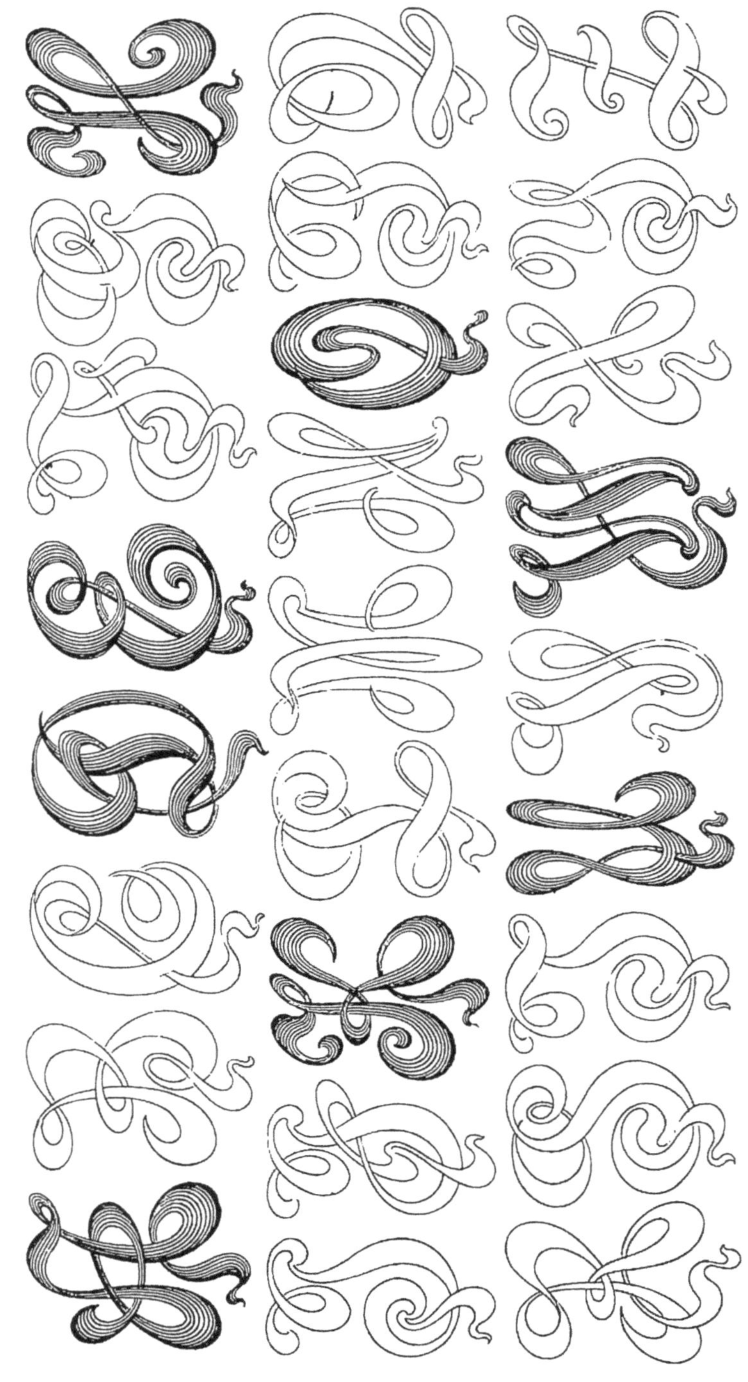

Vault Editions Ltd

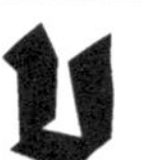
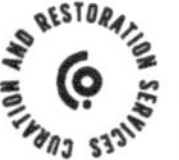

CURATION AND RESTORATION SERVICES

PRACTICE
MAKES
PERFECT

INDUSTRY STD

VAULTEDITIONS.COM

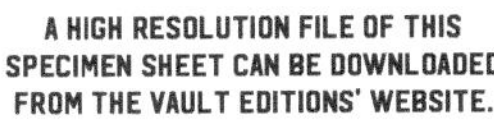

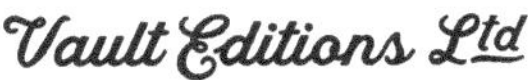

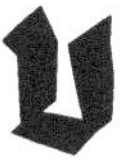

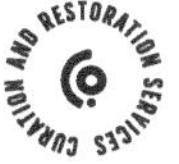

INDUSTRY STD

VAULTEDITIONS.COM

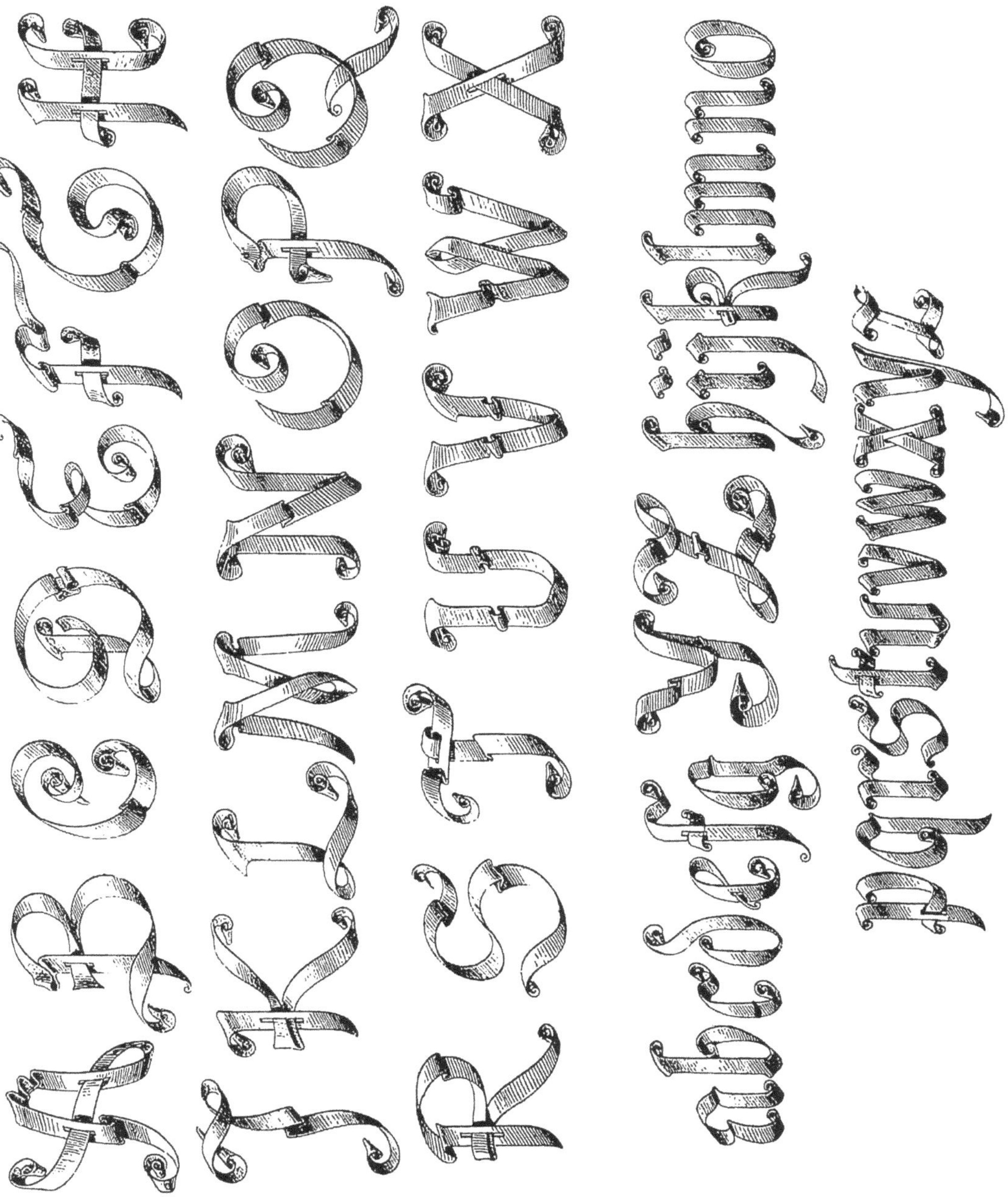

13

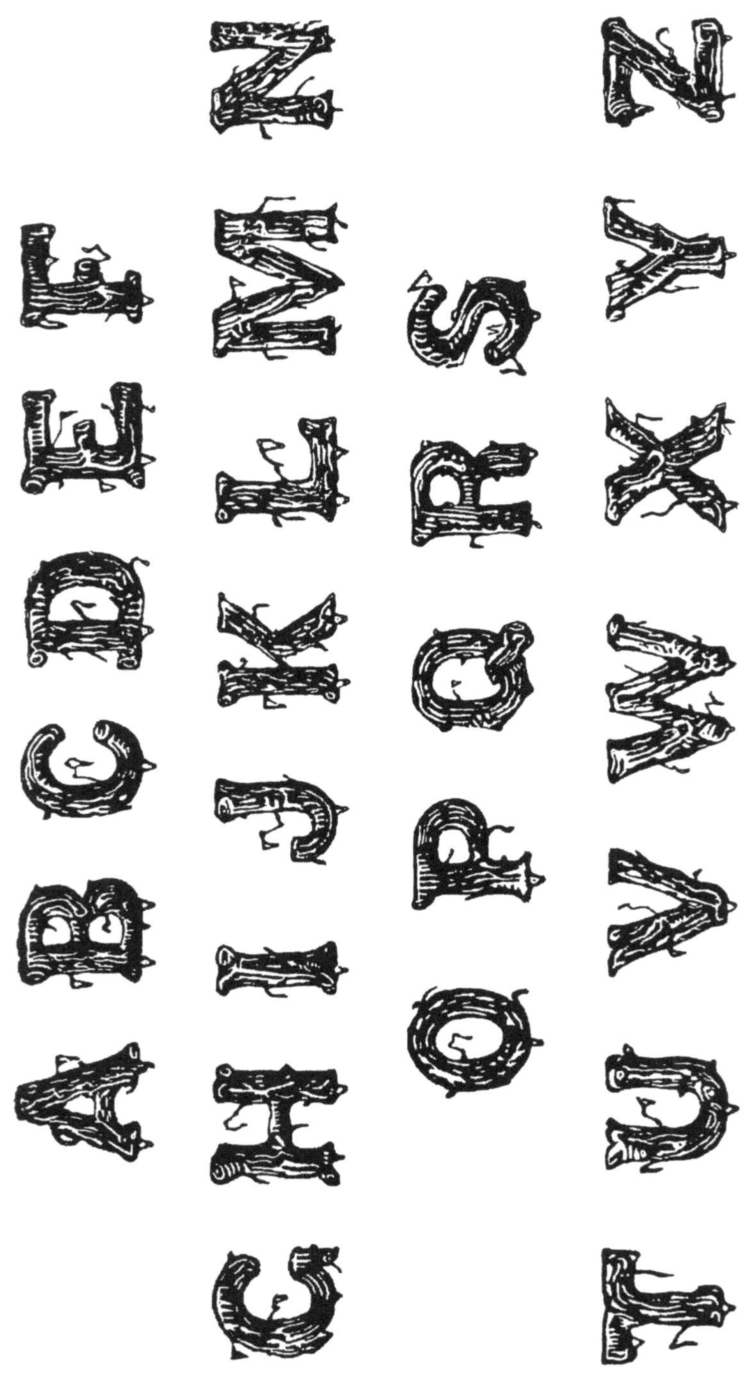

Vault Editions Ltd

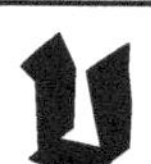

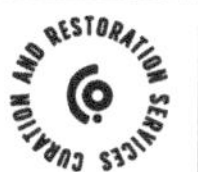

PRACTICE
MAKES
PERFECT
T R D   M R K

INDUSTRY STD
VAULTEDITIONS.COM

14

ABCDEFG
HIJKLM
NOPQRSTU
VWXYZ

Vault Editions Ltd

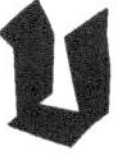
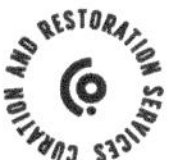

CURATION AND RESTORATION SERVICES

PRACTICE
MAKES
PERFECT

INDUSTRY STD

VAULTEDITIONS.COM

15

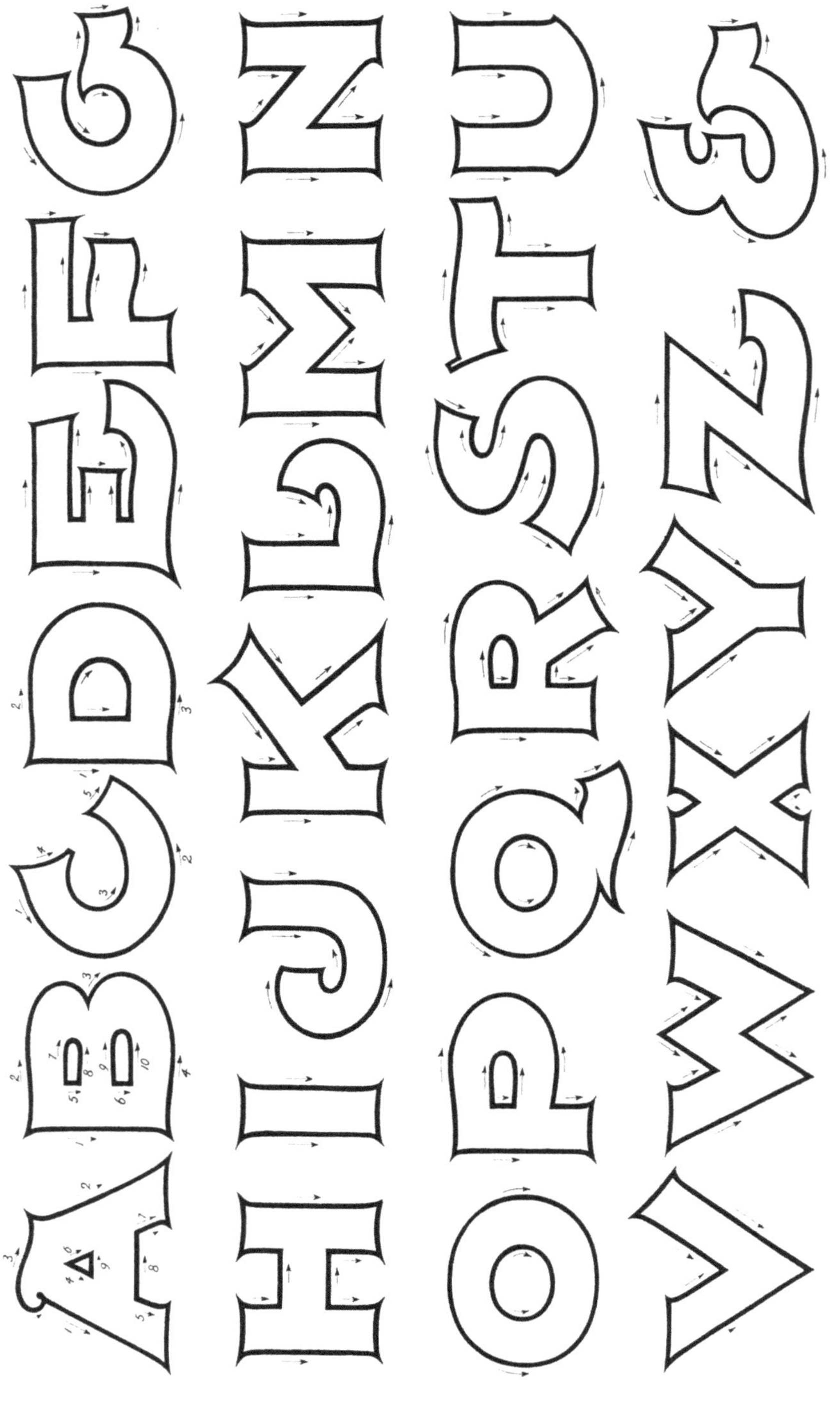

ABCDEFG
HIJKLMN
OPQRSTU
VWXYZ&

Vault Editions Ltd

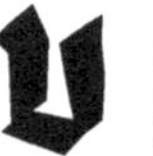

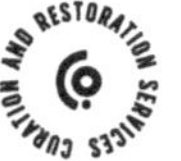

INDUSTRY STD

VAULTEDITIONS.COM

ABCDEFGHIJ
KLMNOPQRS
TUVWXYZ&

Vault Editions Ltd

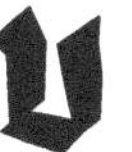
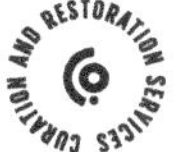

INDUSTRY STD

VAULTEDITIONS.COM

17

ABCDEFGHIJKL
MNOPQRSTUVW
XYZ & 1234567890
abcdefghijklmnopqrstuvwxyz

Vault Editions Ltd

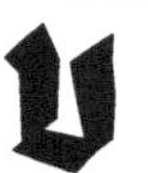

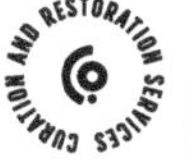

INDUSTRY STD

VAULTEDITIONS.COM

ABCDEFGHIJ
KLMNOPQRS
TUVWXYZ&
abcdefghij klmnopqr
stuvwxyz

Vault Editions Ltd

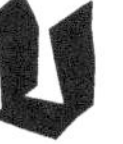

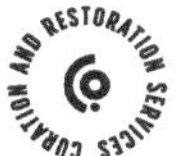

19

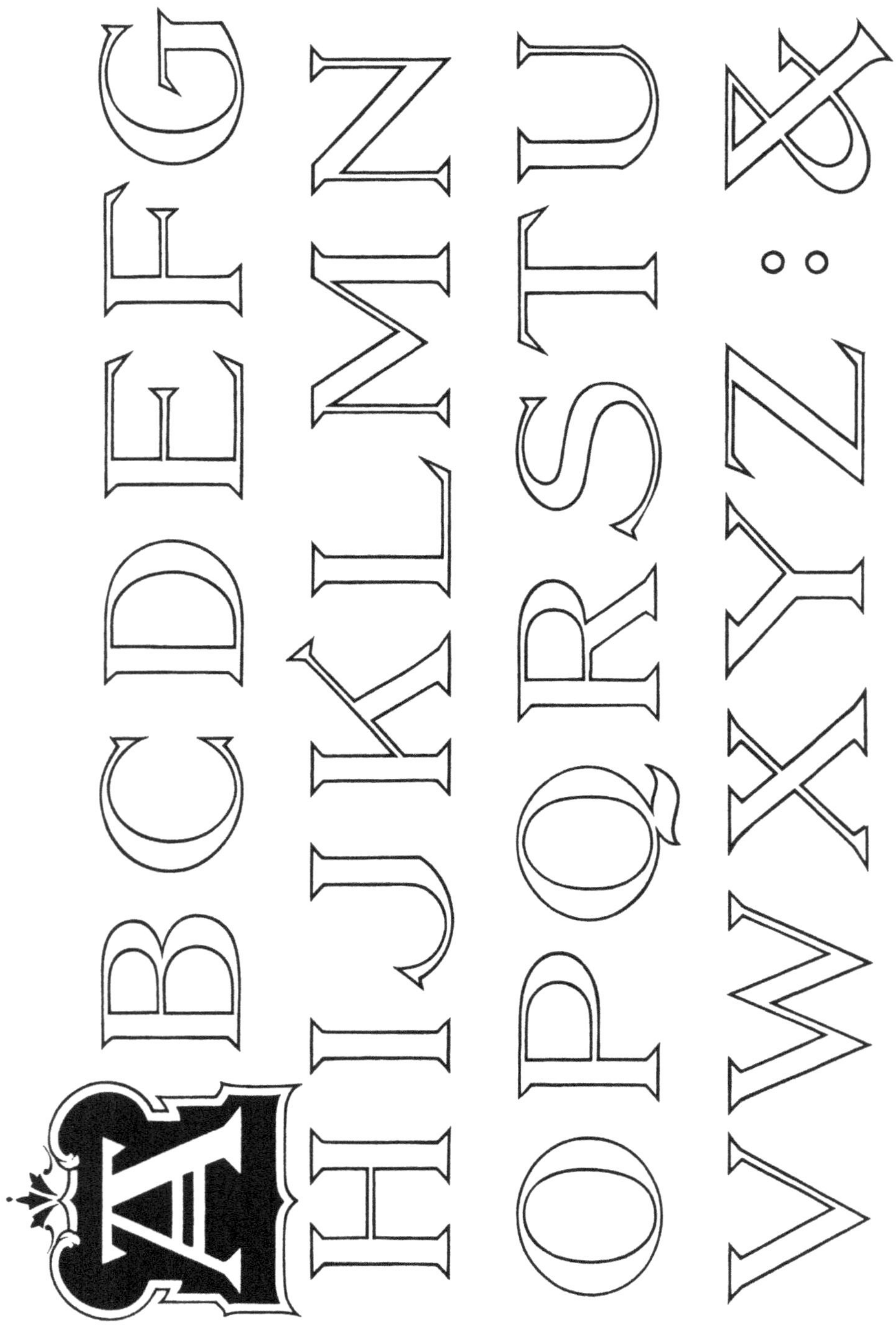

ABCD EFG
HIJKLMN
OPQ RST U
VW XYZ :. &

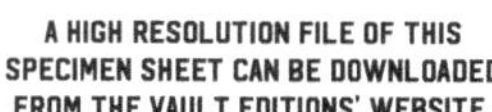

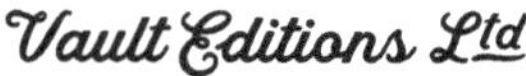

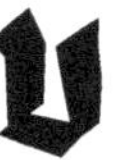

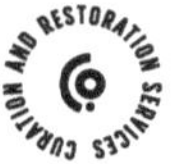

INDUSTRY STD

VAULTEDITIONS.COM

abcdefghijklm
nopqrstuvwxyz
1234567890

A HIGH RESOLUTION FILE OF THIS SPECIMEN SHEET CAN BE DOWNLOADED FROM THE VAULT EDITIONS' WEBSITE.

Vault Editions Ltd

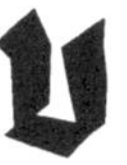

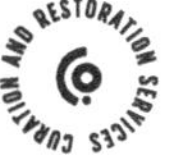

COATING AND RESTORATION SERVICES

PRACTICE MAKES PERFECT
TRD · MRK

INDUSTRY STD

VAULTEDITIONS.COM

UPPER CASE ←→ **WEIGHT: LIGHT** ←→ **PUBLISHED: 1903**

21

ABCDEFGHI
JKLMNOPQR
STUVWXYZ&
123456789

A HIGH RESOLUTION FILE OF THIS SPECIMEN SHEET CAN BE DOWNLOADED FROM THE VAULT EDITIONS' WEBSITE.

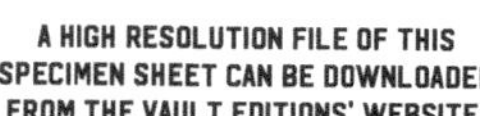

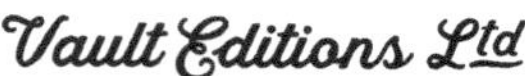

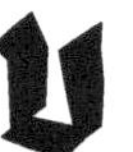

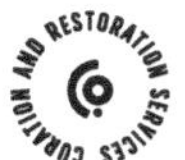

PRACTICE
MAKES
PERFECT
T R D
M R K

INDUSTRY STD

VAULTEDITIONS.COM

ABCDEFG
HIJKLMN
OPQRSTU
VWXYZ&

Vault Editions Ltd

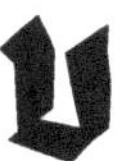

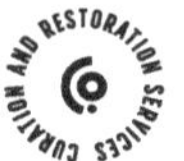

PRACTICE MAKES PERFECT

INDUSTRY STD

VAULTEDITIONS.COM

23

A B C D E
F G H I J K
L M N O

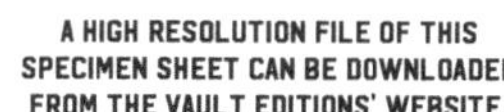

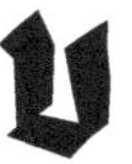

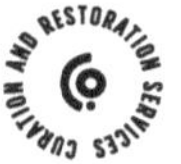

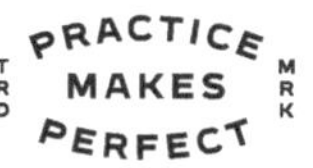

INDUSTRY STD

VAULTEDITIONS.COM

24

PQRST UVWX ZY

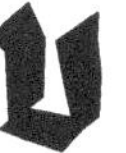
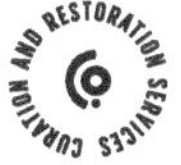

Vault Editions Ltd

PRACTICE MAKES PERFECT

INDUSTRY STD

VAULTEDITIONS.COM

25

ABCDEFG HIJKLMN OPQRSTU

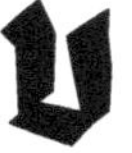

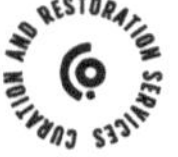

VWXYZ

abcdefghijklmno

pqrstuvwxyz

UPPER CASE ← → **WEIGHT: REGULAR** ← → **PUBLISHED: 1903**

27

A B C D E F G
H I J K L M N
O P Q R S T U
V W X X Y Z

Vault Editions Ltd

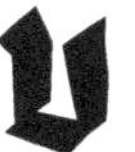

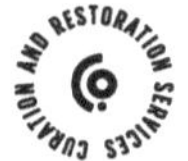

PRACTICE
MAKES
PERFECT
T R D   M R K

INDUSTRY STD

VAULTEDITIONS.COM

abcdefghijk
lmnopqrsst
uvwxyz

Vault Editions Ltd

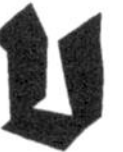

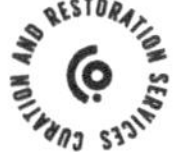

CURATION AND RESTORATION SERVICES

PRACTICE MAKES PERFECT
TRD MRK

INDUSTRY STD

VAULTEDITIONS.COM

29

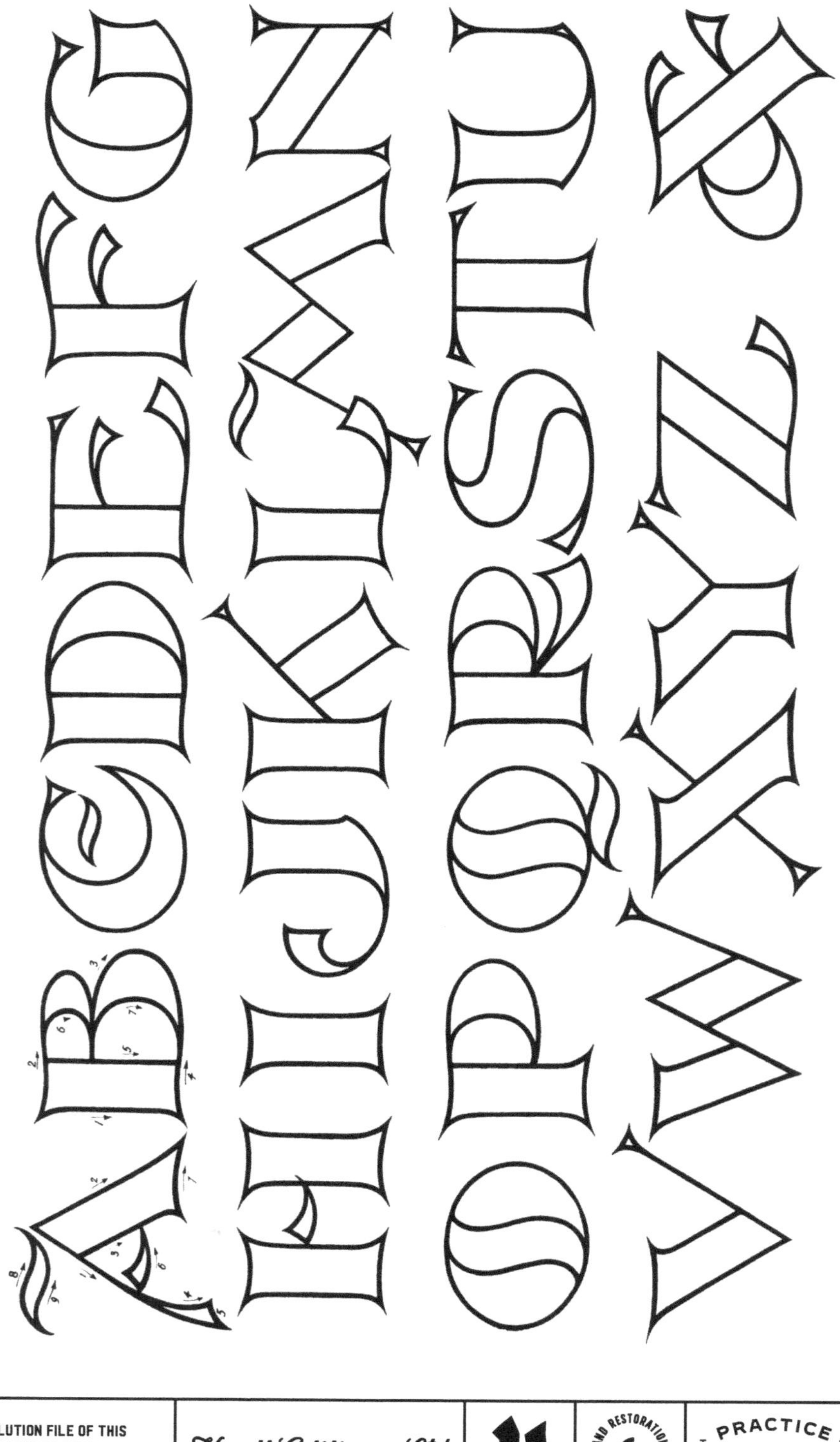

ABCDEFG
HIJKLMN
OPQRSTU
VWXYZ&

Vault Editions Ltd

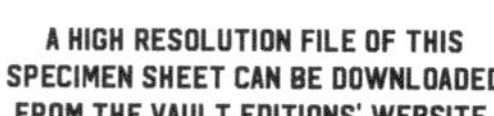
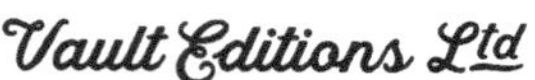
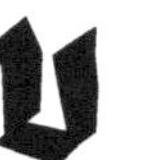
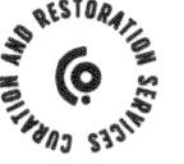

CURATION AND RESTORATION SERVICES

PRACTICE
MAKES
PERFECT

INDUSTRY STD

VAULTEDITIONS.COM

abcdefghijklm
nopqrstuvwxyz
1234567890

Vault Editions Ltd

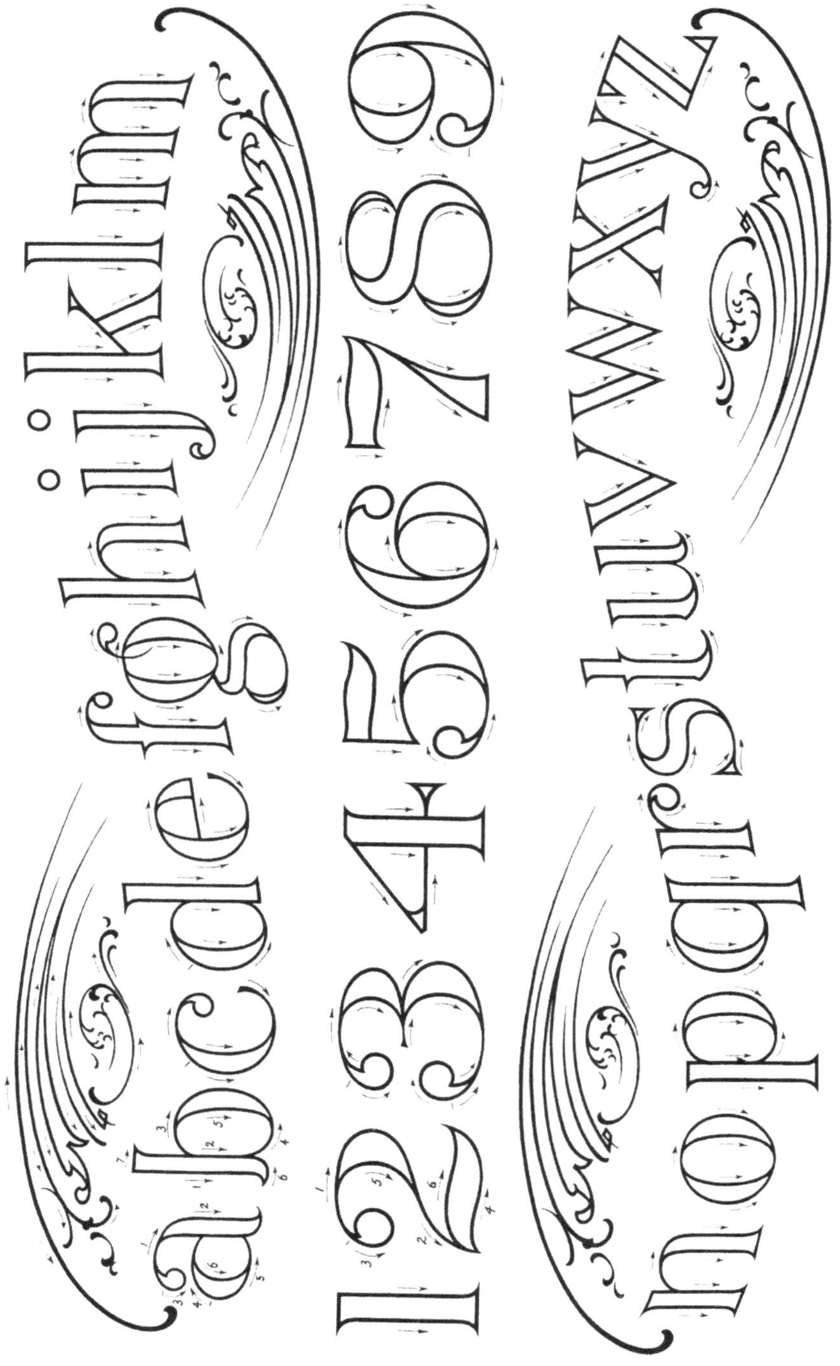

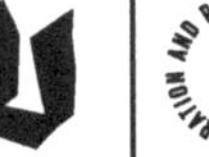

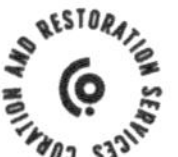

PRACTICE MAKES PERFECT
T R D — M R K

INDUSTRY STD

VAULTEDITIONS.COM

31

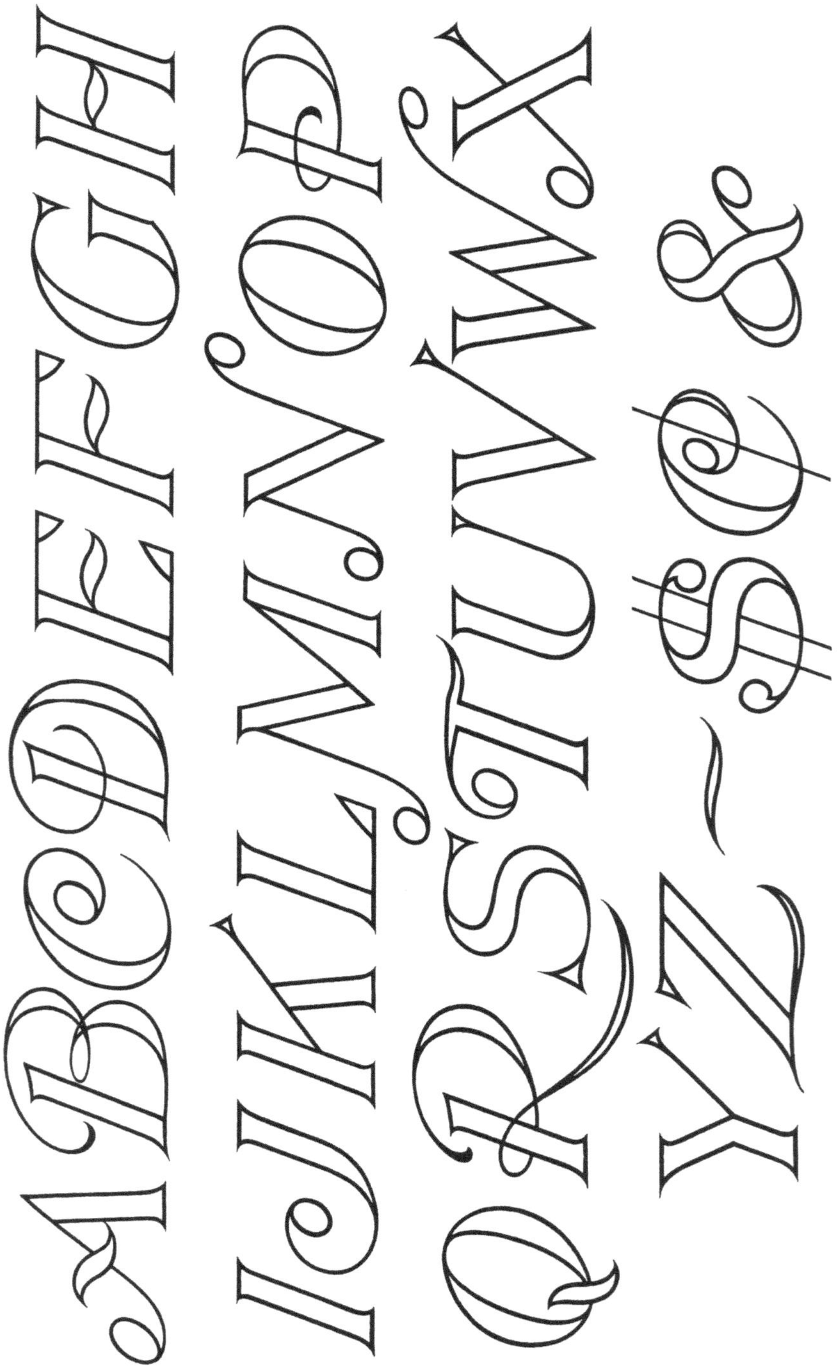

A B C D E F G H
I J K L M N O P
Q R S T U V W X
Y Z & -

Vault Editions Ltd

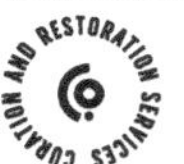

PRACTICE MAKES PERFECT

INDUSTRY STD

VAULTEDITIONS.COM

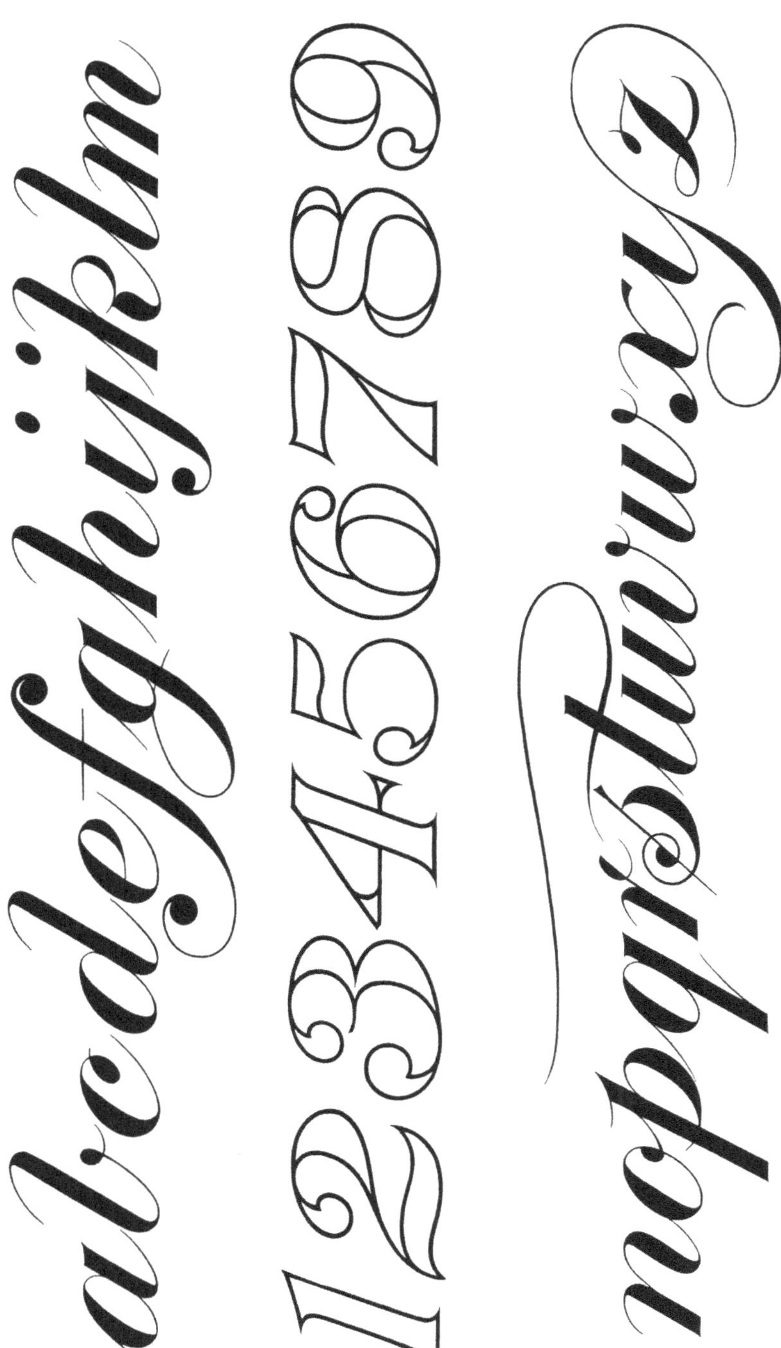

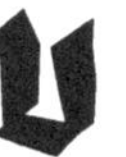

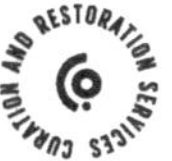

33

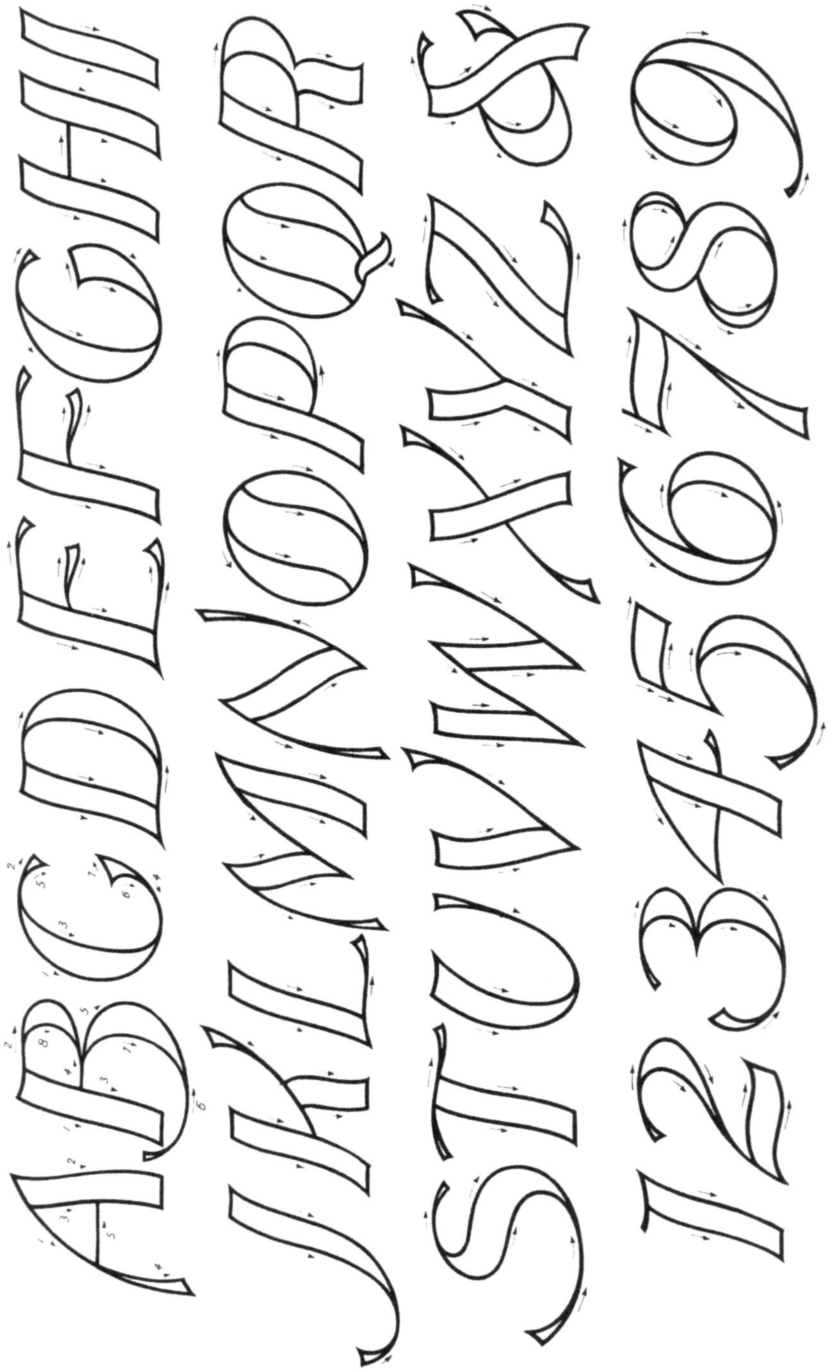

Vault Editions Ltd

CURATION AND RESTORATION SERVICES

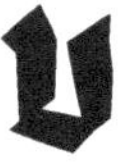
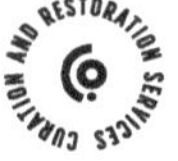

INDUSTRY STD

VAULTEDITIONS.COM

35

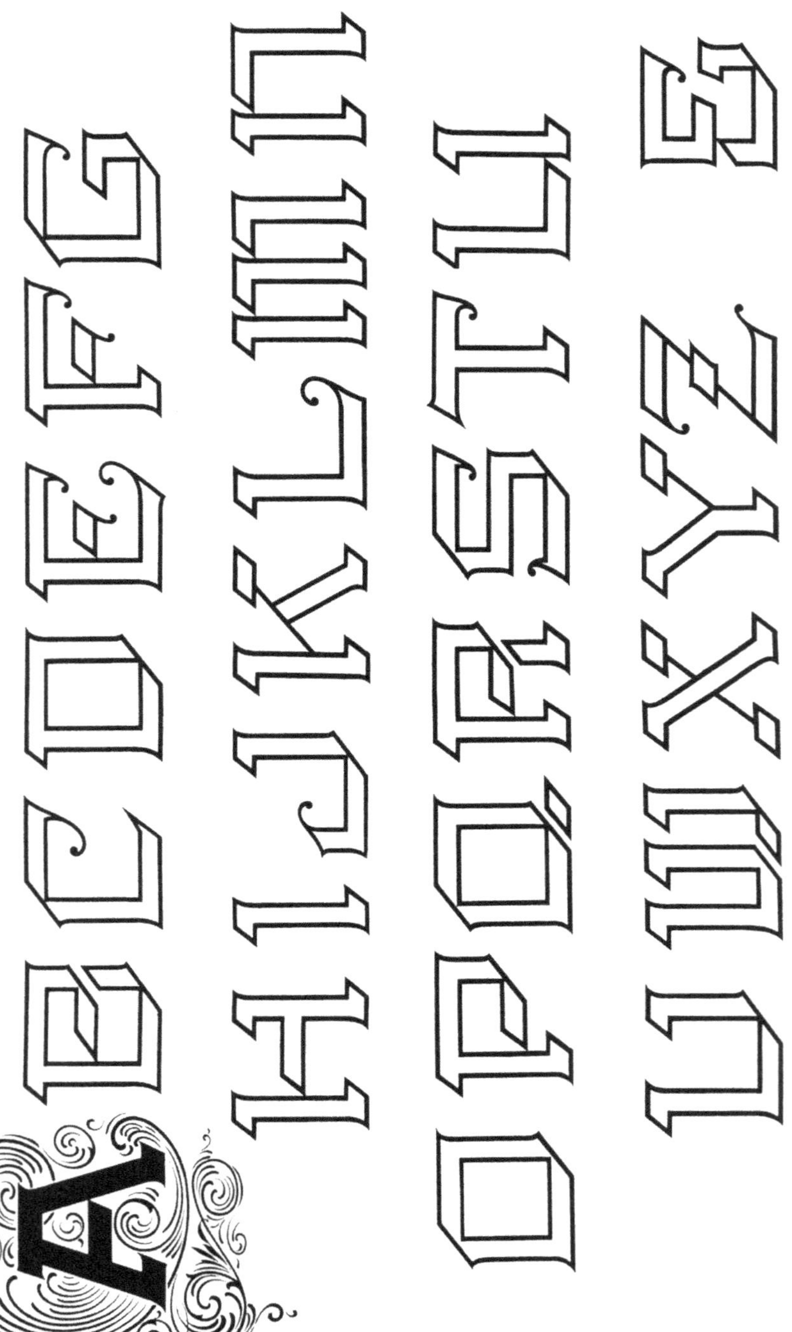

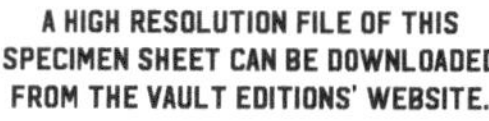

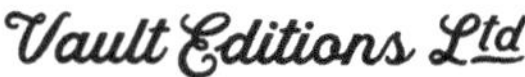

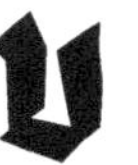

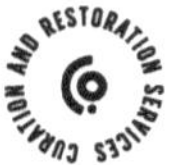

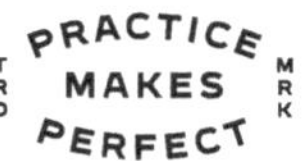

INDUSTRY STD
VAULTEDITIONS.COM

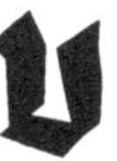
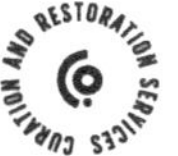

Vault Editions Ltd

CURATION AND RESTORATION SERVICES CO.

TRD PRACTICE MAKES PERFECT MRK

INDUSTRY STD

VAULTEDITIONS.COM

37

ABCDEFGHIJKL
MNOPQRSTUV
WXYZ & 67890
12345
abcdefghijklmnopqrstuvwxyz

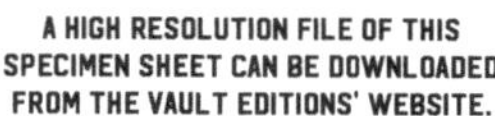

Vault Editions Ltd

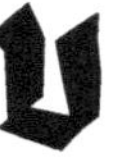

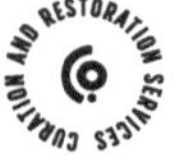

PRACTICE
MAKES
PERFECT
T·R·D · M·R·K

INDUSTRY STD

VAULTEDITIONS.COM

ABCDEFGHIJKL
MNOPQRSTUVW
12345~XYZ~67890
abcdefghijklmnopqrst
uvwxyz

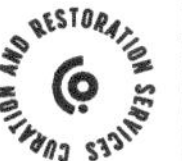

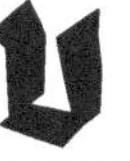

39

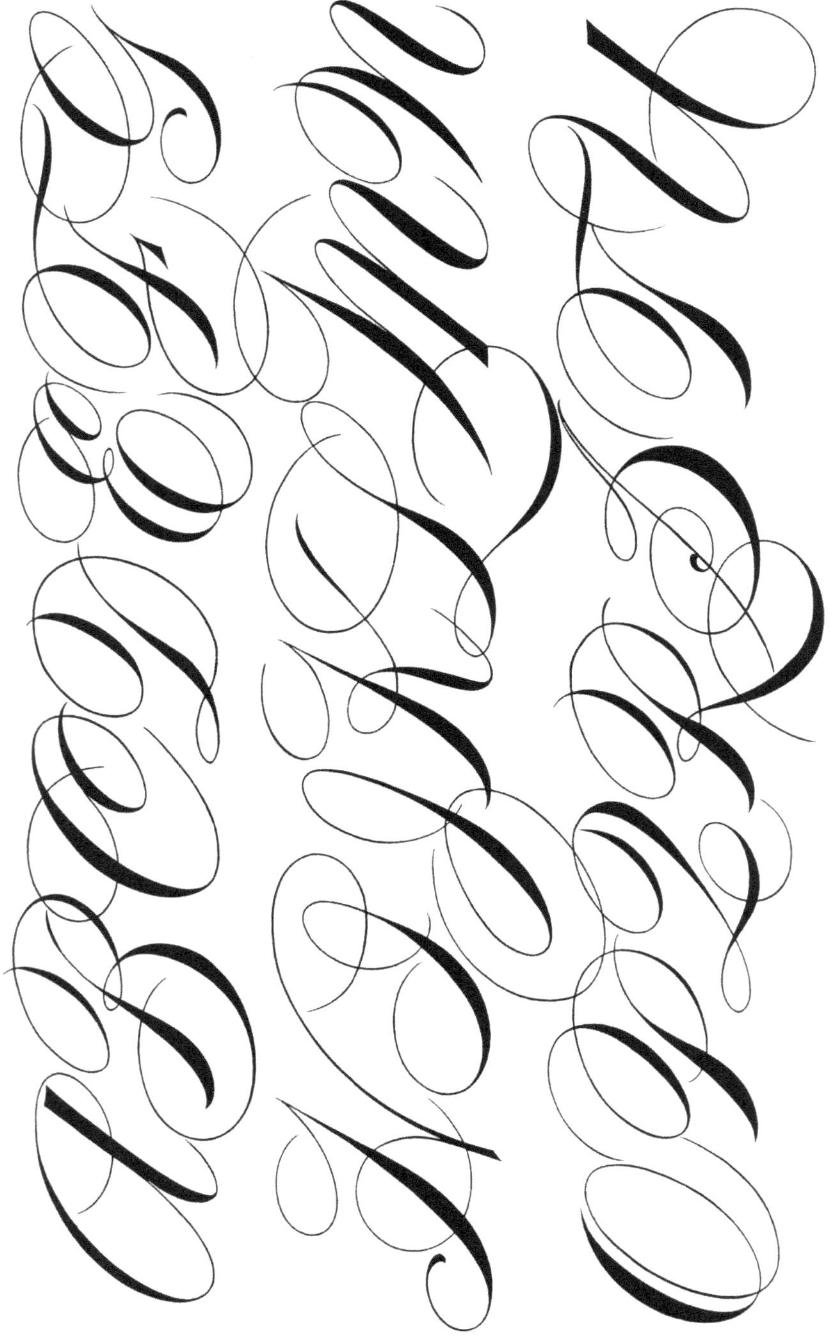

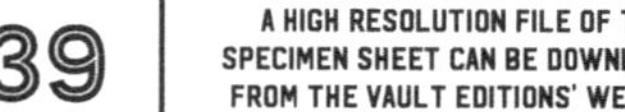

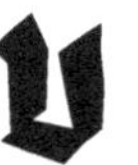

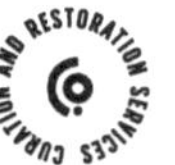

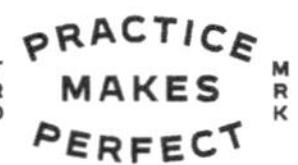

INDUSTRY STD

VAULTEDITIONS.COM

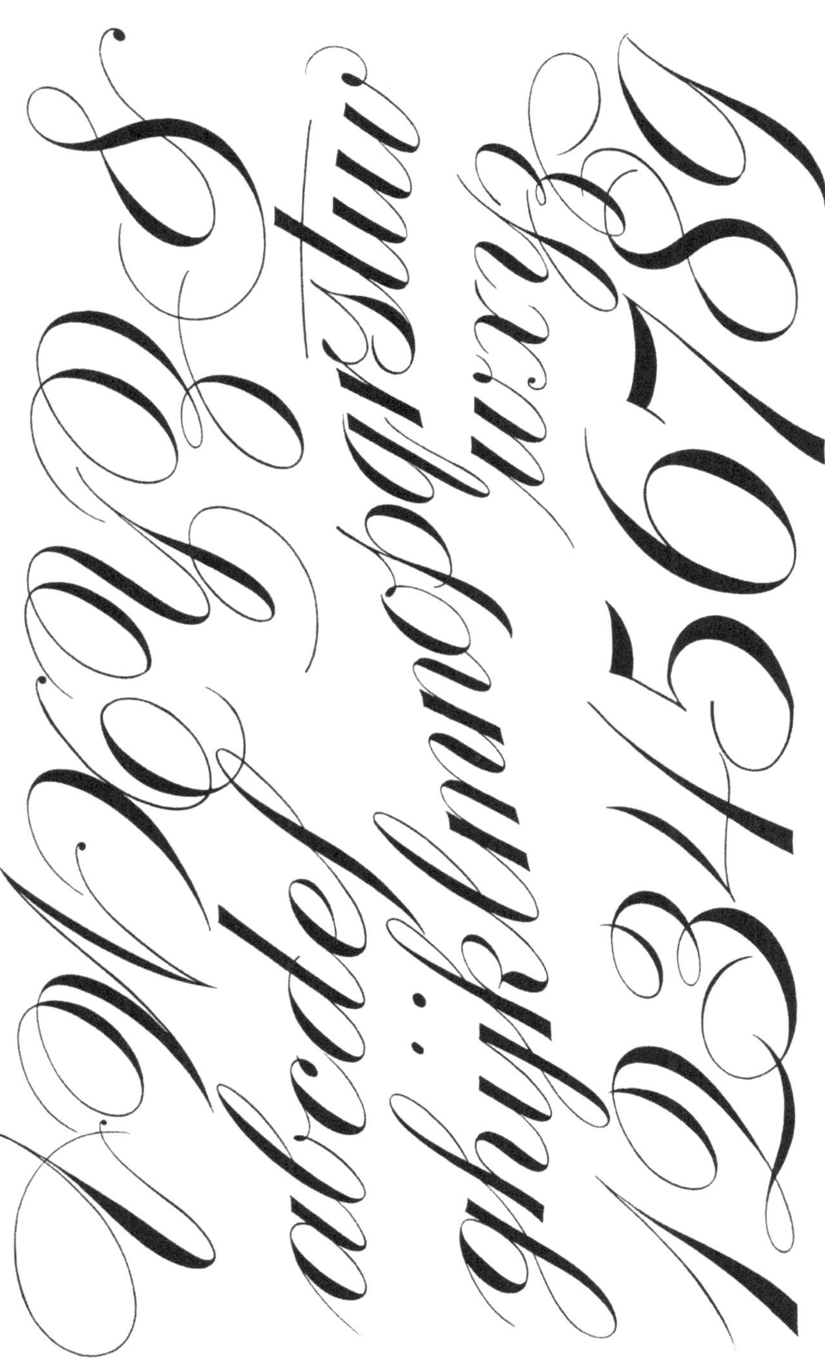

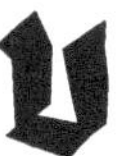
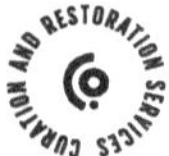

41

ABCDEFGHIJ
KLMNOPQRS
TUVWXYZ
1234567890
abcdefghijklmnopqrsfuvwxyzl
ijxmnsjalpounxfl

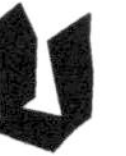

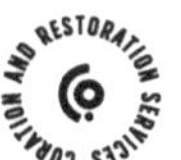

42

ABCDEFGHIJK
LMNOPQRSTUV
WXYZ

abcdefghijklmnopqrs
tuvwxyz

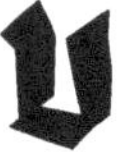
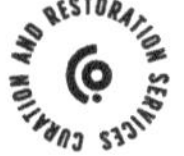

43

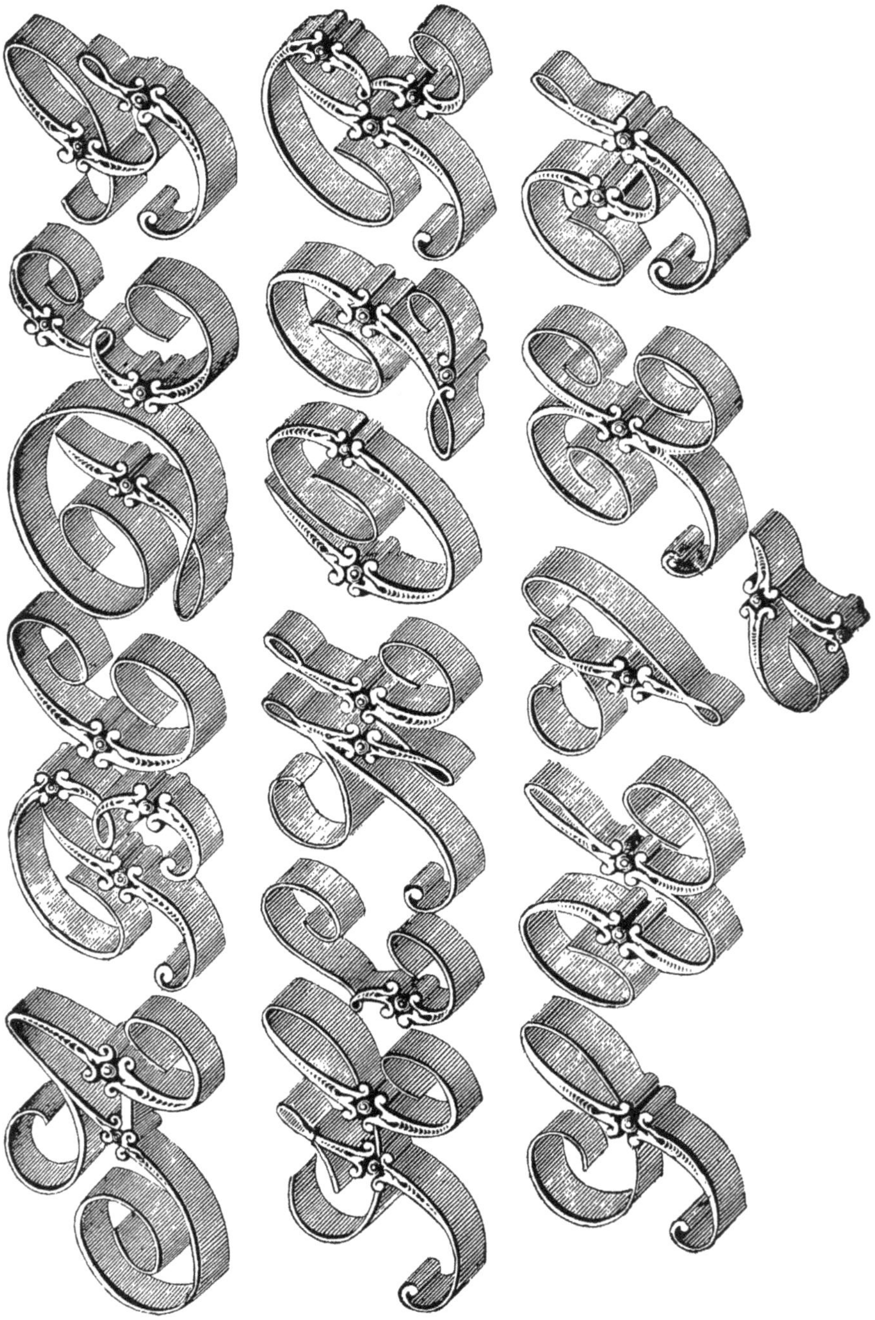

Vault Editions Ltd

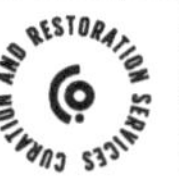

INDUSTRY STD

VAULTEDITIONS.COM

44

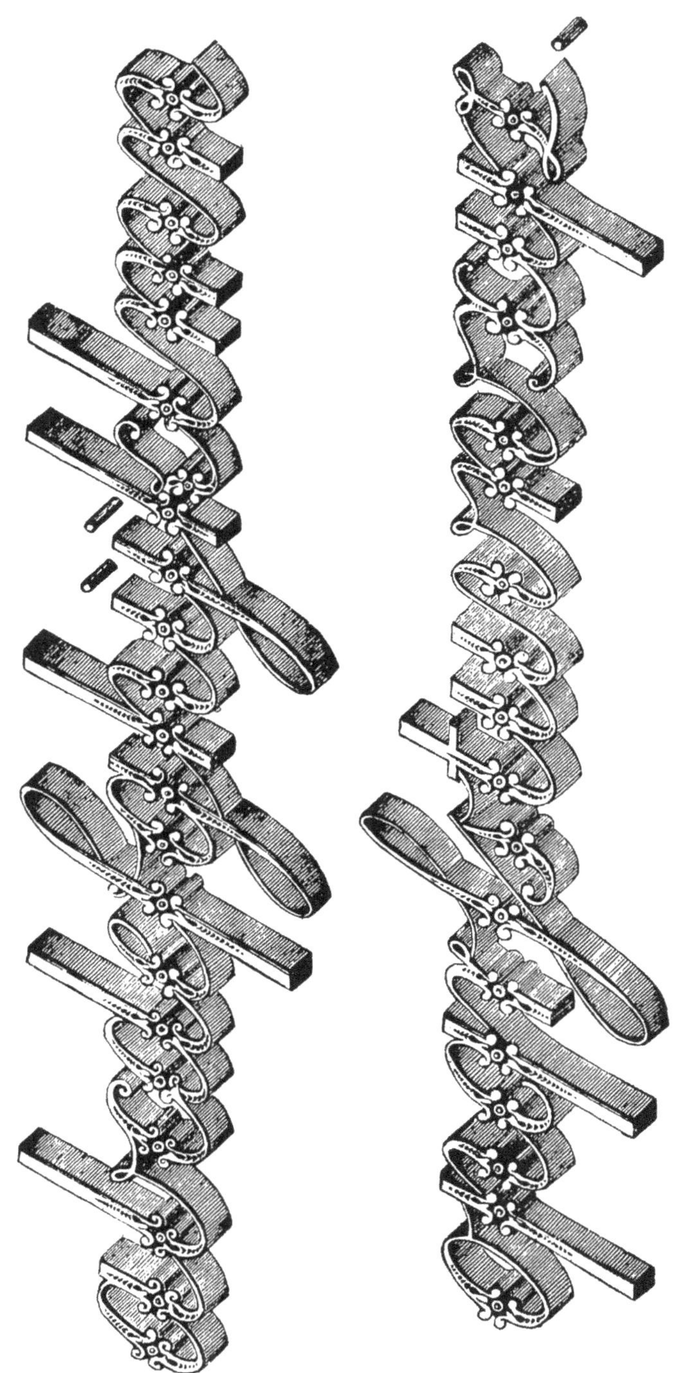

Vault Editions Ltd

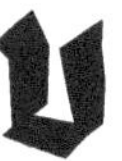
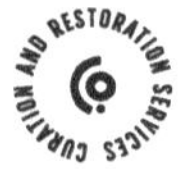

CURATION AND RESTORATION SERVICES

PRACTICE MAKES PERFECT
TRD MRK

INDUSTRY STD

VAULTEDITIONS.COM

45

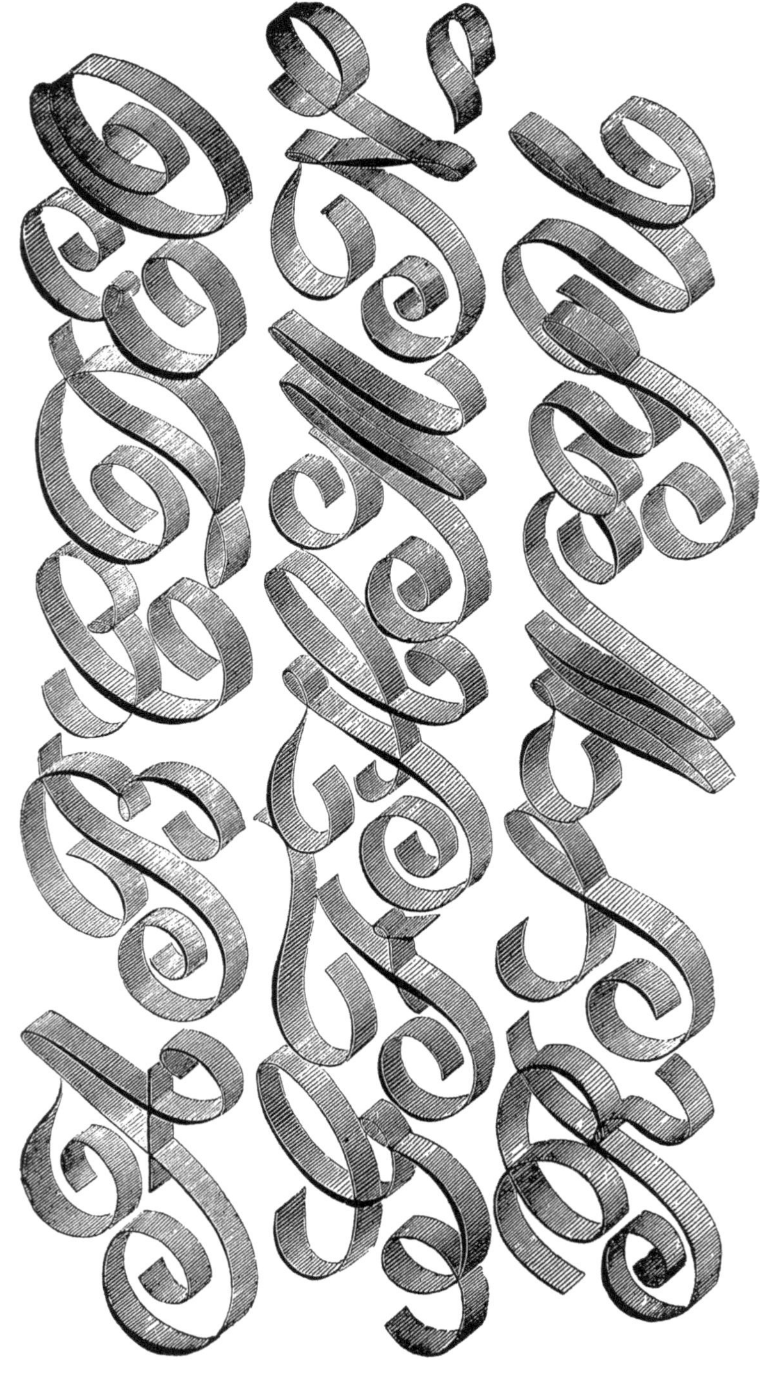

Vault Editions Ltd

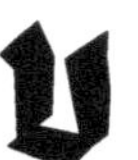
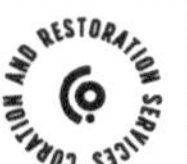

DESIGNER

FREEMAN DELAMOTTE

THE SIGN PAINTER AND

LETTERING ARTIST'S REFERENCE BOOK

TYPEFACE

ITALIAN SHADED

UPPER & LOWER CASE ⟷ WEIGHT: REGULAR ⟷ PUBLISHED: 1872

46

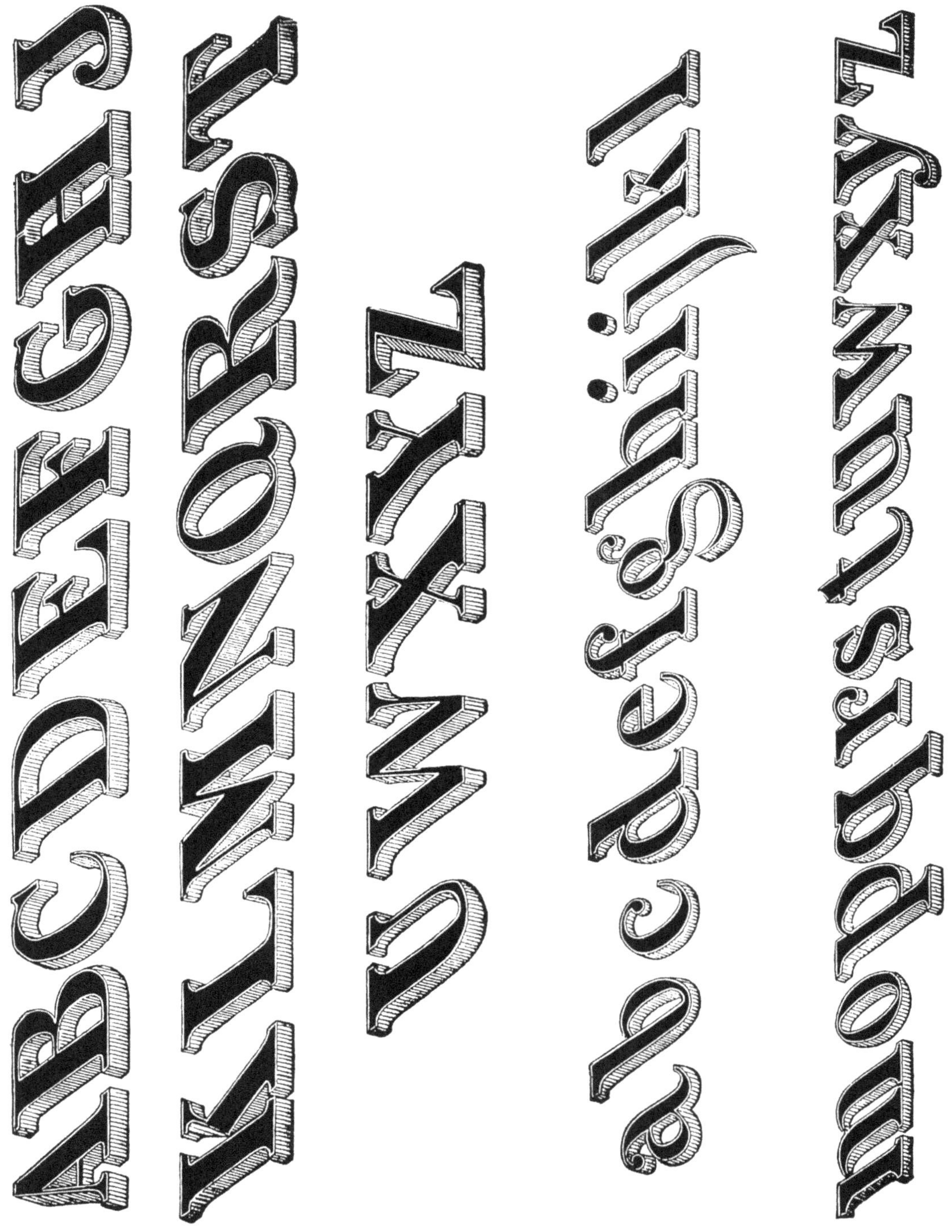

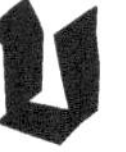

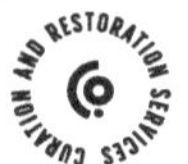

47

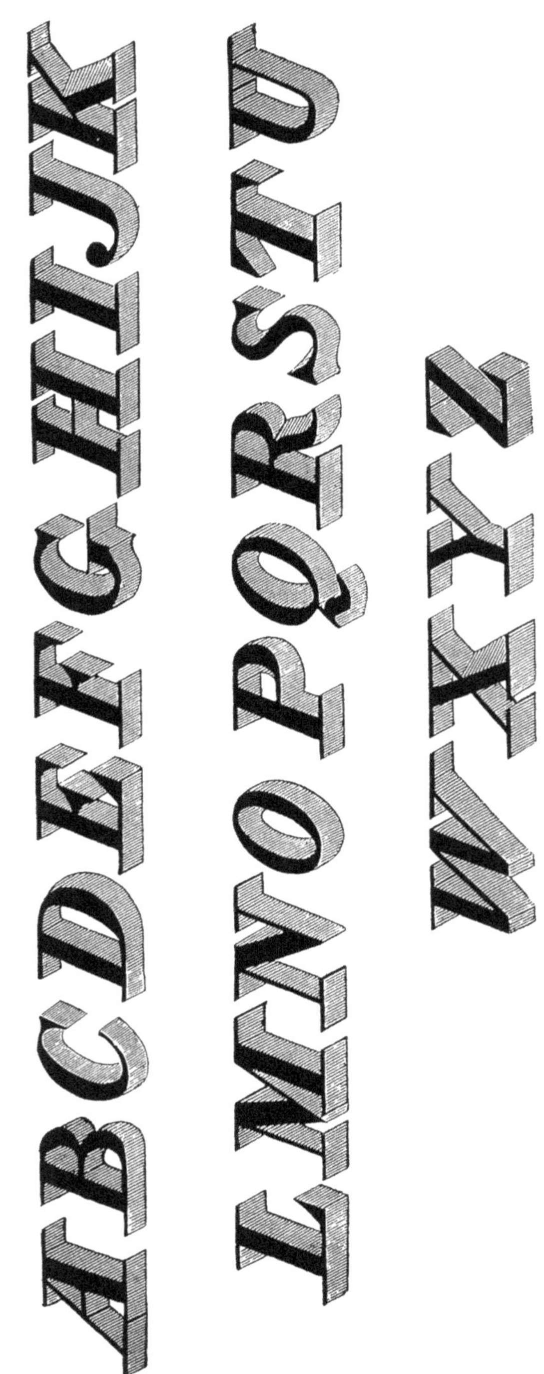

Vault Editions Ltd

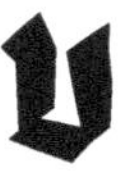

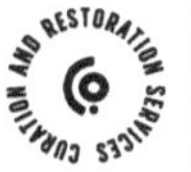

PRACTICE MAKES PERFECT

INDUSTRY STD

VAULTEDITIONS.COM

48

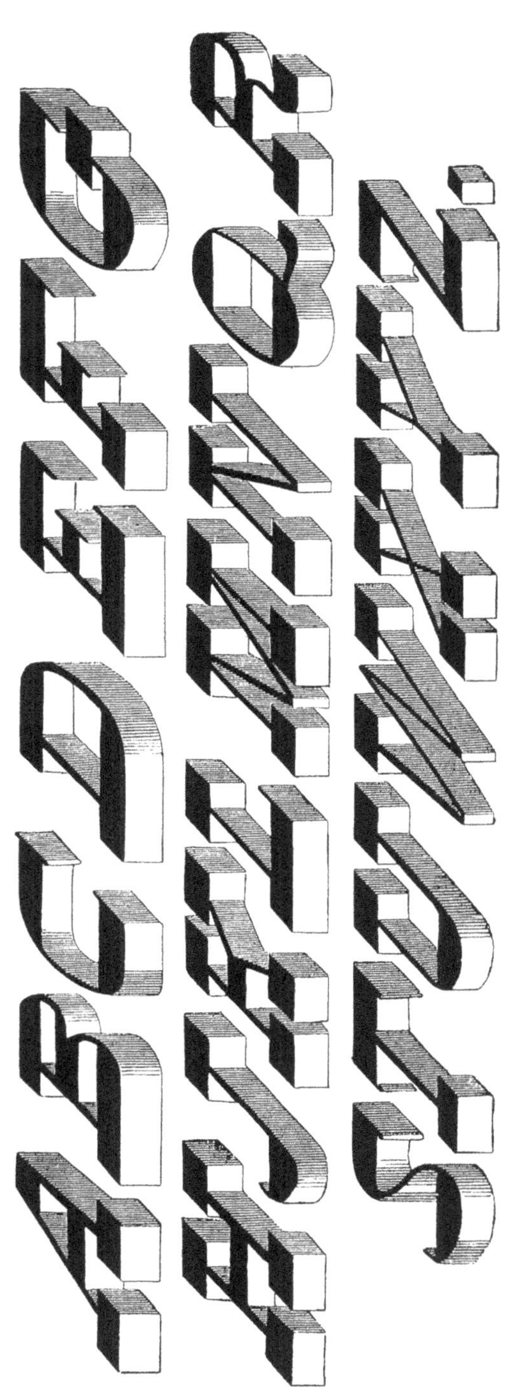

Vault Editions Ltd

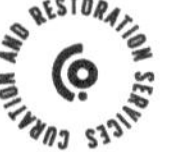

CURATION AND RESTORATION SERVICES COATING

PRACTICE MAKES PERFECT
TRD MRK

INDUSTRY STD

VAULTEDITIONS.COM

49

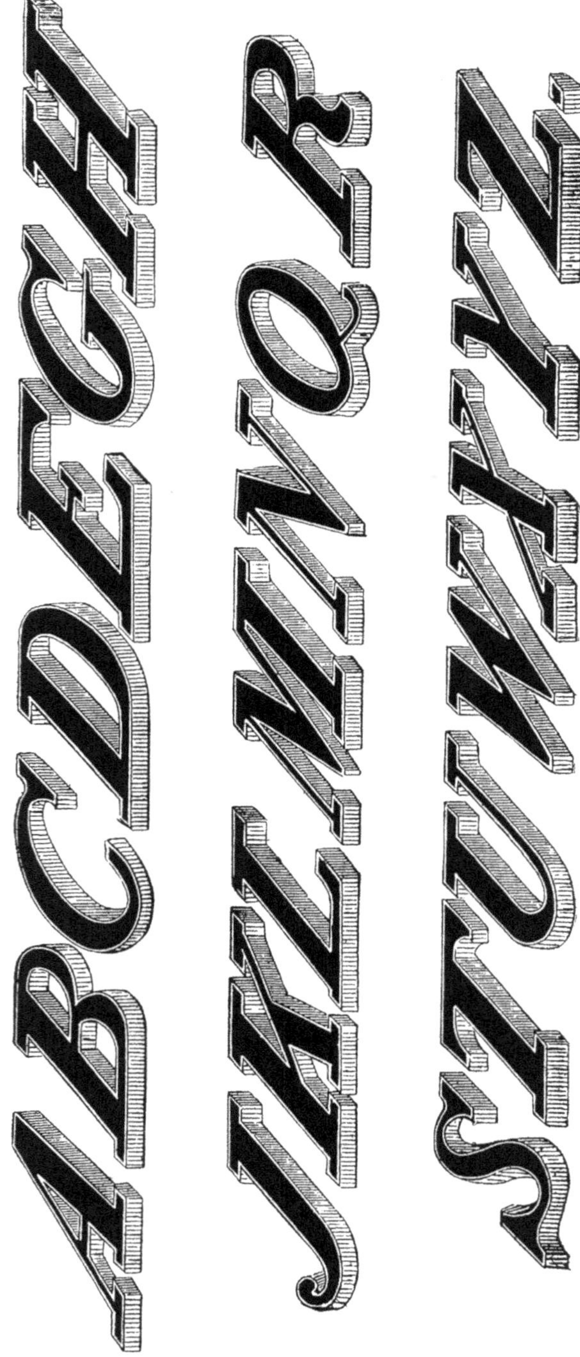

A HIGH RESOLUTION FILE OF THIS
SPECIMEN SHEET CAN BE DOWNLOADED
FROM THE VAULT EDITIONS' WEBSITE.

Vault Editions Ltd

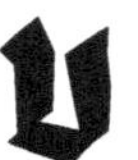

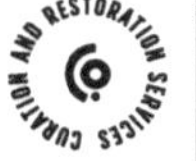
CURATION AND RESTORATION SERVICES

PRACTICE
MAKES
PERFECT
TRD MRK

INDUSTRY STD

VAULTEDITIONS.COM

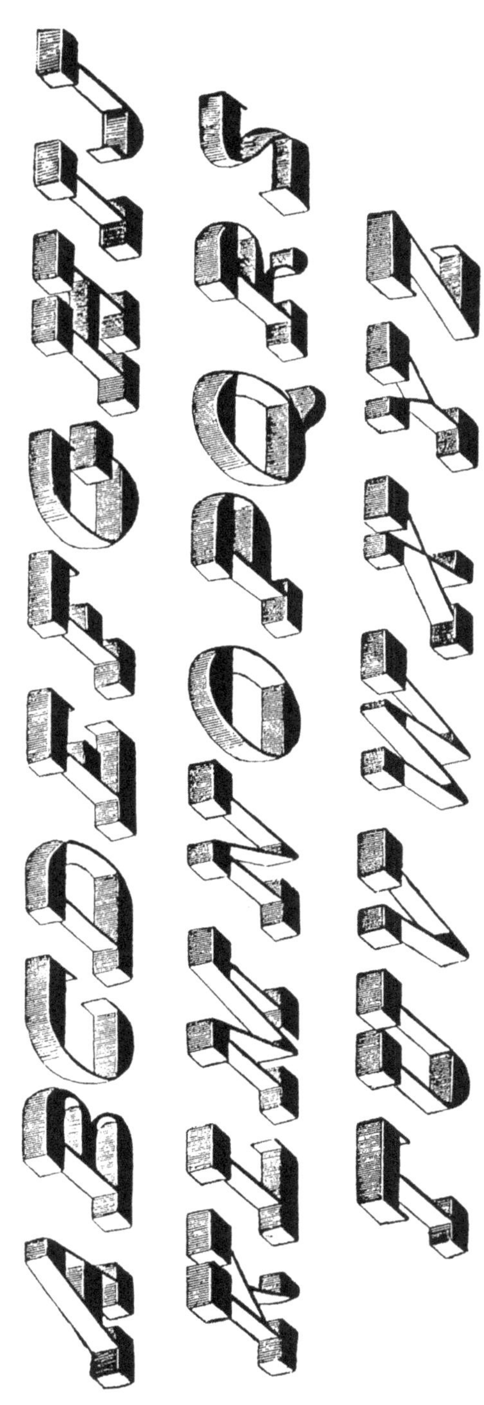

51

ABCDEFGHIJKLN
MPQRSTUVWXYZ

abcdefghijklmnopqrs
tuvwxyz

52

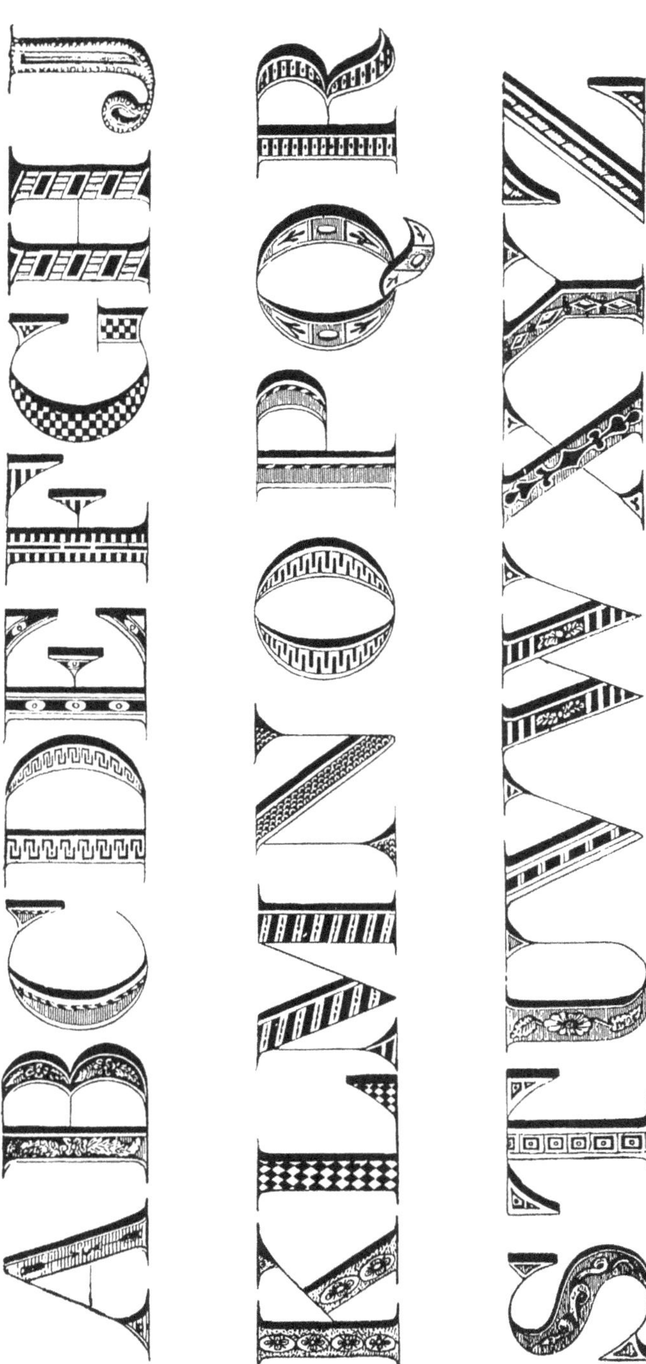

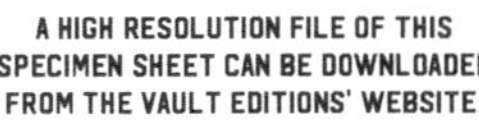

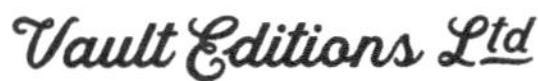
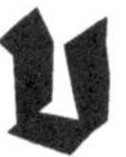
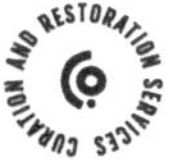

PRACTICE
MAKES
PERFECT

INDUSTRY STD

VAULTEDITIONS.COM

53

A B C D E F G H I
J K L M N O P Q R S
T U V W X Y Z

Vault Editions Ltd

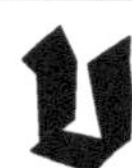
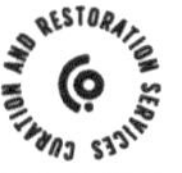

INDUSTRY STD

VAULTEDITIONS.COM

54

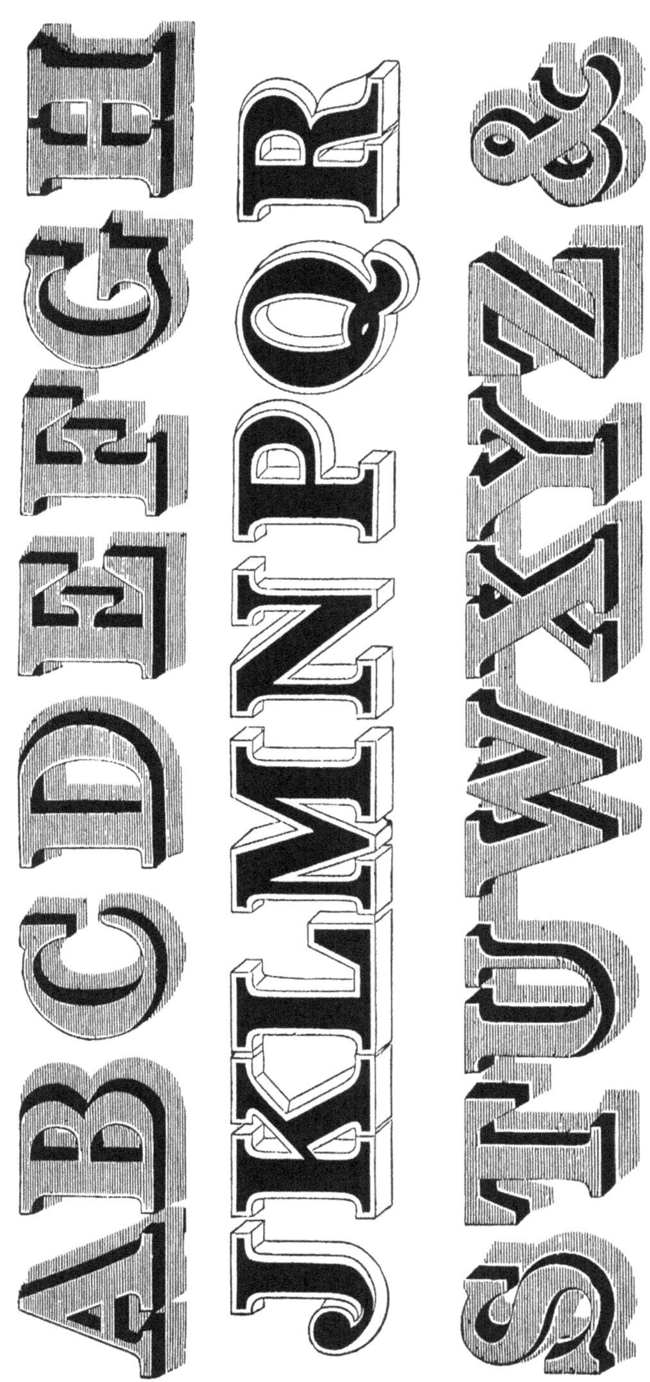

Vault Editions Ltd

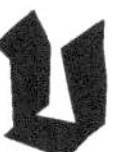

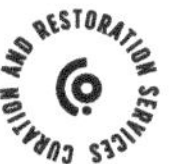

PRACTICE MAKES PERFECT

INDUSTRY STD

VAULTEDITIONS.COM

55

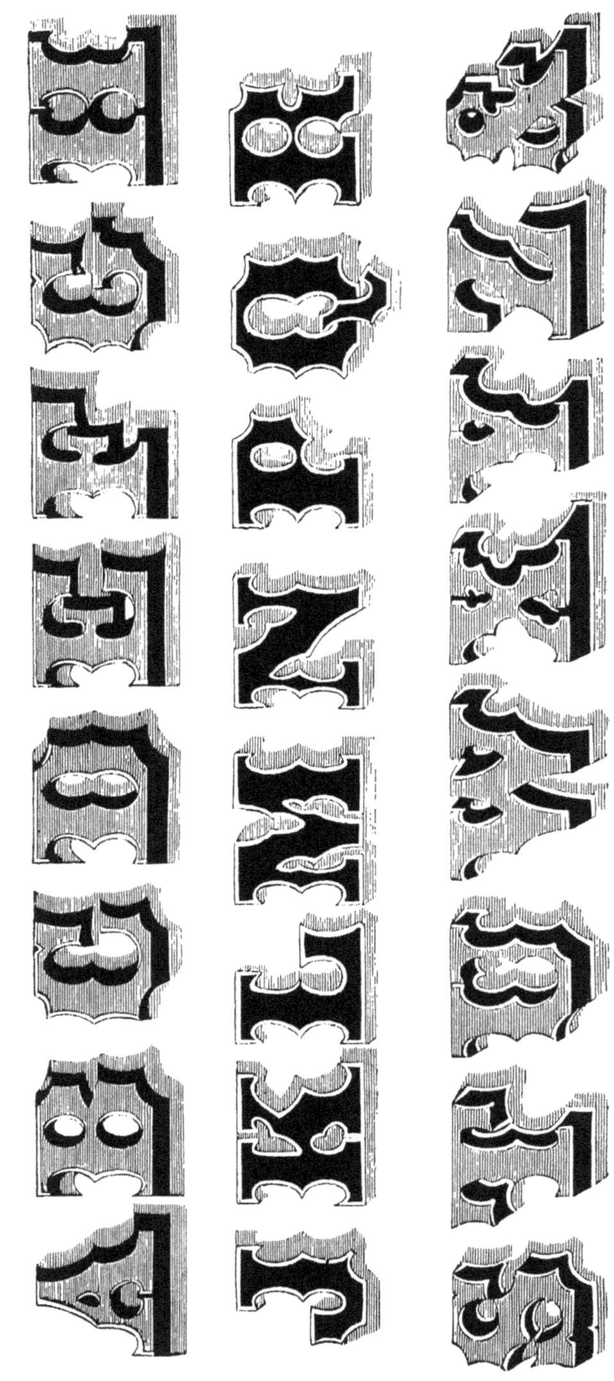

56

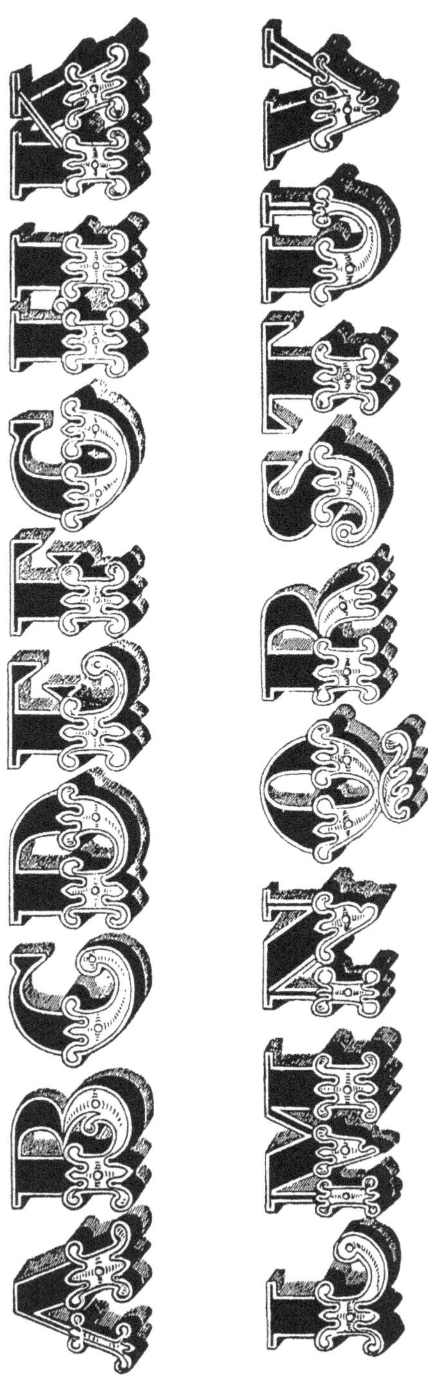
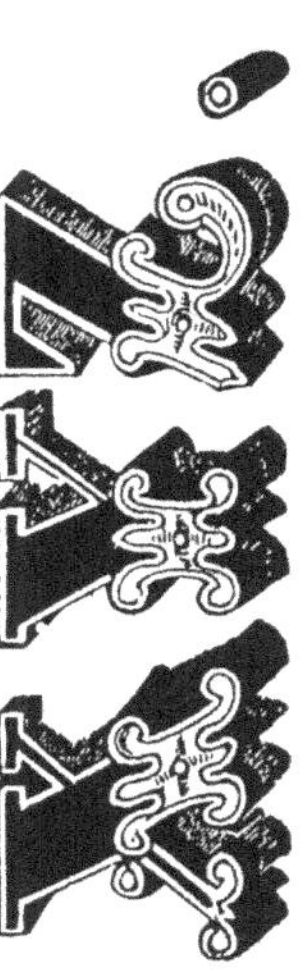

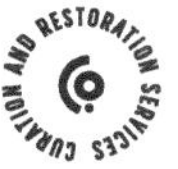

57

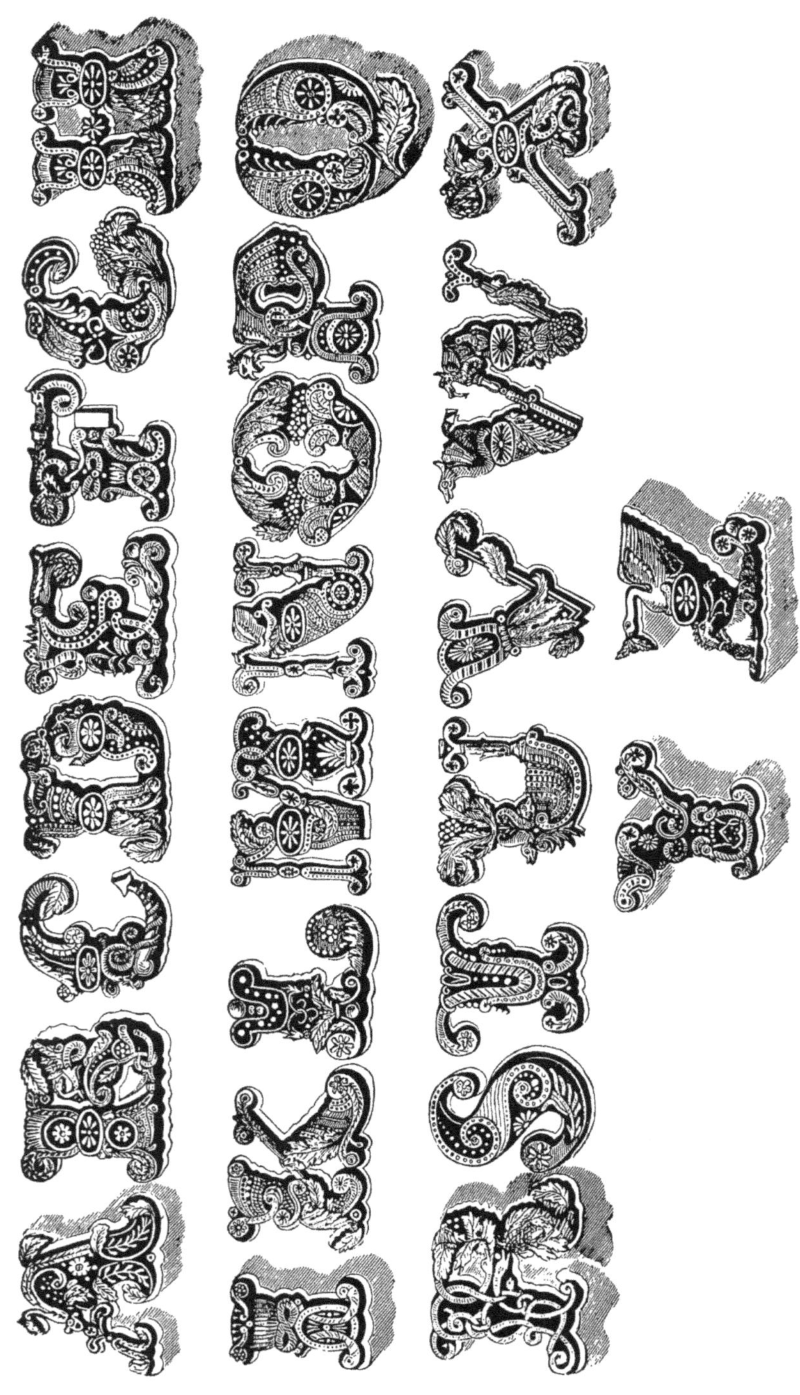

Vault Editions Ltd

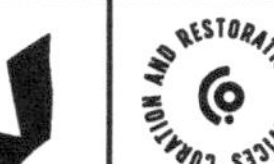

CURATION AND RESTORATION SERVICES

PRACTICE MAKES PERFECT
T R D   M R K

INDUSTRY STD

VAULTEDITIONS.COM

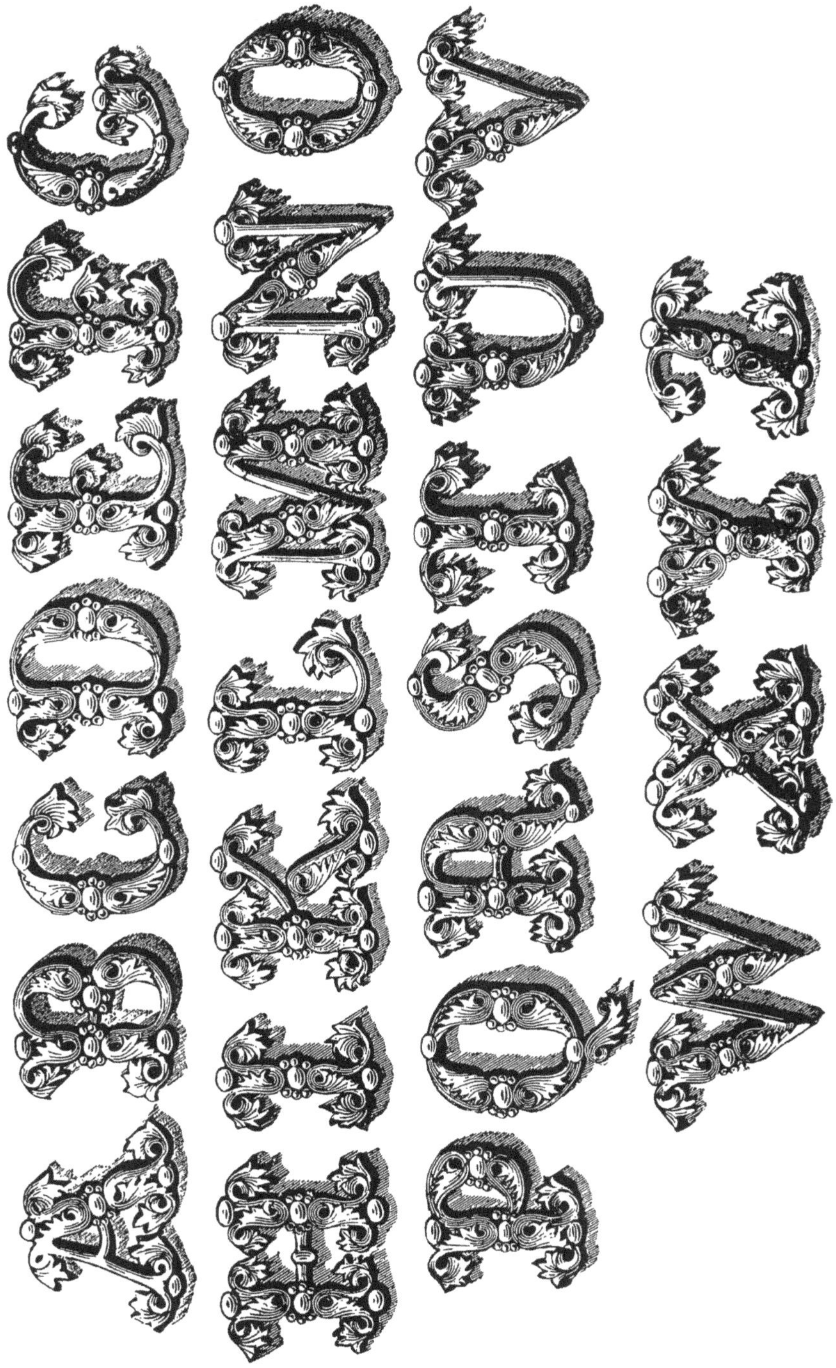

58

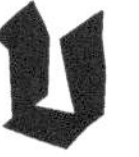
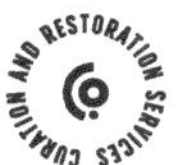

Vault Editions Ltd

PRACTICE MAKES PERFECT

INDUSTRY STD

VAULTEDITIONS.COM

59

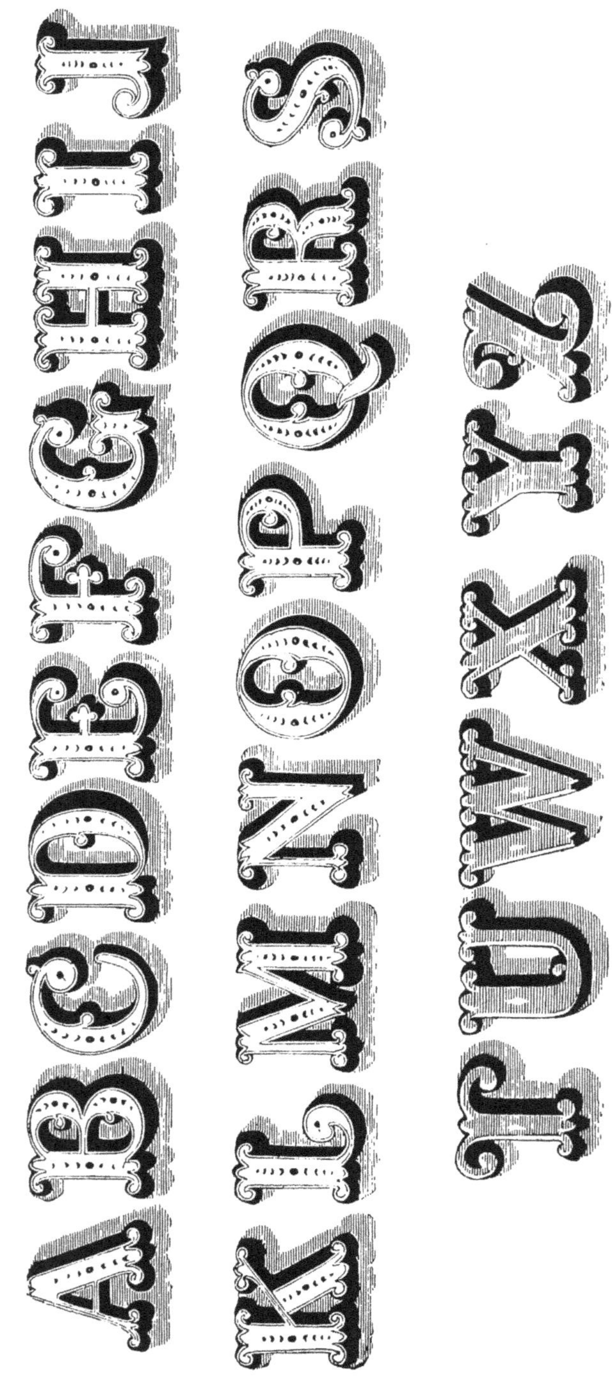

A HIGH RESOLUTION FILE OF THIS SPECIMEN SHEET CAN BE DOWNLOADED FROM THE VAULT EDITIONS' WEBSITE.

Vault Editions Ltd

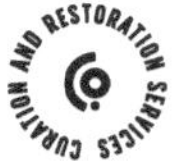

PRACTICE MAKES PERFECT

INDUSTRY STD

VAULTEDITIONS.COM

60

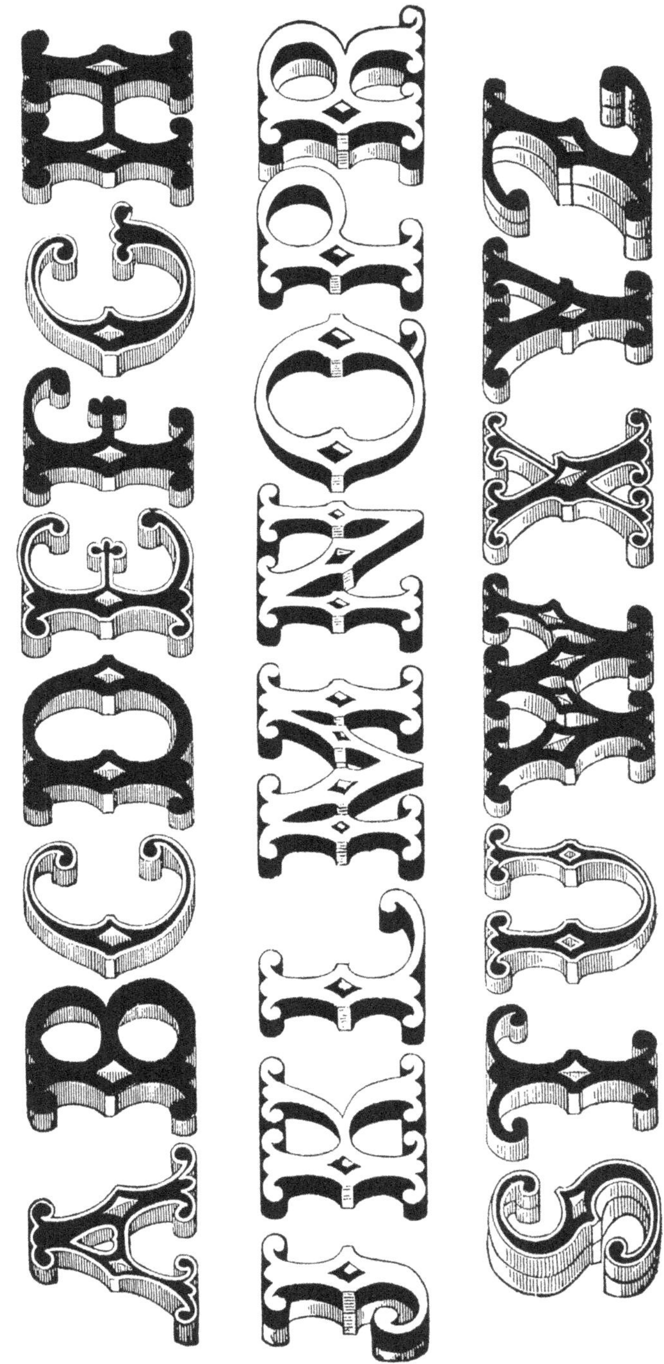

Vault Editions Ltd

CURATION AND RESTORATION SERVICES

PRACTICE MAKES PERFECT
TRD • MRK

INDUSTRY STD

VAULTEDITIONS.COM

61

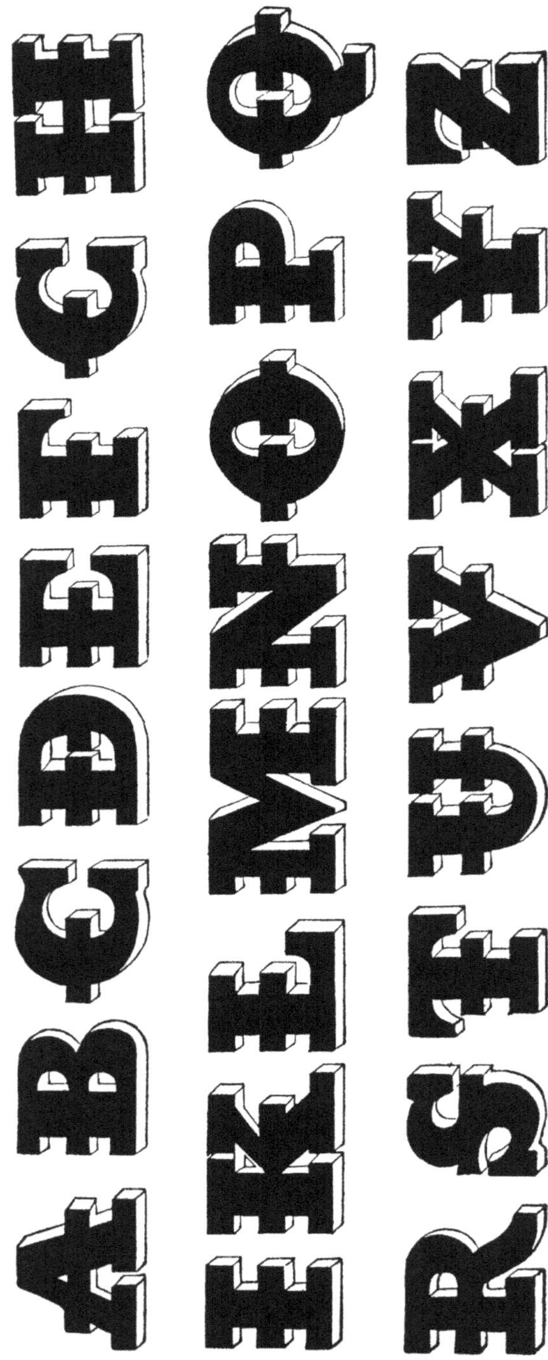

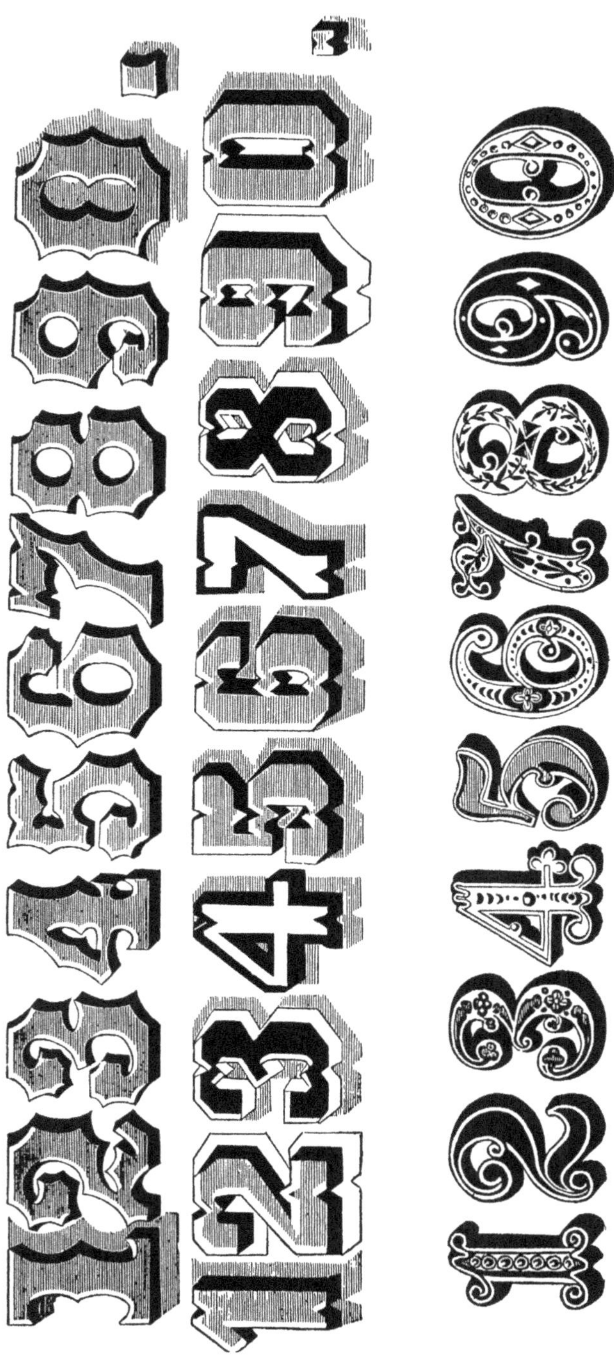

Vault Editions Ltd

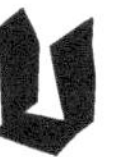
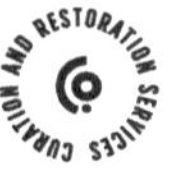

PRACTICE MAKES PERFECT

INDUSTRY STD

VAULTEDITIONS.COM

63

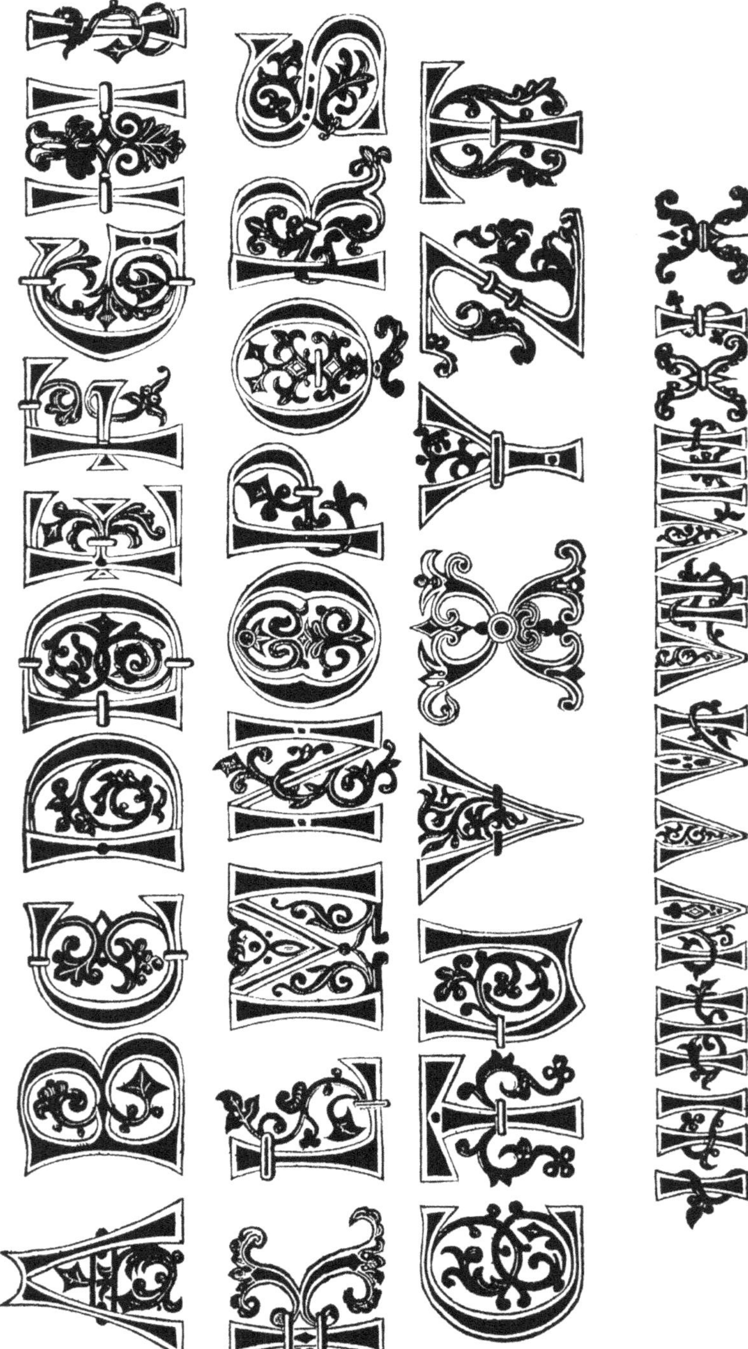

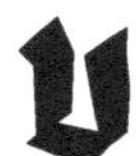
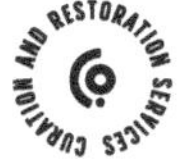

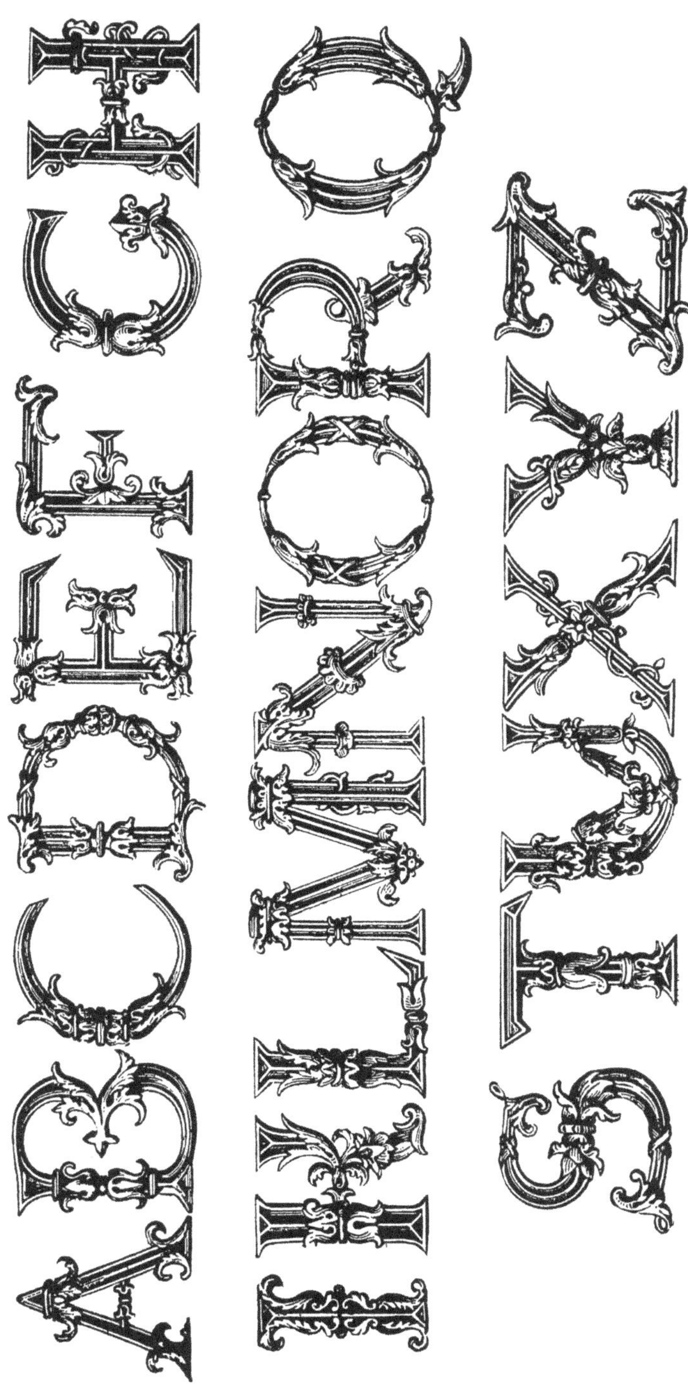

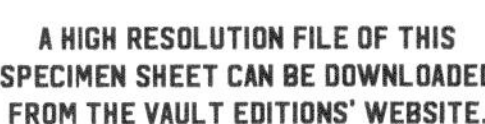
Vault Editions Ltd

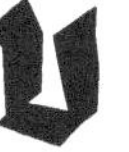

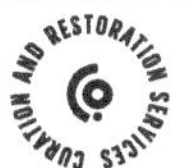

PRACTICE MAKES PERFECT

INDUSTRY STD

VAULTEDITIONS.COM

65

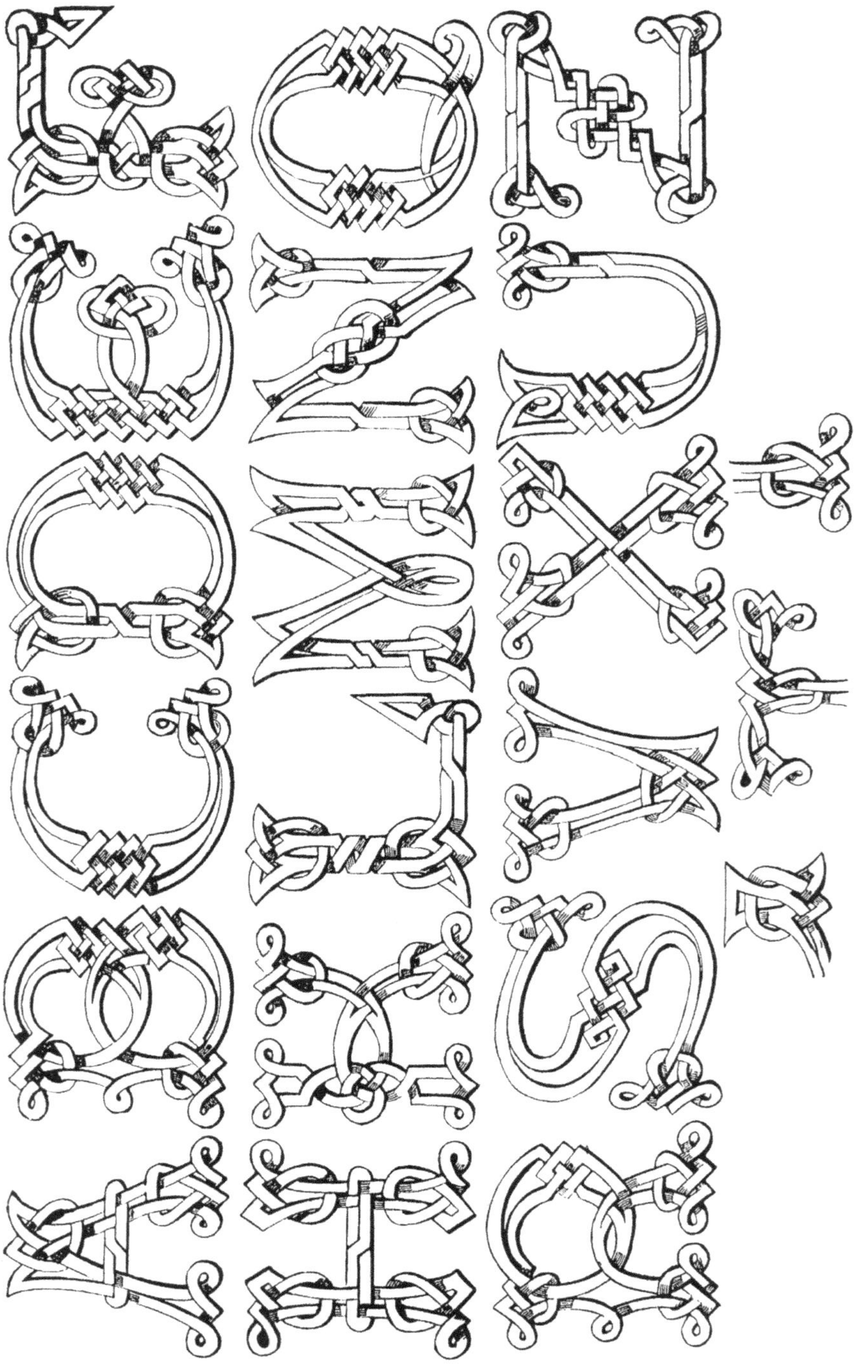

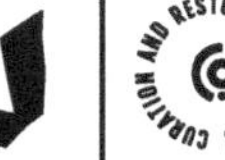

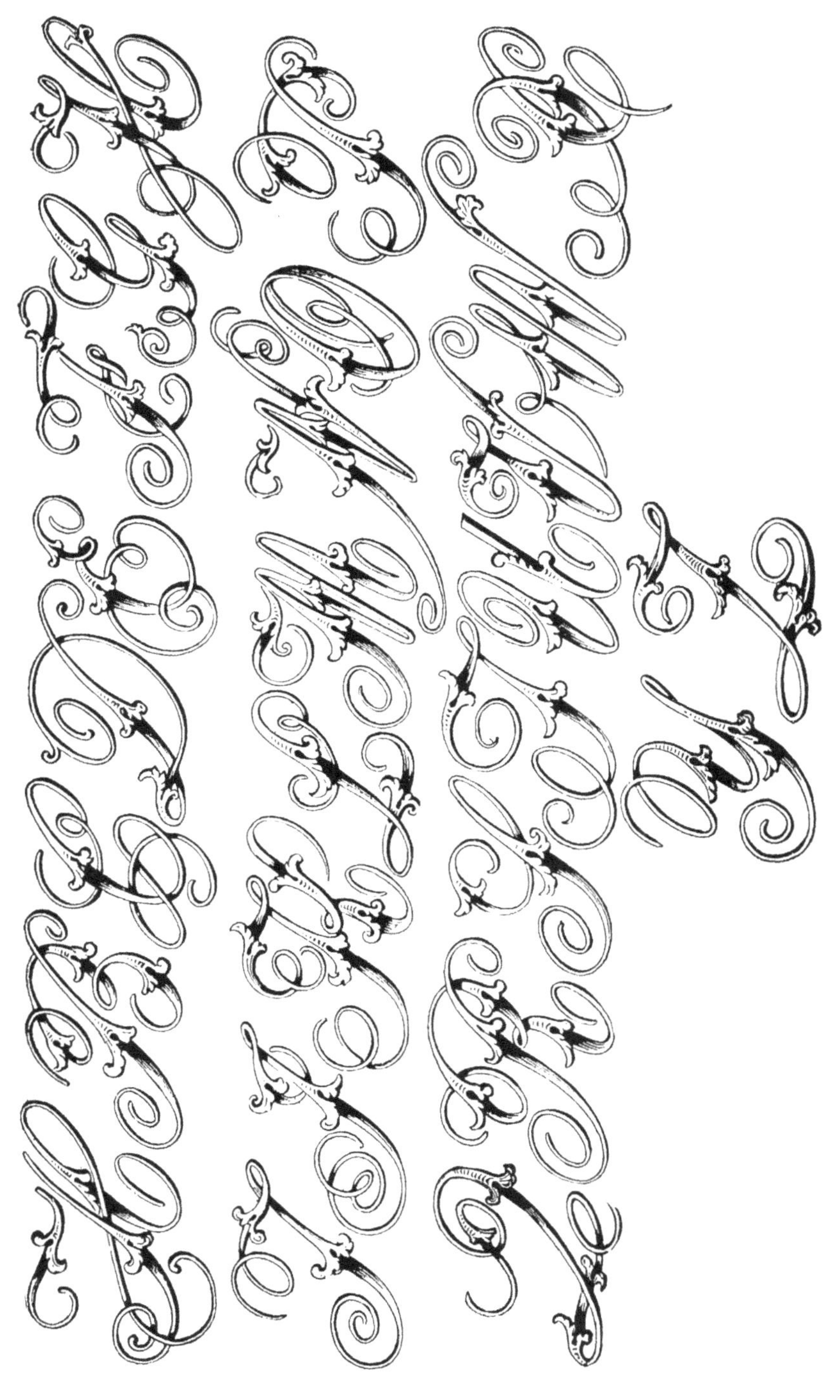

67

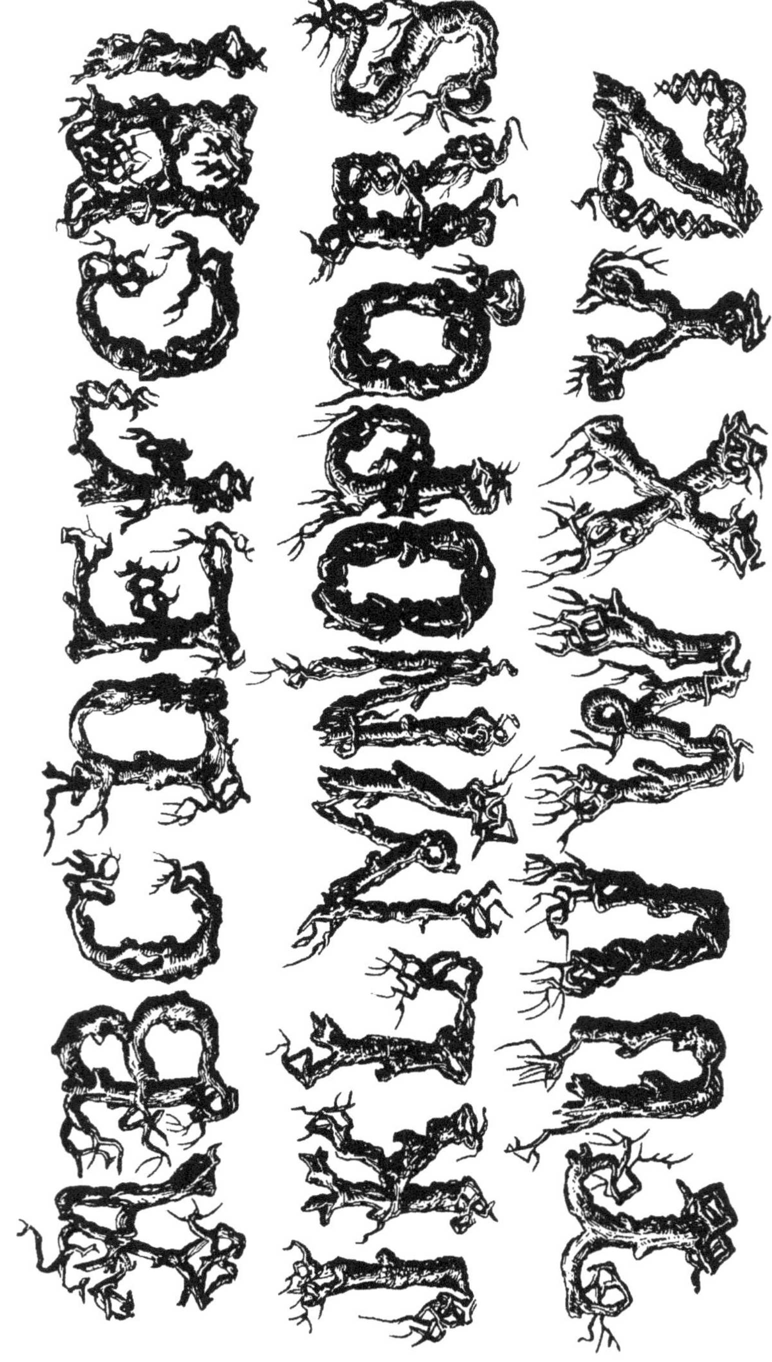

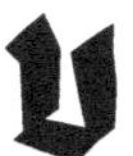
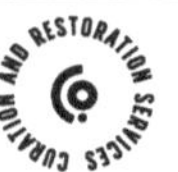

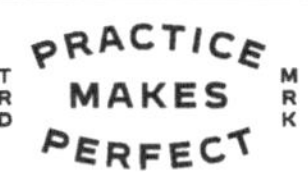

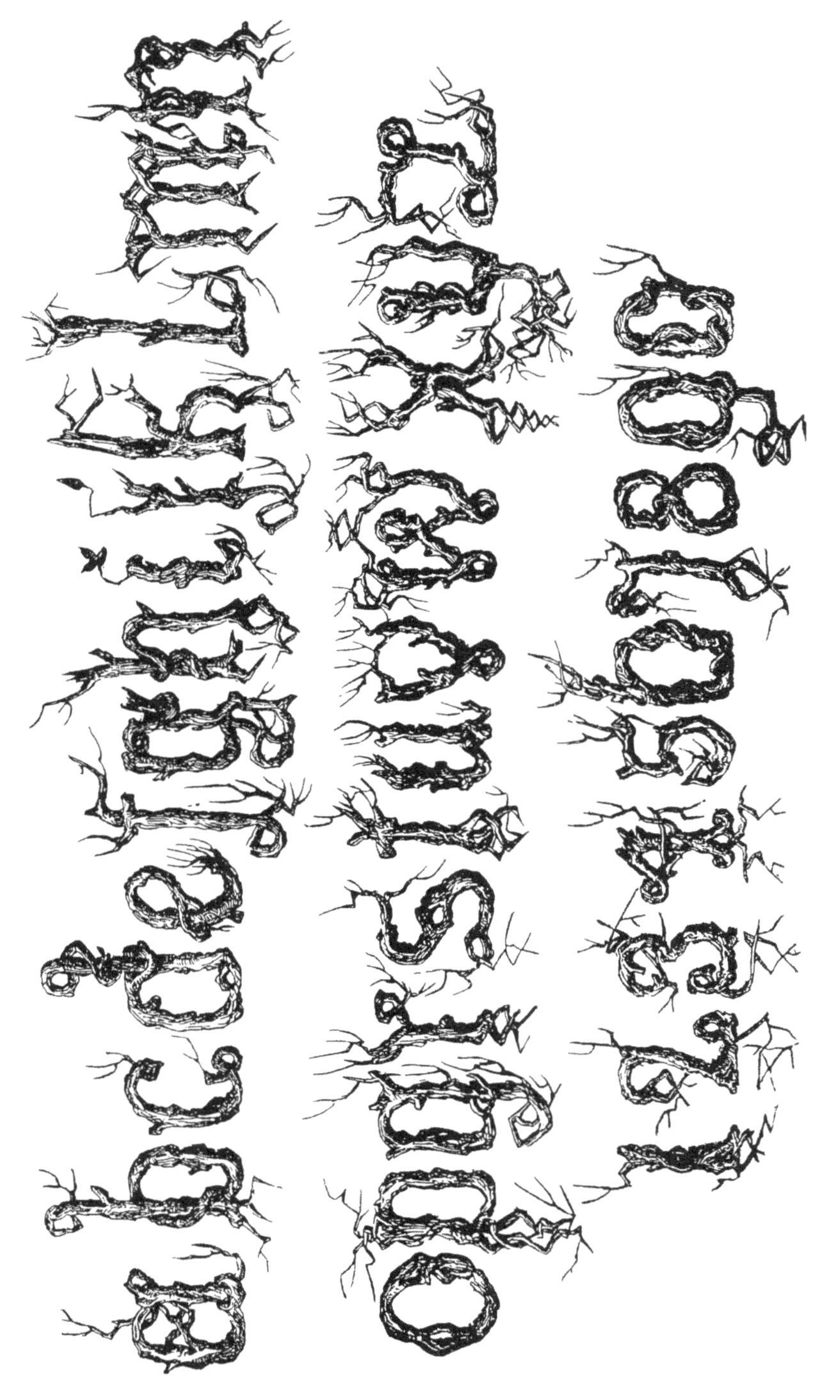

69

ABCDEFG
HIJKLMN
PQRSTUVW
XYZ
1234567890&

A HIGH RESOLUTION FILE OF THIS SPECIMEN SHEET CAN BE DOWNLOADED FROM THE VAULT EDITIONS' WEBSITE.

Vault Editions Ltd

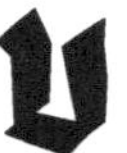

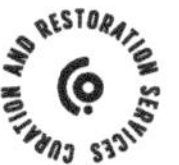

CURATION AND RESTORATION SERVICES

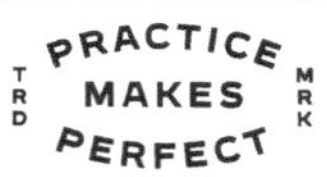

INDUSTRY STD

VAULTEDITIONS.COM

70

ABCDEFGHIJK
LMNOPQRS
TUVWXYZ&.-
abcdefghijklmnopqrstuvw
xyz
1234567890

71

ABCDEFGHIJ
KLMNOPQR
STUVWXYZ

abcdefghijklm
nopqrstuwxxyz

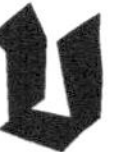

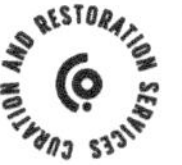

CURATION AND RESTORATION SERVICES

PRACTICE MAKES PERFECT — TRD — MRK

INDUSTRY STD

VAULTEDITIONS.COM

UPPER | LOWER | NUMERALS   ←→   WEIGHT: REGULAR   ←→   PUBLISHED: 1883

72

ABCDEFGHIJ
KLMNOPQRS
TUVWXYZ&
abcdefghijklmnopqrstuvwxyz3
1234567890

A HIGH RESOLUTION FILE OF THIS SPECIMEN SHEET CAN BE DOWNLOADED FROM THE VAULT EDITIONS' WEBSITE.

Vault Editions Ltd

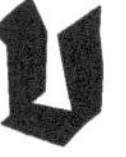

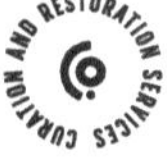

CURATION AND RESTORATION SERVICES

PRACTICE MAKES PERFECT — TRD — MRK

INDUSTRY STD

VAULTEDITIONS.COM

73

ABCDEFGHIJ
KLMNOPQRS
TUVWXYZ&

abcddefghhijkklmnmn
opqrrsftuvwwxyyz3

Vault Editions Ltd

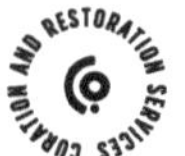

PRACTICE MAKES PERFECT

INDUSTRY STD

VAULTEDITIONS.COM

UPPER | LOWER | NUMERALS | WEIGHT: REGULAR | PUBLISHED: 1883

74

ABCDEFGHIJK
LMNOPQRSTU
VWXYZ&
abcdefghijklmnopqrs
tuvwxyz" 1234567890

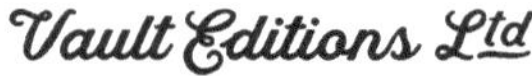

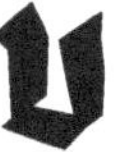

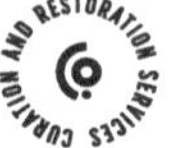

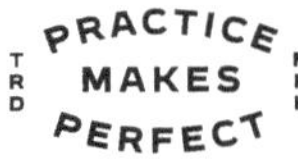

INDUSTRY STD

VAULTEDITIONS.COM

75

ABCDEFGHIJ
KLMNOPQRS
TUVWXYZ&
abcdefghijklmnopqrst
uvwxyz

Vault Editions Ltd

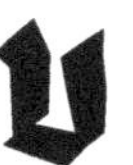
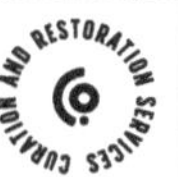

CURATION AND RESTORATION SERVICES

PRACTICE
MAKES
PERFECT

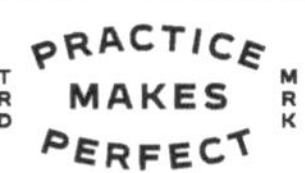

INDUSTRY STD

VAULTEDITIONS.COM

76

UPPER & LOWER CASE   WEIGHT: REGULAR   PUBLISHED: 1883

77

A HIGH RESOLUTION FILE OF THIS SPECIMEN SHEET CAN BE DOWNLOADED FROM THE VAULT EDITIONS' WEBSITE.

Vault Editions Ltd

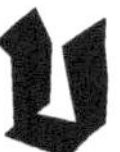

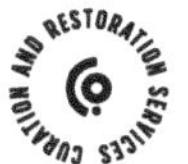

INDUSTRY STD

VAULTEDITIONS.COM

78

ABCDEFGH
IJKLMNOPQ
RSTUVWXYZ
abcdefghijklmno
pqrstuvwxyz &
123456789

Vault Editions Ltd

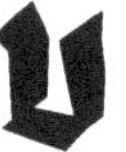

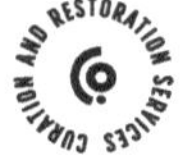

INDUSTRY STD

VAULTEDITIONS.COM

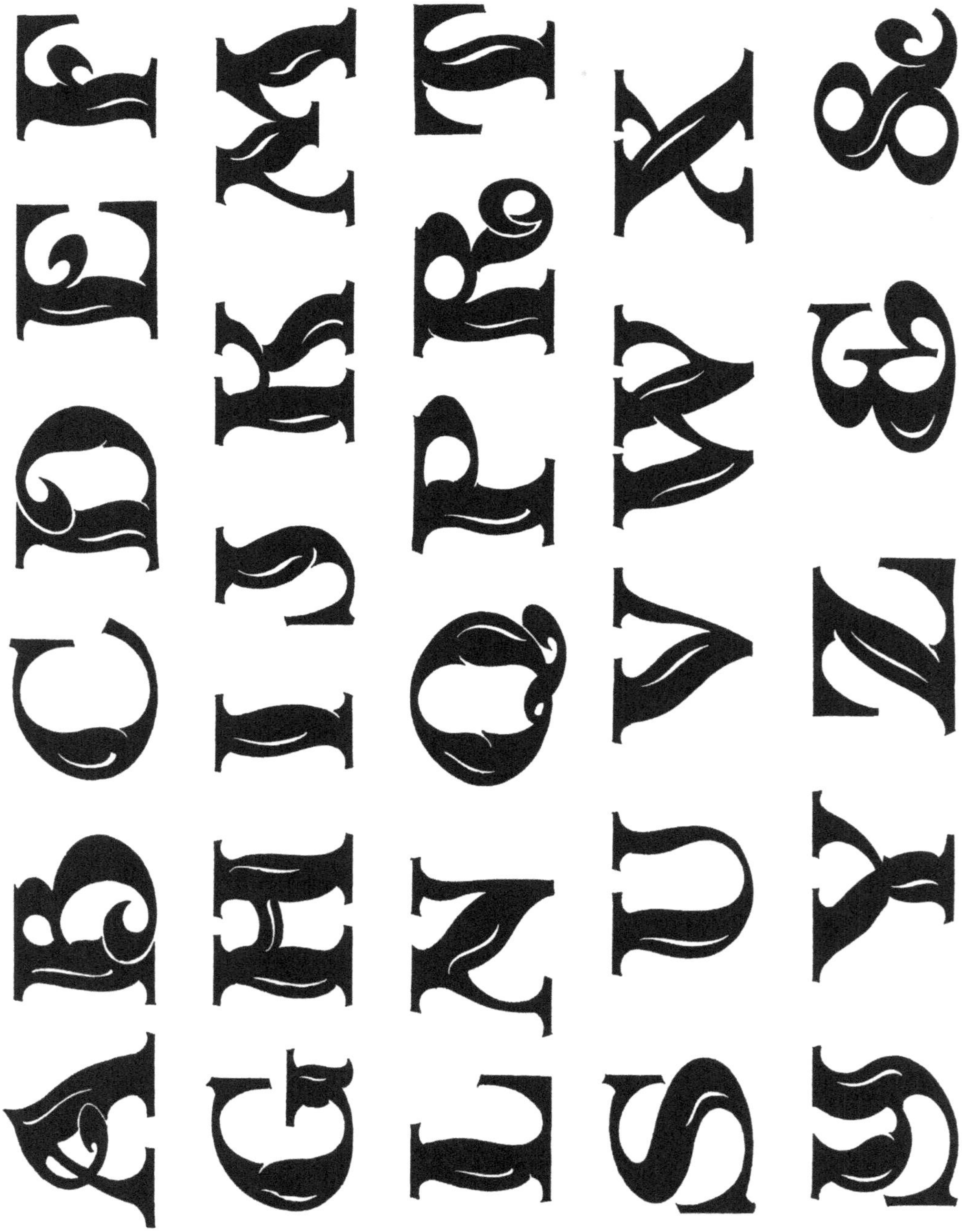

79

A B C D E F
G H I J K M
L N O P R Q T
S U V W X
Y Z &

Vault Editions Ltd

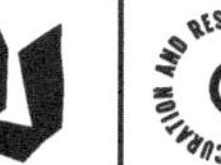
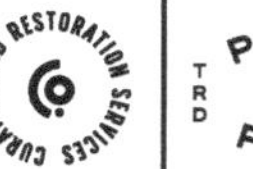

CURATION AND RESTORATION SERVICES

INDUSTRY STD

VAULTEDITIONS.COM

80

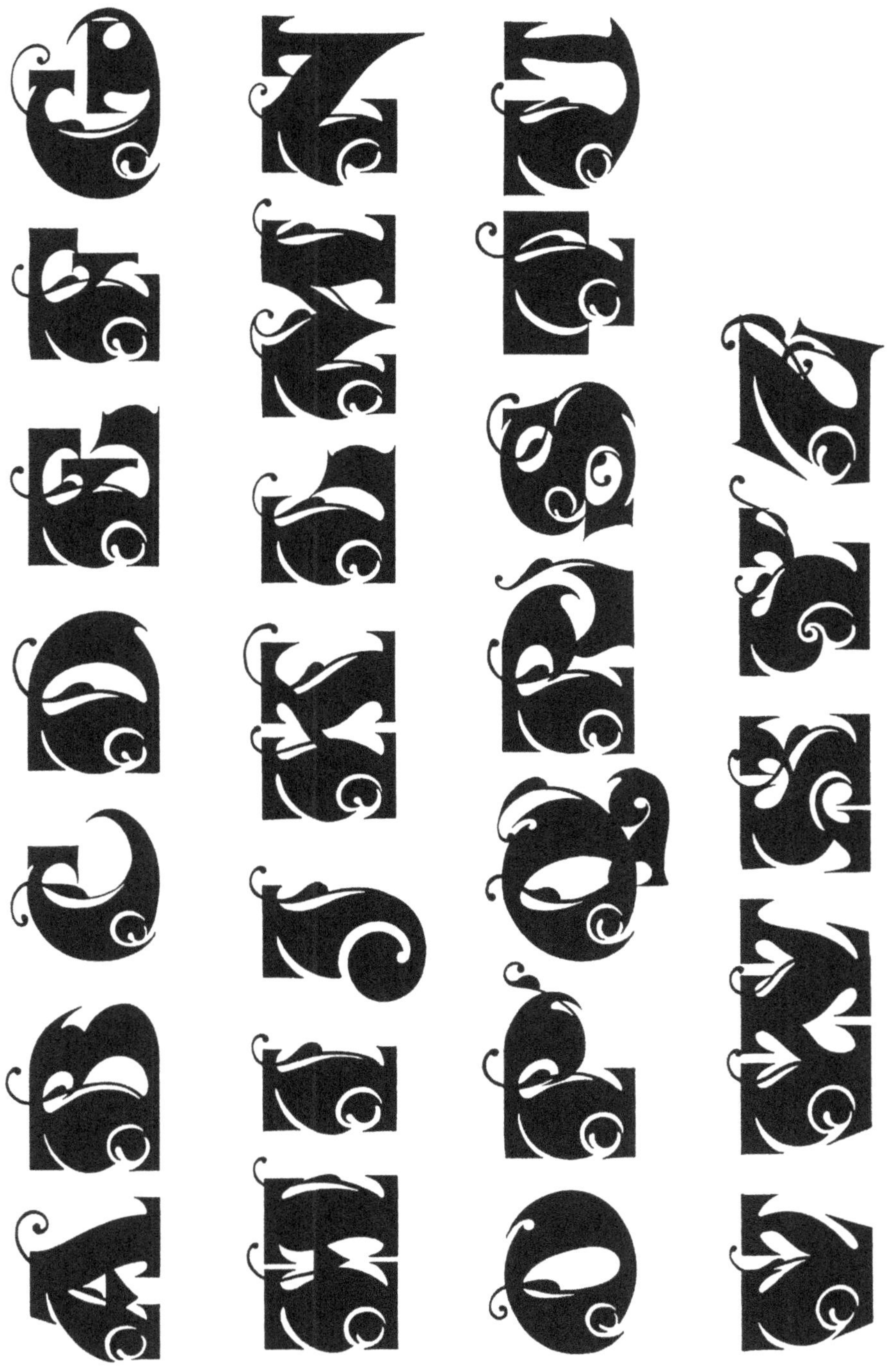

A HIGH RESOLUTION FILE OF THIS SPECIMEN SHEET CAN BE DOWNLOADED FROM THE VAULT EDITIONS' WEBSITE.

Vault Editions Ltd

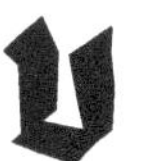

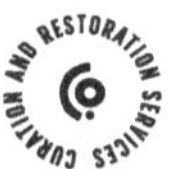

INDUSTRY STD

VAULTEDITIONS.COM

81

A B C D E F G H I J K L M N O P Q R S T U V W X Y Z

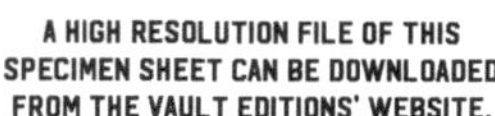

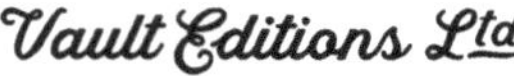

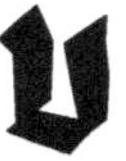

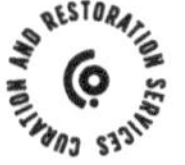

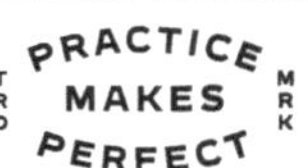

INDUSTRY STD

VAULTEDITIONS.COM

·DESIGNER·
JOHN O. OHNIMUS

THE SIGN PAINTER'S
LETTERING ARTIST'S
REFERENCE BOOK

·TYPEFACE·
ORNAMENTAL ROMAN & ITALICS

UPPER & LOWER CASE ⟷ WEIGHT: REGULAR ⟷ PUBLISHED: C. 1906

ABCDEFGHIJ
KLMNOPQR
STUVWXYZ&
abcdefghijklmnopqrstuvw
xyz

A HIGH RESOLUTION FILE OF THIS SPECIMEN SHEET CAN BE DOWNLOADED FROM THE VAULT EDITIONS' WEBSITE.

Vault Editions Ltd

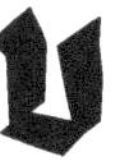
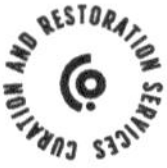

CURATION AND RESTORATION SERVICES

PRACTICE MAKES PERFECT — TRD · MRK

INDUSTRY STD

VAULTEDITIONS.COM

83

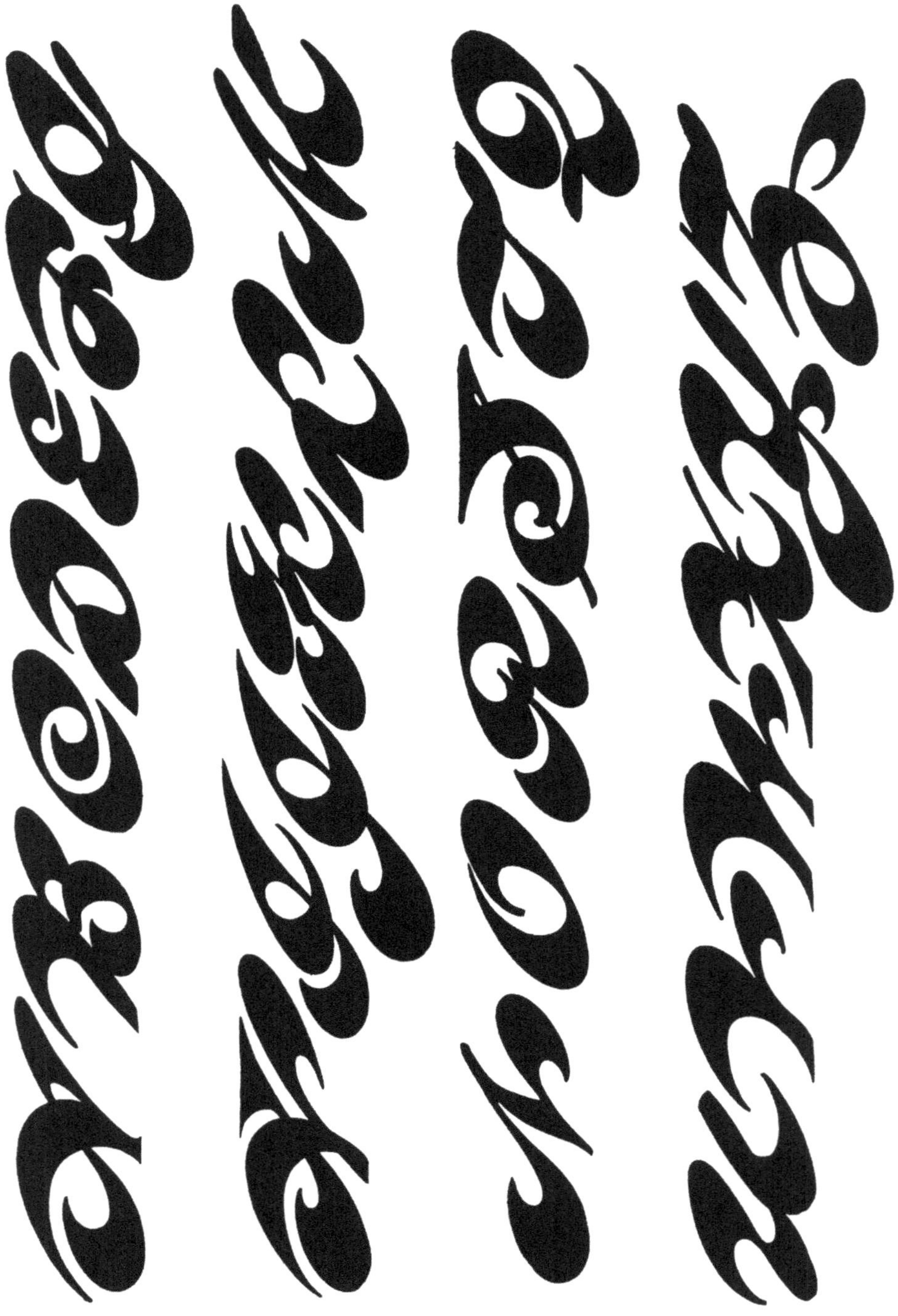

Vault Editions Ltd

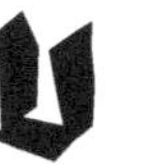

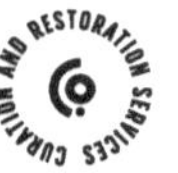

PRACTICE MAKES PERFECT

INDUSTRY STD

VAULTEDITIONS.COM

ABCDEF
GHIJKLM
NOPRTSU
VWXZ&Y

85

ABCDEFGHI
JKLMNOPQR
STUVWXYZ&
1234567890

Vault Editions Ltd

CURATION AND RESTORATION SERVICES

PRACTICE MAKES PERFECT
TRD · MRK

INDUSTRY STD

VAULTEDITIONS.COM

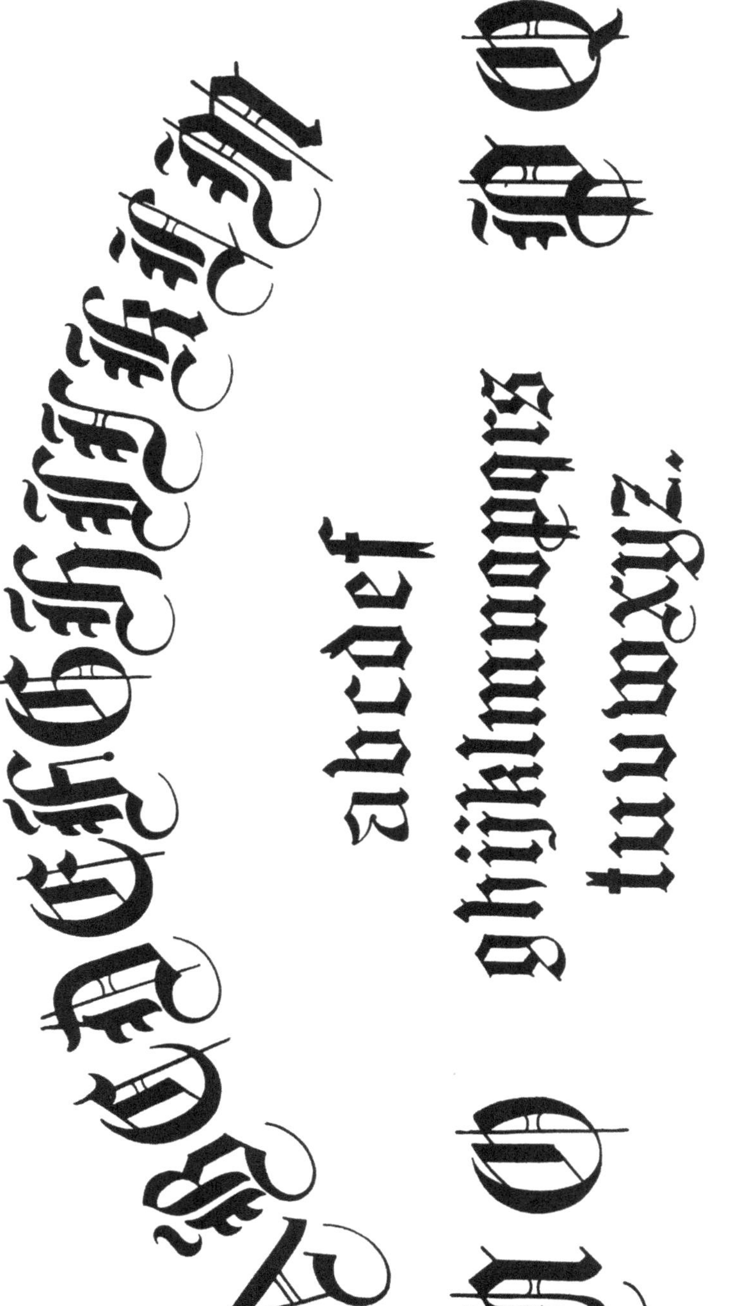

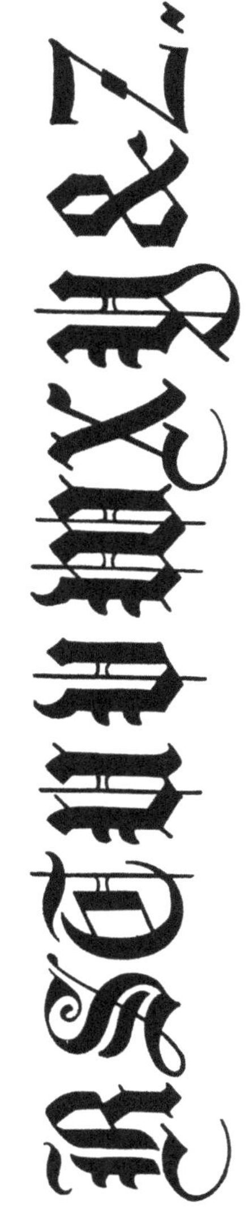

Vault Editions Ltd

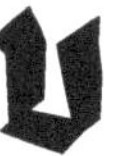
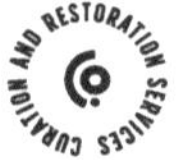

PRACTICE MAKES PERFECT

INDUSTRY STD

VAULTEDITIONS.COM

87

A B C D E

F G H

I J K L M

N O P Q

R S T U V

W X Y Z

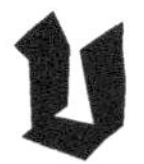
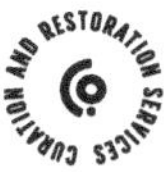

A B C D
E F G
H I J K
L M N O
P Q R
S T U V
W X Y Z

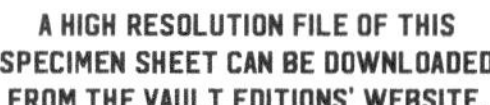

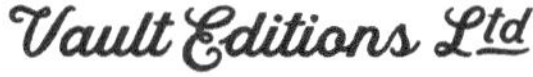

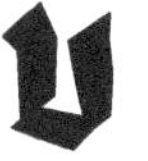

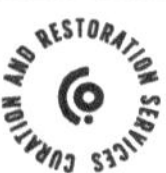

INDUSTRY STD

VAULTEDITIONS.COM

· DESIGNER ·
JAMES CALLINGHAM

THE SIGN PAINTER &
LETTERING ARTIST'S
REFERENCE BOOK

· TYPEFACE ·
BROADGAUGE ORNATE

UPPER CASE | WEIGHT: REGULAR | PUBLISHED: 1890

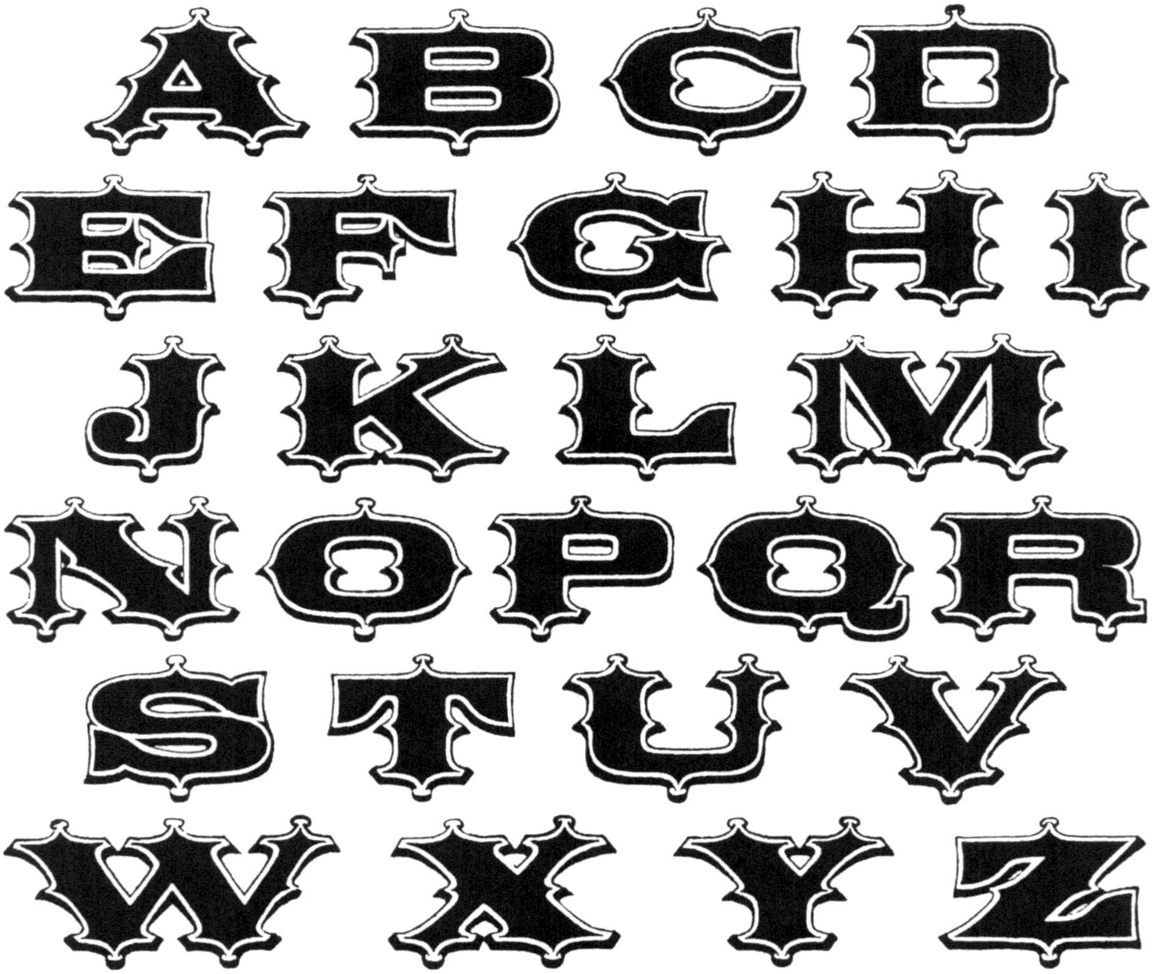

A B C D
E F G H I
J K L M
N O P Q R
S T U V
W X Y Z

Vault Editions Ltd

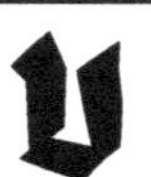

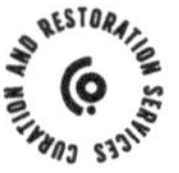

CURATION AND RESTORATION SERVICES

T·R·D **PRACTICE MAKES PERFECT** M·R·K

INDUSTRY STD

VAULTEDITIONS.COM

A B C D E F
G H I J K
L M N O P Q
R S T U
V W X Y Z

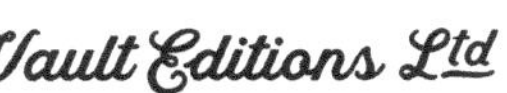

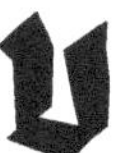

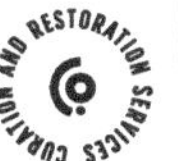

PRACTICE MAKES PERFECT

INDUSTRY STD

VAULTEDITIONS.COM

91

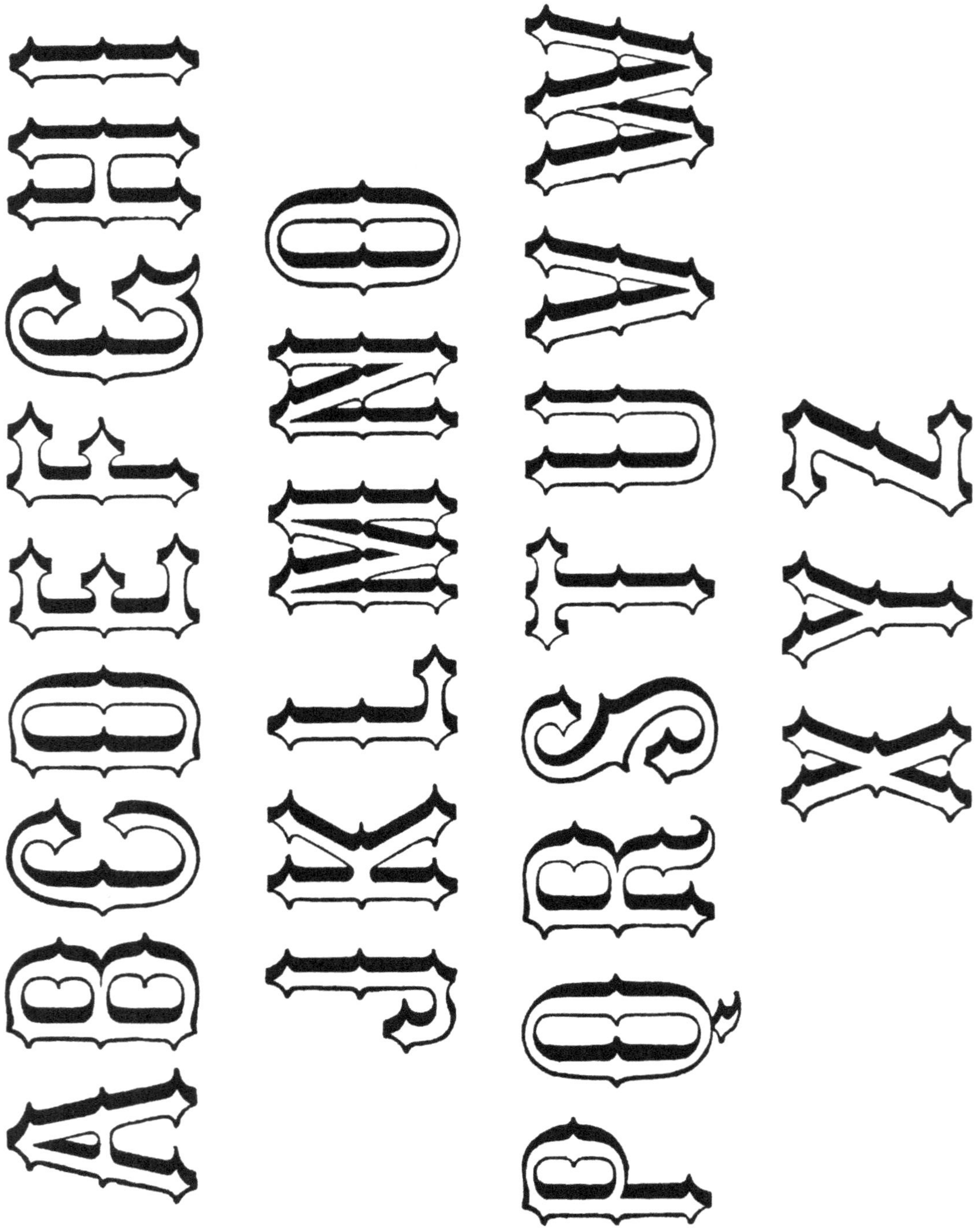

ABCDEFGHI
JKLMNO
PQRSTU
VWXYZ

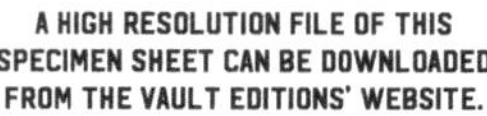

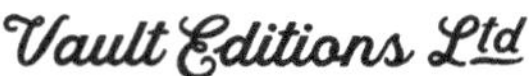

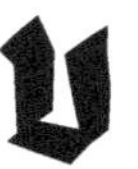

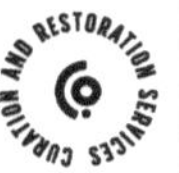

INDUSTRY STD

VAULTEDITIONS.COM

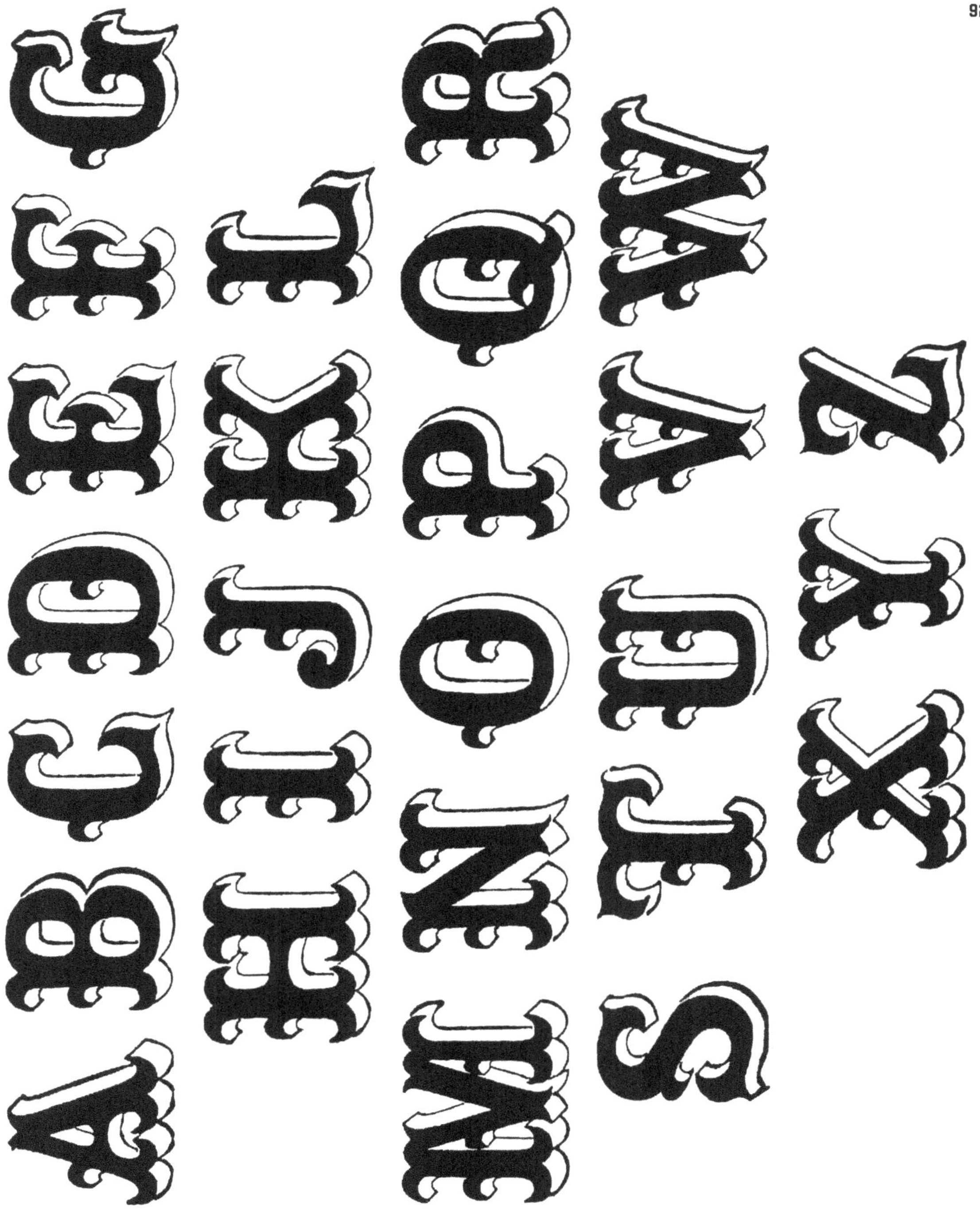

93

A B C D E
F G H I
J K L M N
O P Q R
S T U V W
X Y Z

Vault Editions Ltd

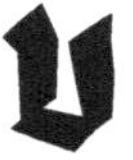

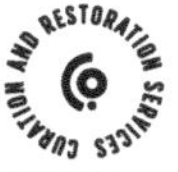

INDUSTRY STD

VAULTEDITIONS.COM

94

ABCDE
FGHI
JKLMN
OPQR
STUVW
XYZ

Vault Editions Ltd

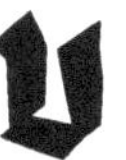

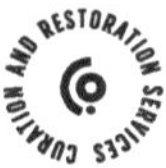

CURATION AND RESTORATION SERVICES

PRACTICE
MAKES
PERFECT
T R D · M R K

INDUSTRY STD

VAULTEDITIONS.COM

95

ABCDEFGHIJKL
MNOPQRSTUVW
XYZ 123456789

Vault Editions Ltd

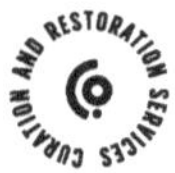

CREATION AND RESTORATION SERVICES CO.

PRACTICE
MAKES
PERFECT
TRD · MRK

INDUSTRY STD

VAULTEDITIONS.COM

abcdefghijklmn
opqrstuvwxy&
§@©/¶ß¢

A HIGH RESOLUTION FILE OF THIS SPECIMEN SHEET CAN BE DOWNLOADED FROM THE VAULT EDITIONS' WEBSITE.

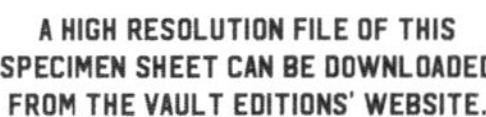

Vault Editions Ltd

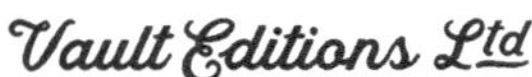
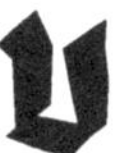
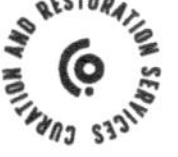

PRACTICE MAKES PERFECT

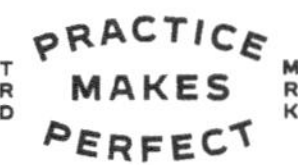

INDUSTRY STD

VAULTEDITIONS.COM

97

ABCDEFGHIJ
KLMNOPQRST
UVWXYZ &?!¿¡;,'

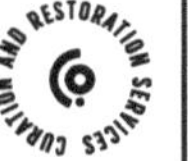

SIGN PAINTER
LETTERING ARTISTS
REFERENCE BOOK

abcdefghijkl
mnopqrstuv
wxyz

Vault Editions Ltd

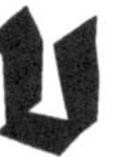

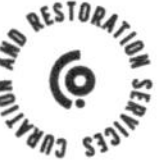

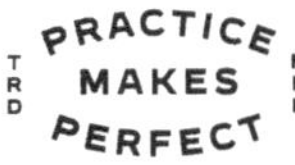

INDUSTRY STD

VAULTEDITIONS.COM

99

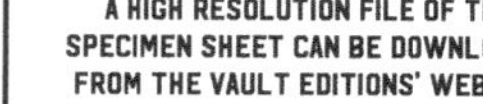

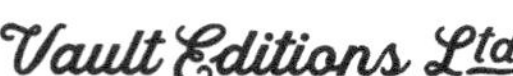

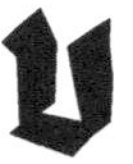

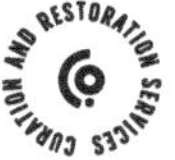

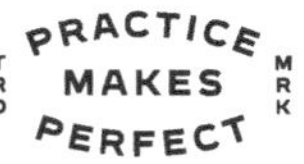

INDUSTRY STD

VAULTEDITIONS.COM

.DESIGNER.
J. G. BISSELL

THE SIGN PAINTER
LETTERING
ARTISTS'
REFERENCE BOOK

.TYPEFACE.
SINGLE STROKE
ALPHABET

LOWER CASE & NUMERALS ⟷ WEIGHT: REGULAR ⟷ PUBLISHED: 1913

abcdefghijkl
mnopqrstuvw
xyz 123456789 $¢

Vault Editions Ltd

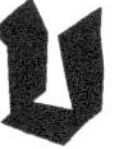
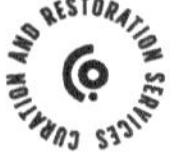

CURATION AND RESTORATION SERVICES

PRACTICE MAKES PERFECT
TRD · MRK

INDUSTRY STD

VAULTEDITIONS.COM

101

A B C D E
F G H I J
K L M N O
P Q R S T
U V W X Y
Z & S R H

Vault Editions Ltd

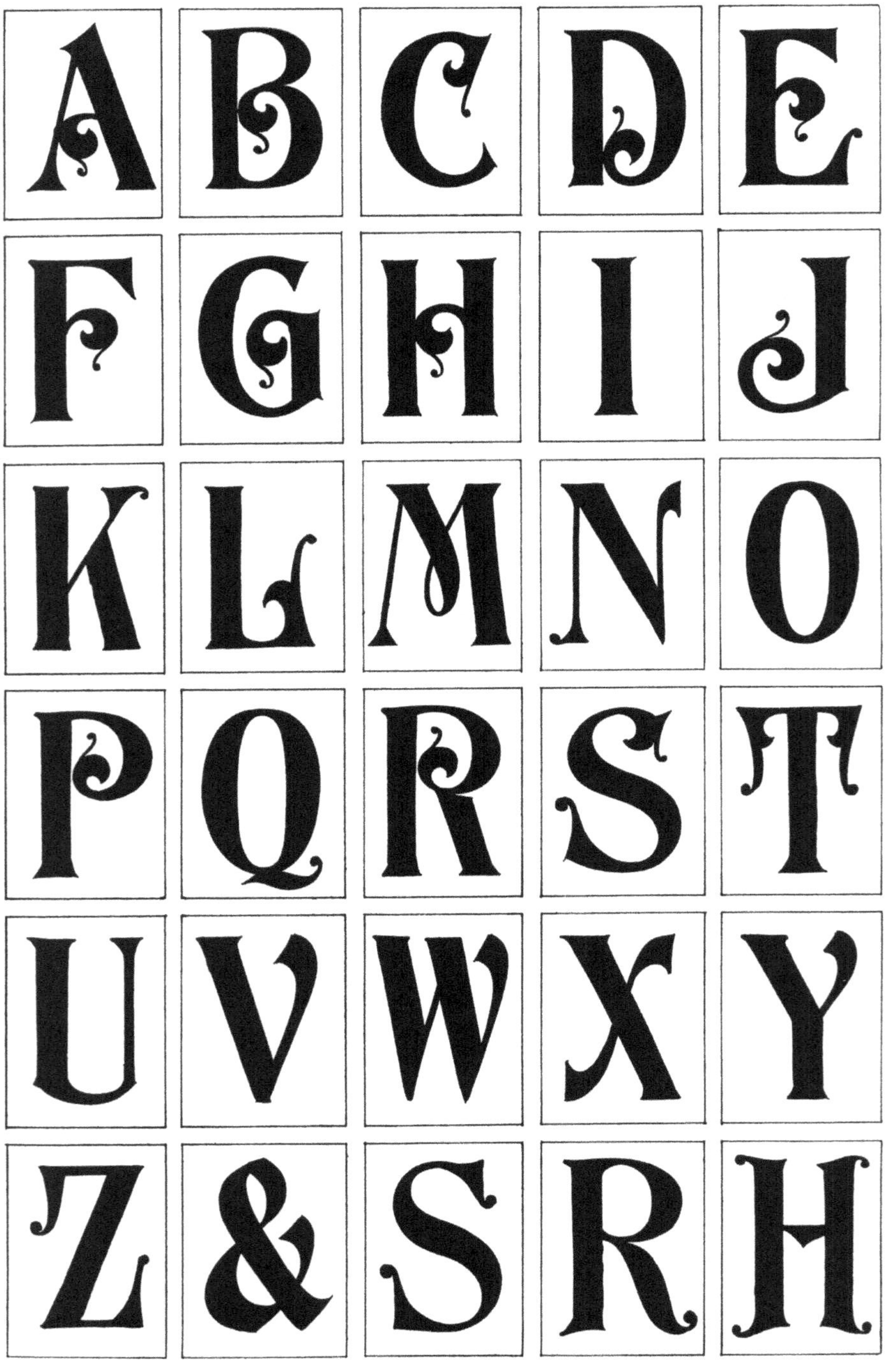

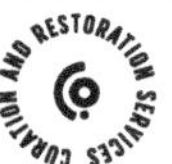

CURATION AND RESTORATION SERVICES

PRACTICE MAKES PERFECT

INDUSTRY STD

VAULTEDITIONS.COM

102

 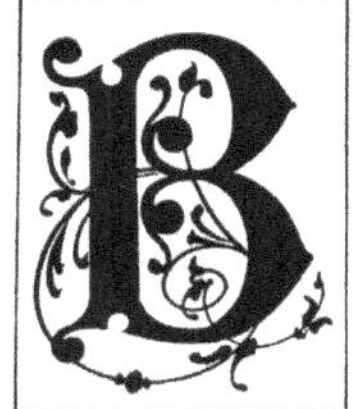 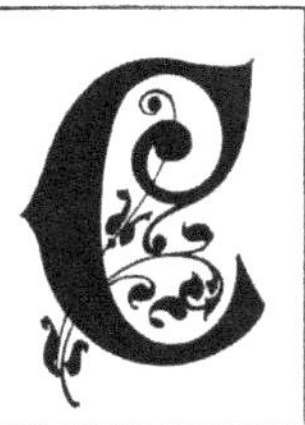 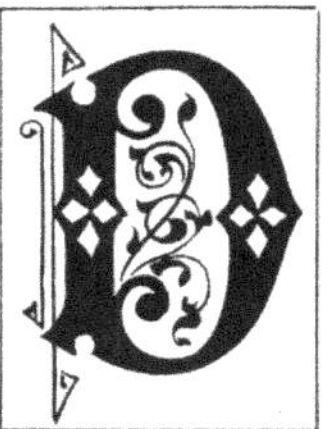 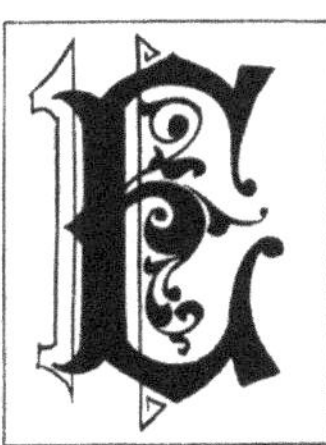
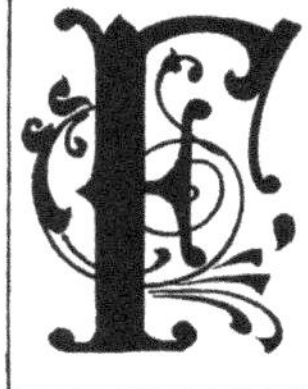 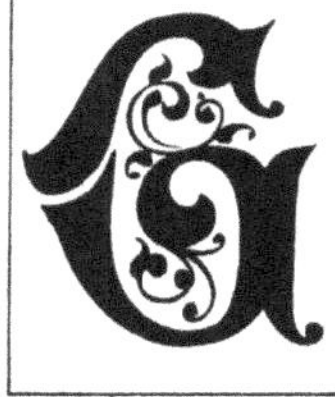 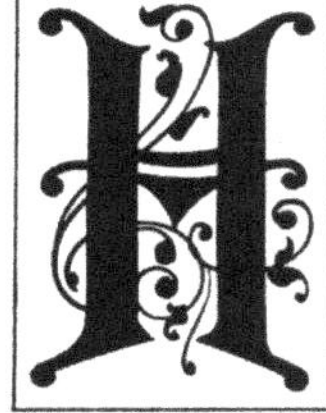 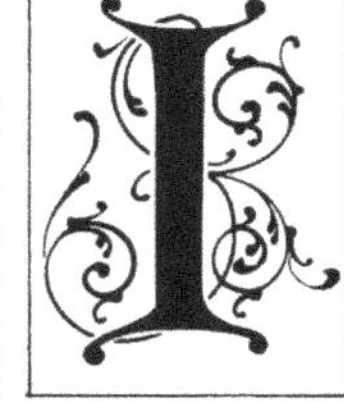 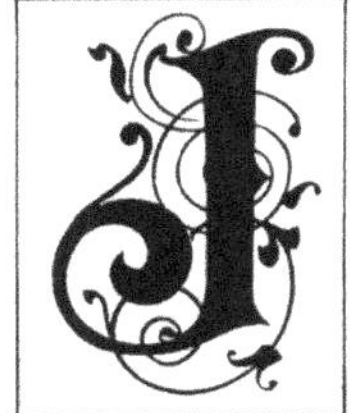
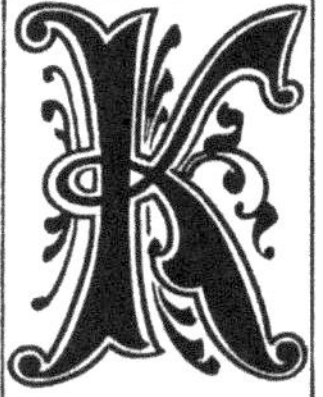 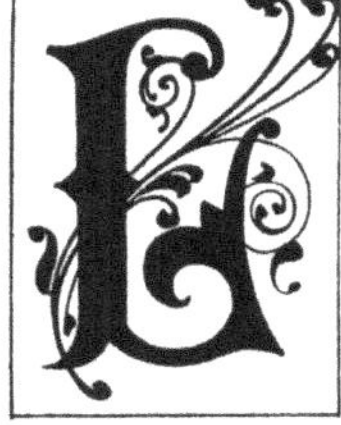 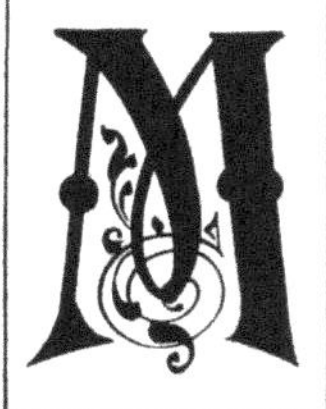 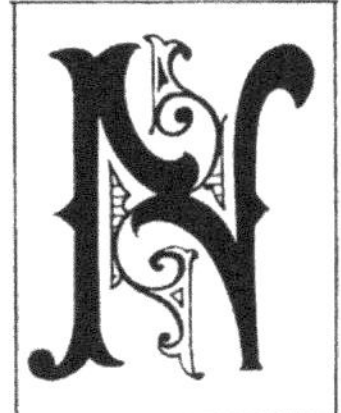 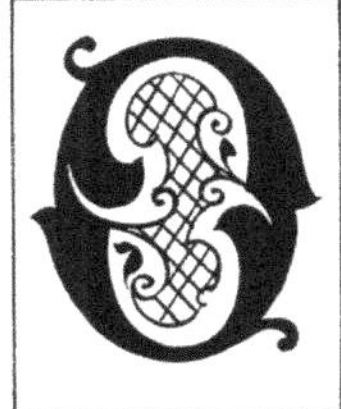
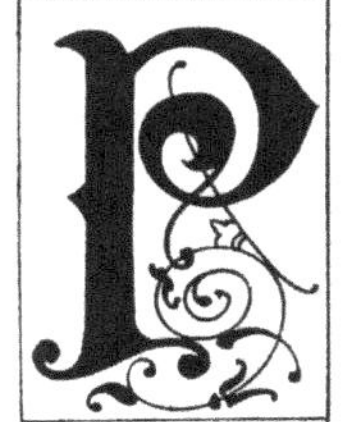 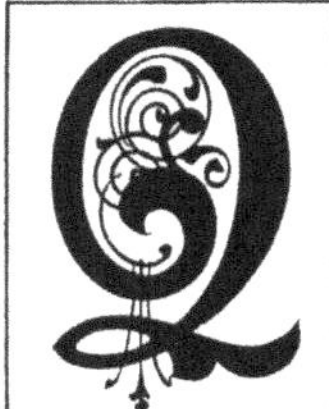 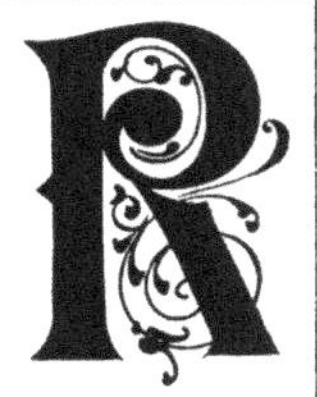  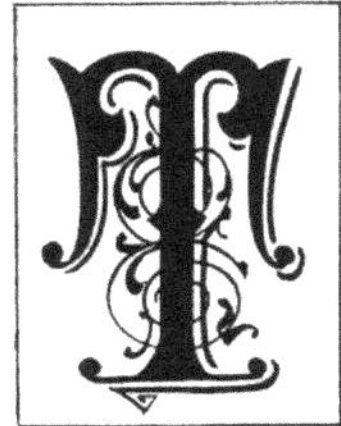
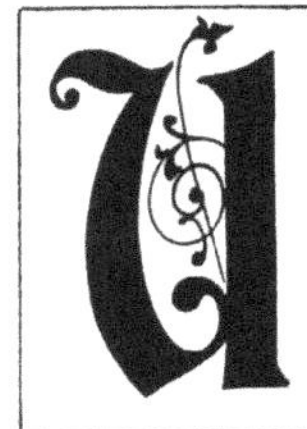  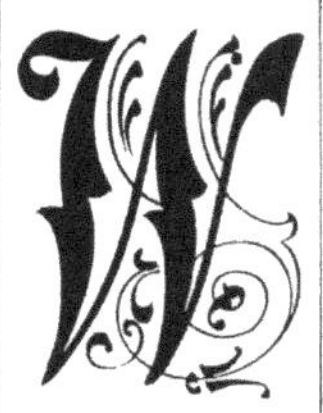  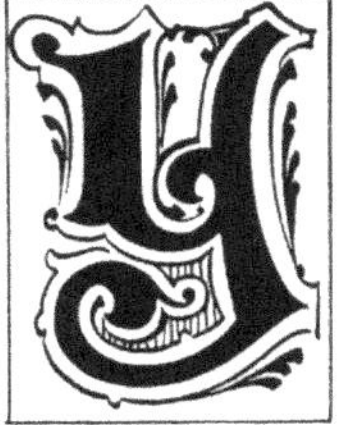
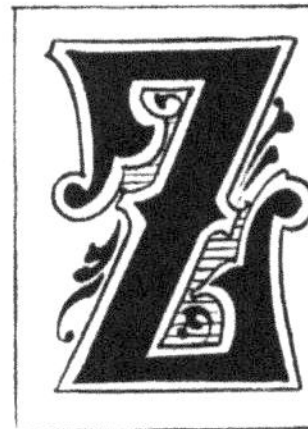 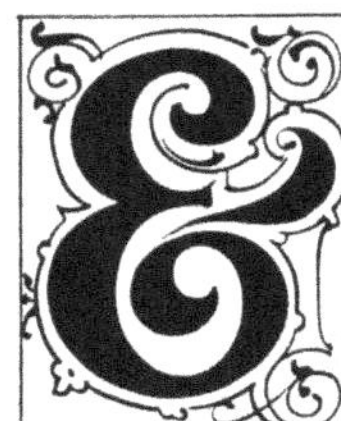 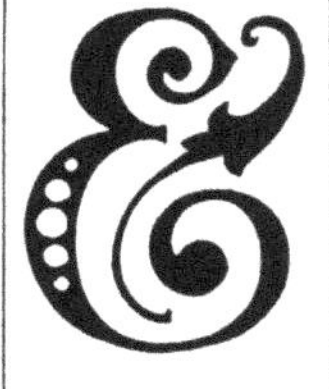 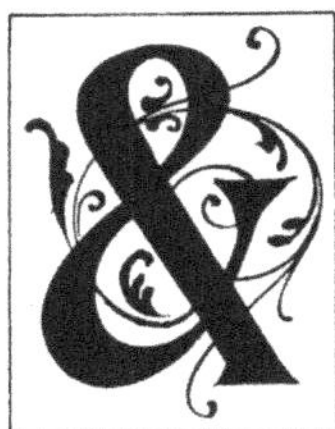 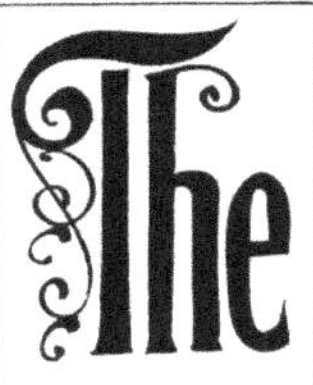

103

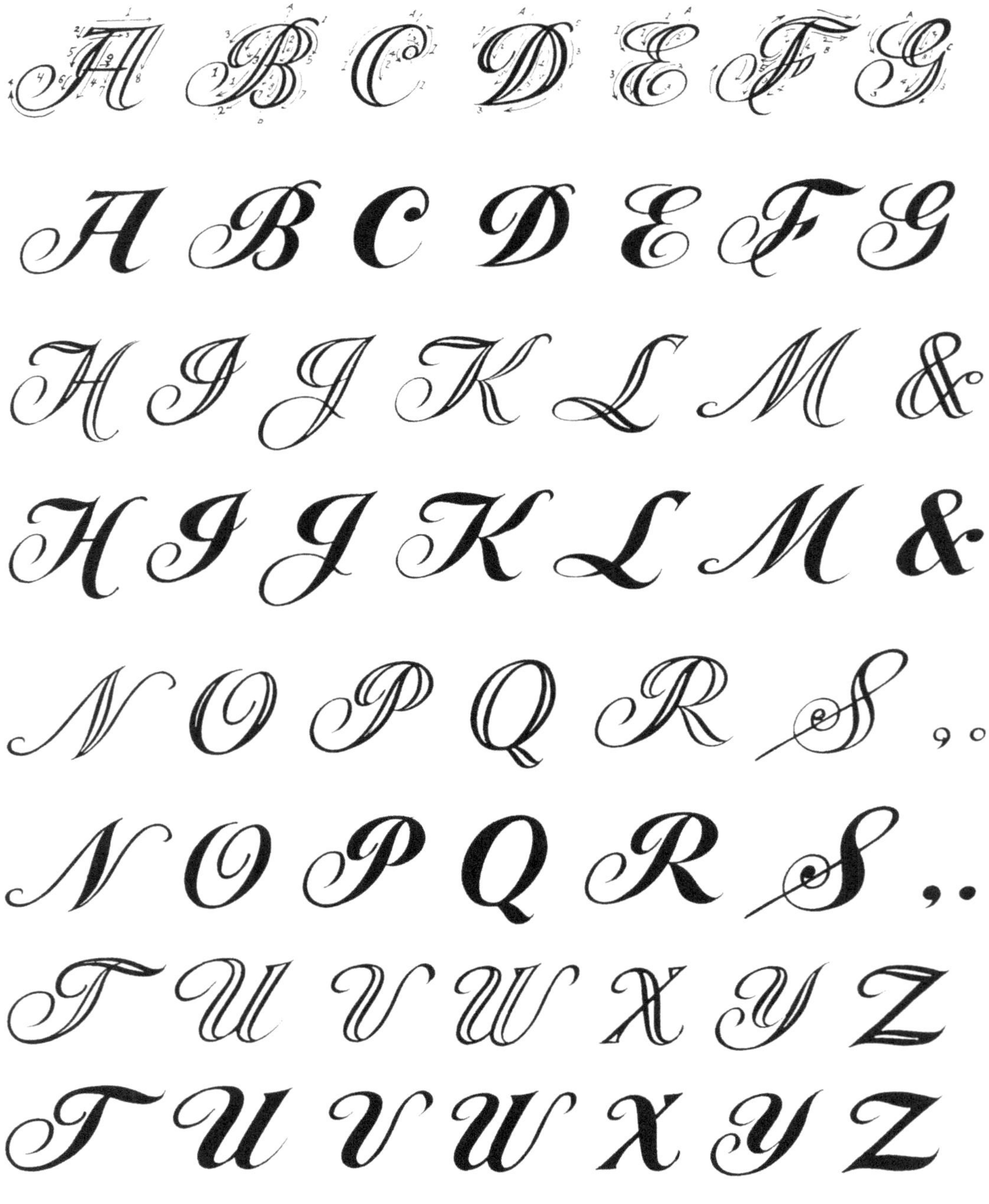

A B C D E F G

A B C D E F G

H I J K L M &

H I J K L M &

N O P Q R S ,.

N O P Q R S ,.

T U V W X Y Z

T U V W X Y Z

Vault Editions Ltd

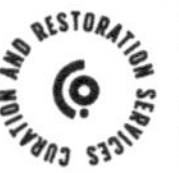

PRACTICE MAKES PERFECT

INDUSTRY STD

VAULTEDITIONS.COM

104

a b c d e f g

a b c d e f g

h i j k l m n

h i j k l m n

o p q r s t

o p q r s t

u v w x y z

u v w x y z

Vault Editions Ltd

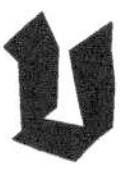

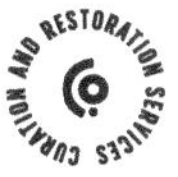

CURATION AND RESTORATION SERVICES

PRACTICE MAKES PERFECT

INDUSTRY STD

VAULTEDITIONS.COM

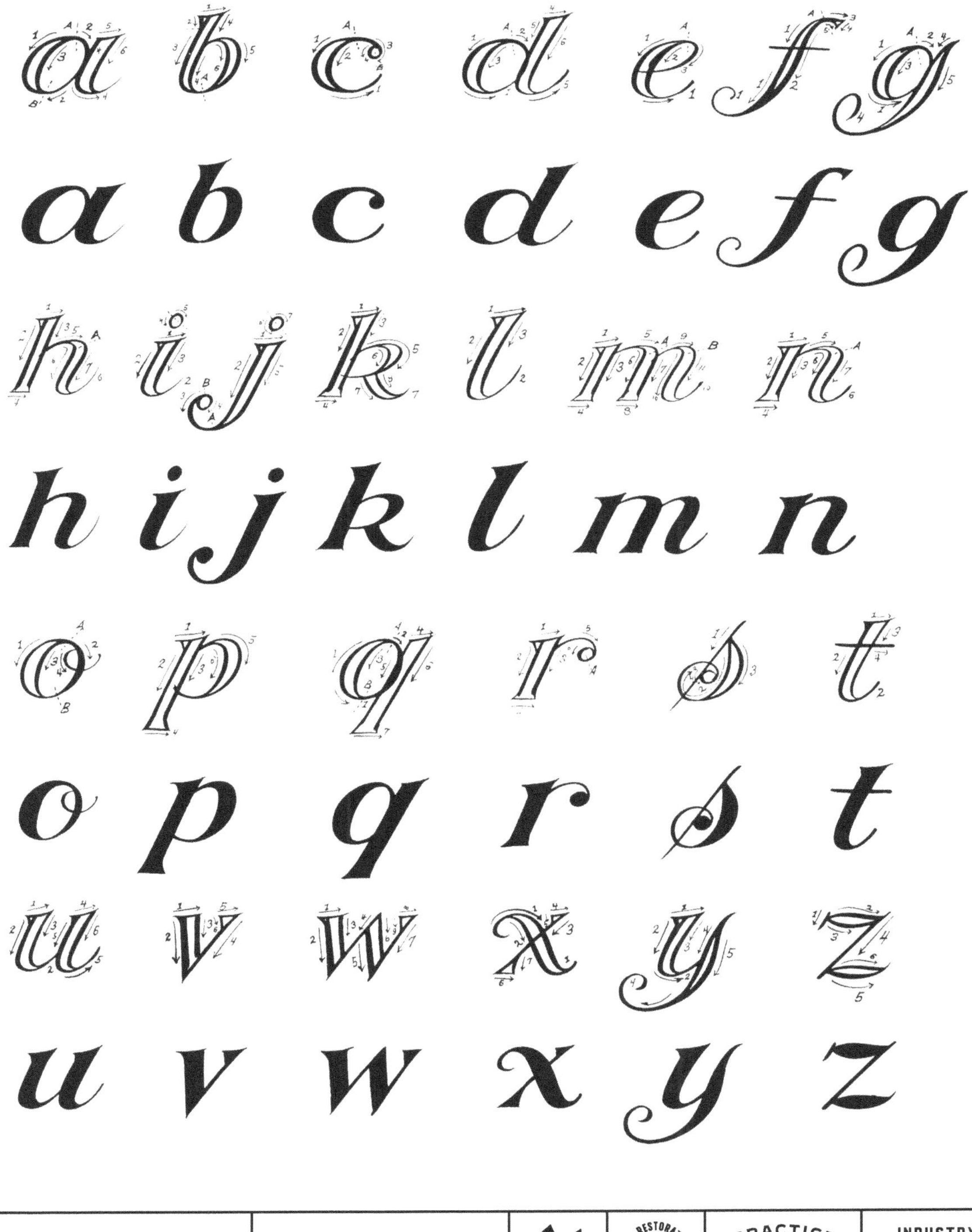

105

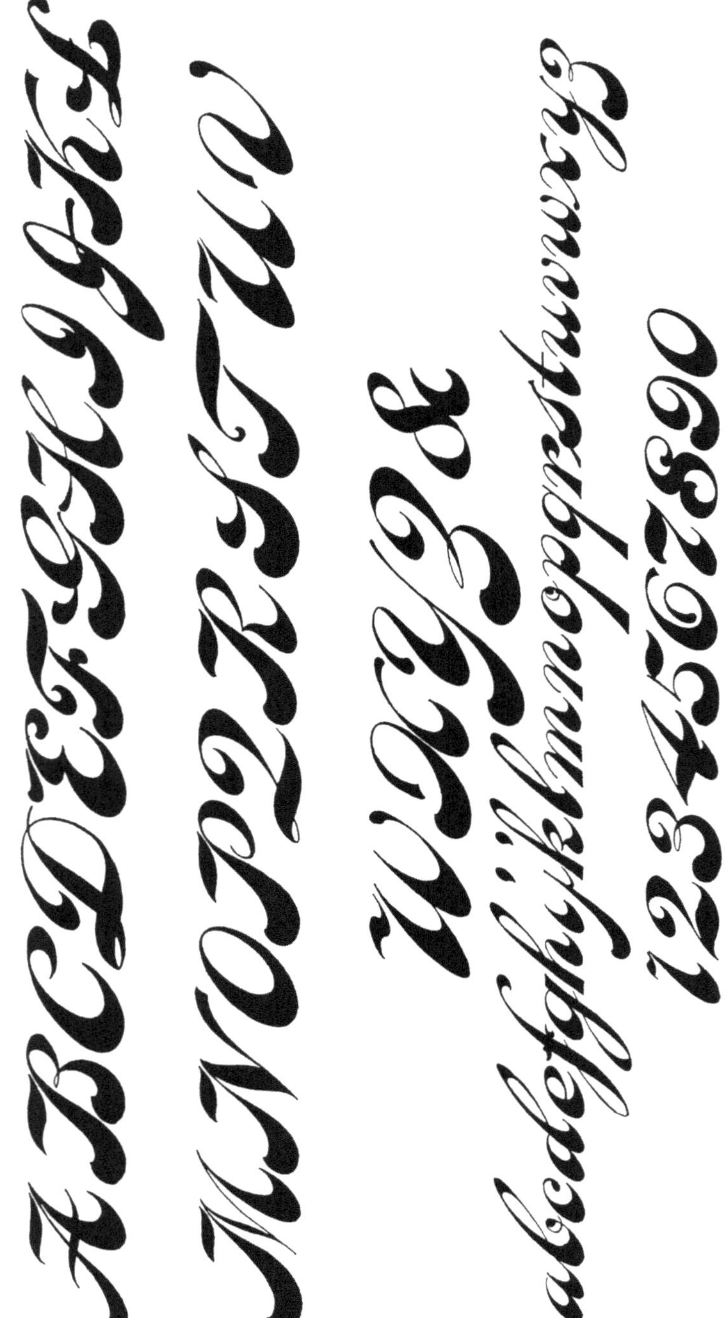

Vault Editions Ltd

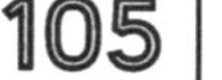

CURATION AND RESTORATION SERVICES

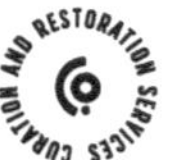

PRACTICE MAKES PERFECT
T·R·D   M·R·K

INDUSTRY STD

VAULTEDITIONS.COM

.SIGN PAINTER.
LETTERING ARTIST'S
REFERENCE BOOK

ABCDEF
GHIJKLMN
OPQRST
UVWXYZ&

A HIGH RESOLUTION FILE OF THIS
SPECIMEN SHEET CAN BE DOWNLOADED
FROM THE VAULT EDITIONS' WEBSITE.

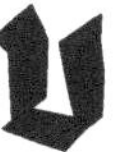
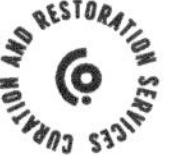

Vault Editions Ltd

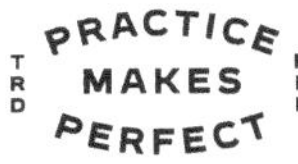

CURATION AND RESTORATION SERVICES

PRACTICE
MAKES
PERFECT
T·R·D M·R·K

INDUSTRY STD

VAULTEDITIONS.COM

107

Vault Editions Ltd

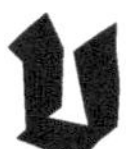

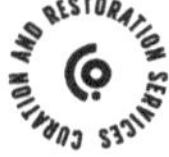

PRACTICE MAKES PERFECT
T R D   M R K

INDUSTRY STD

VAULTEDITIONS.COM

Vault Editions Ltd

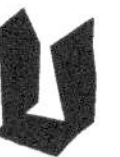
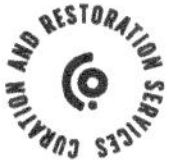
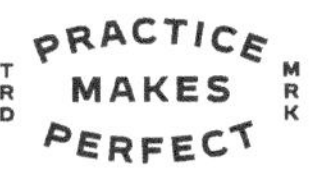

PRACTICE MAKES PERFECT

INDUSTRY STD

VAULTEDITIONS.COM

109

ABCDEFGHIJ
KLMNOPQRS
TUVWXYZ-&
123456789

Vault Editions Ltd

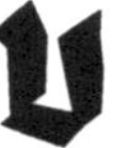

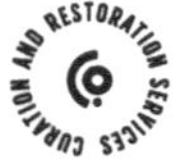

CURATION AND RESTORATION SERVICES

PRACTICE MAKES PERFECT
TRD MRK

INDUSTRY STD

VAULTEDITIONS.COM

ABCDEFGH
IJKLMNOPQ
RSTUVWX
1234567890&YZ

Vault Editions Ltd

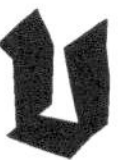
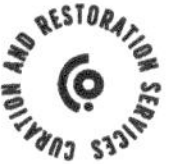

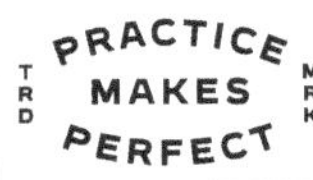

INDUSTRY STD

VAULTEDITIONS.COM

·DESIGNER·
CHARLES JAY STRONG

THE SIGN PAINTER ERA
LETTERING ARTIST'S
REFERENCE BOOK

·TYPEFACE·
ANTIQUE HALF BLOCK

UPPER | LOWER | NUMERALS ←→ WEIGHT: REGULAR ←→ PUBLISHED: C. 1900

ABCDEFGHIJKL
MNOPQRSTUVWX
YZ
1234567890
&
abcdefghijklmn
opqrstuvwxyz

Vault Editions Ltd

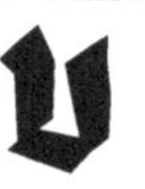
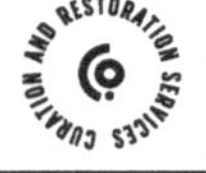

CURATION AND RESTORATION SERVICES

PRACTICE MAKES PERFECT
TRD   MRK

INDUSTRY STD

VAULTEDITIONS.COM

·DESIGNER·

CHARLES JAY STRONG

SIGN PAINTER

LETTERING ARTISTS'

REFERENCE BOOK

·TYPEFACE·

SPUR EGYPTIAN

UPPER | LOWER | NUMERALS   WEIGHT: REGULAR   PUBLISHED: C. 1900

ABCDEFGHIJKL
MNOPQRSTUVWX
YZ 6789
12345 67

abcdefghijklmn
opqrstuvwxyz
&

A HIGH RESOLUTION FILE OF THIS SPECIMEN SHEET CAN BE DOWNLOADED FROM THE VAULT EDITIONS' WEBSITE.

Vault Editions Ltd

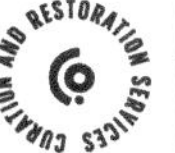

CURATION AND RESTORATION SERVICES

PRACTICE MAKES PERFECT

INDUSTRY STD

VAULTEDITIONS.COM

113

ABCDEFGHI
JKLMNOPQR
STUVWXYZ&
123456789

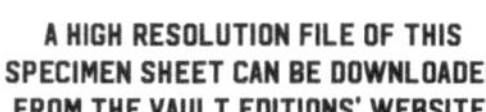

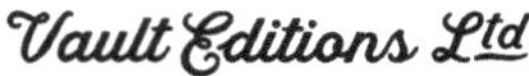

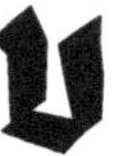

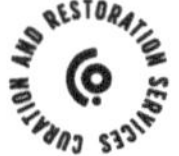

114

ABCDEFGHI
JKLMNOPQR
STUVWXYZ&
123456789

Vault Editions Ltd

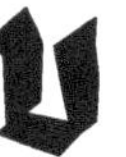

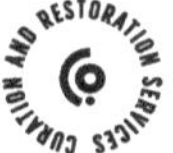

CURATION AND RESTORATION SERVICES

PRACTICE MAKES PERFECT
TRD · MRK

INDUSTRY STD

VAULTEDITIONS.COM

115

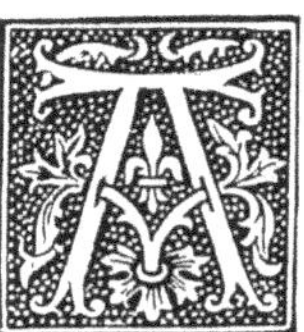 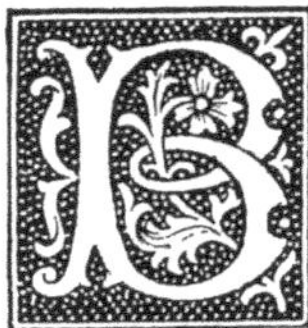 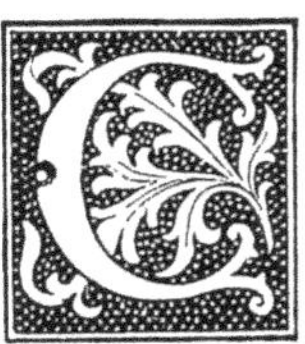  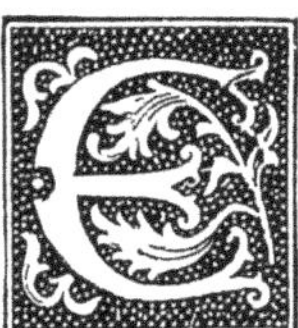

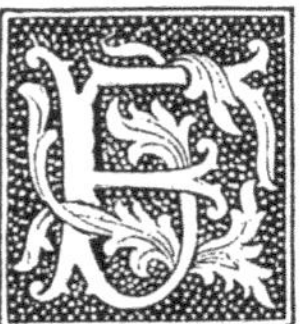  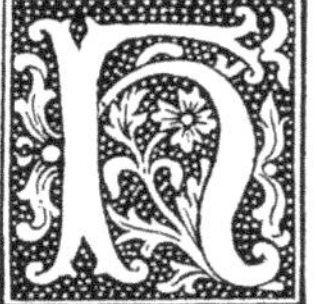 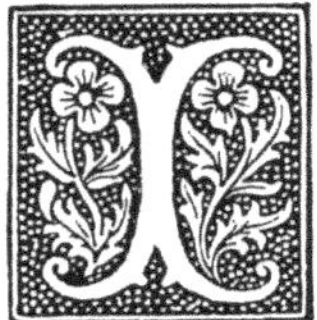 

 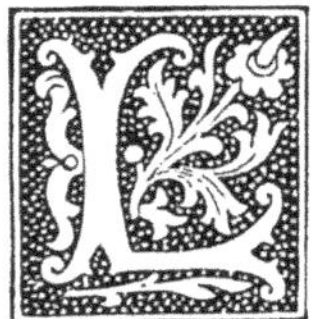 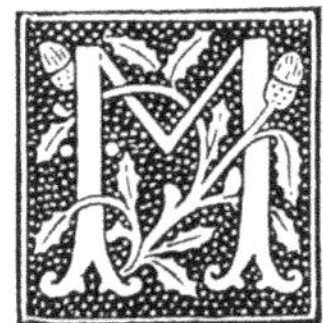  

 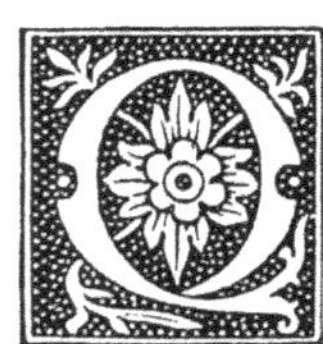 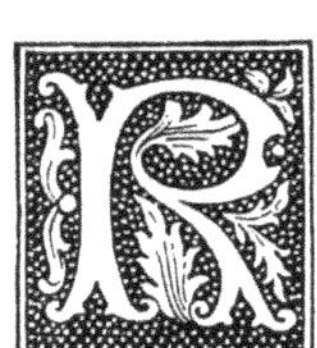 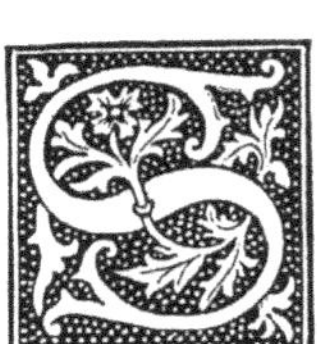 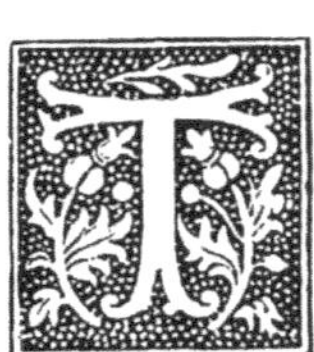

  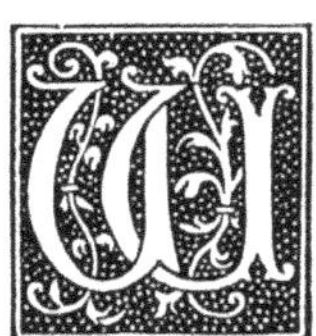 

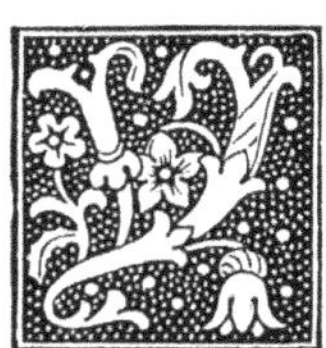 

Vault Editions Ltd

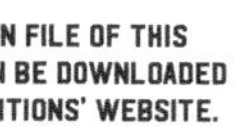

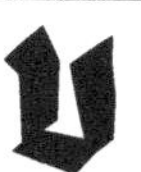 CORATION AND RESTORATION SERVICES

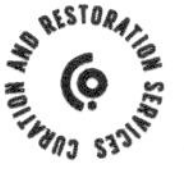

PRACTICE
MAKES
PERFECT
TRD **MRK**

INDUSTRY STD

VAULTEDITIONS.COM

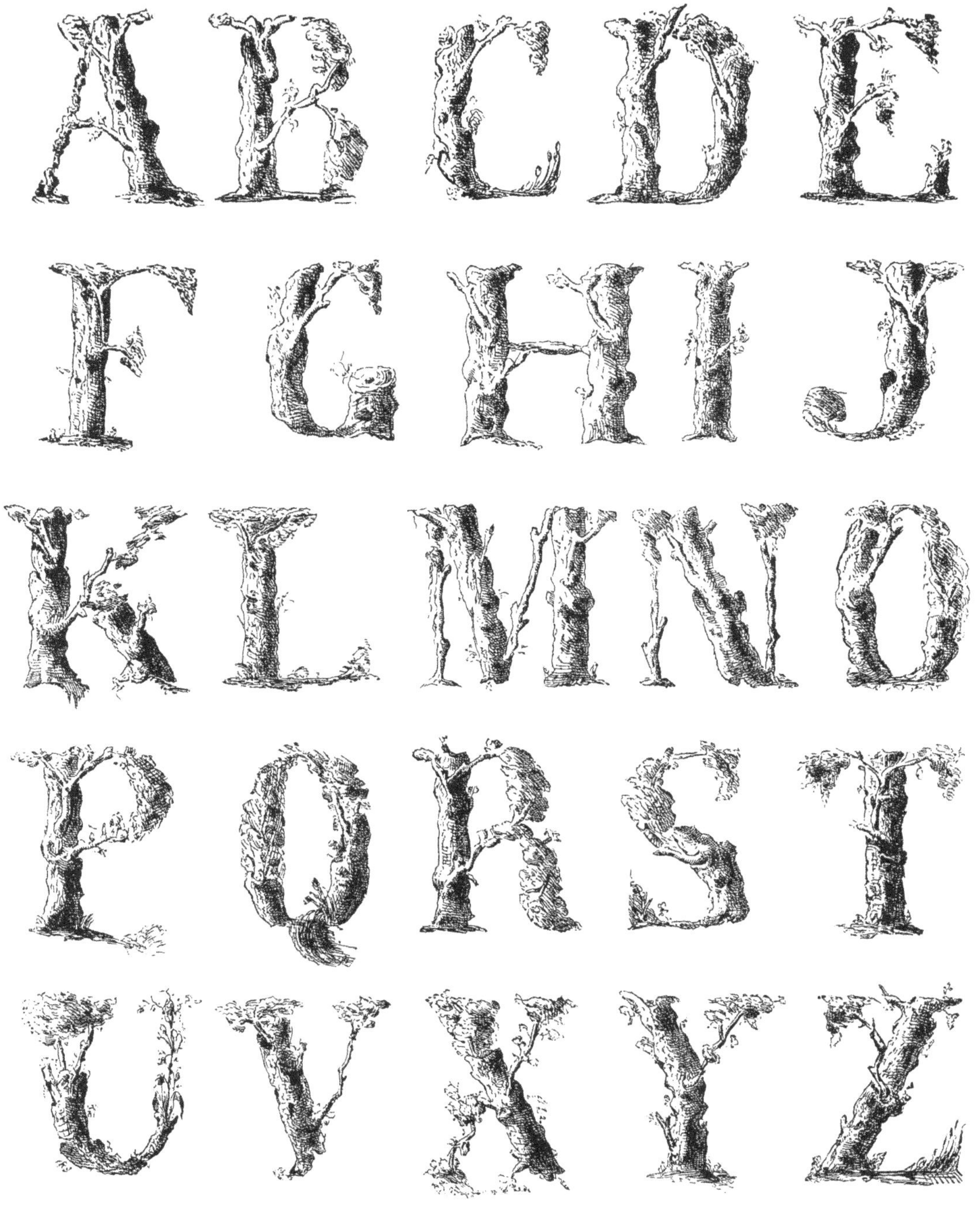

A B C D E

F G H I J

K L M N O

P Q R S T

U V X Y Z

UPPER CASE | **WEIGHT: REGULAR** | **PUBLISHED: 1878**

117

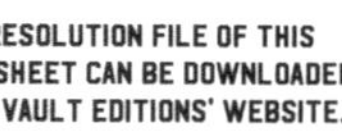

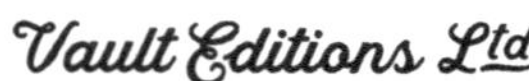

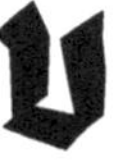

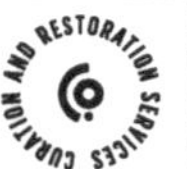

INDUSTRY STD

VAULTEDITIONS.COM

118

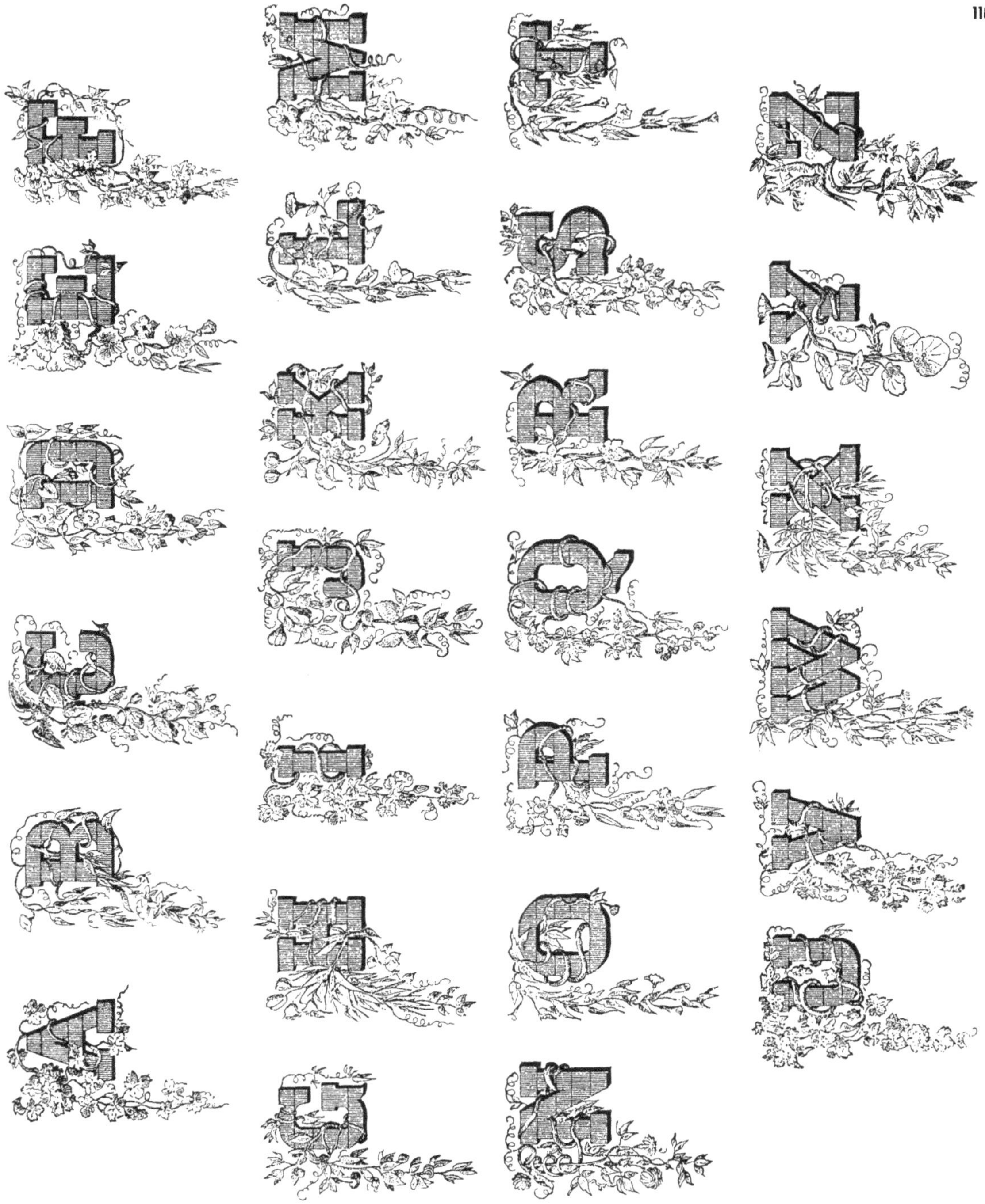

119

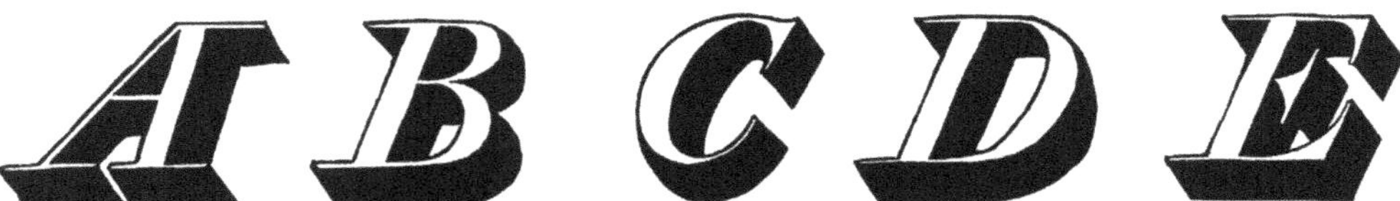

F G H I J K

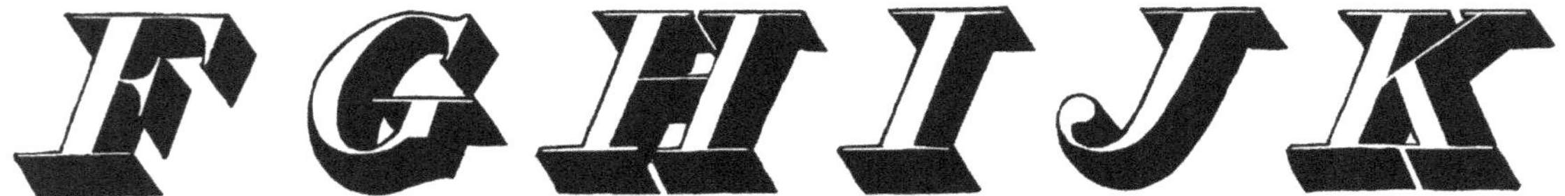

Q R S T U

V W X Y Z.

Vault Editions Ltd

CURATION AND RESTORATION SERVICES

PRACTICE
MAKES
PERFECT
TRD · MRK

INDUSTRY STD

VAULTEDITIONS.COM

SIGN PAINTER
LETTERING ARTISTS
REFERENCE BOOK

UPPER CASE · WEIGHT: REGULAR · PUBLISHED: 1845

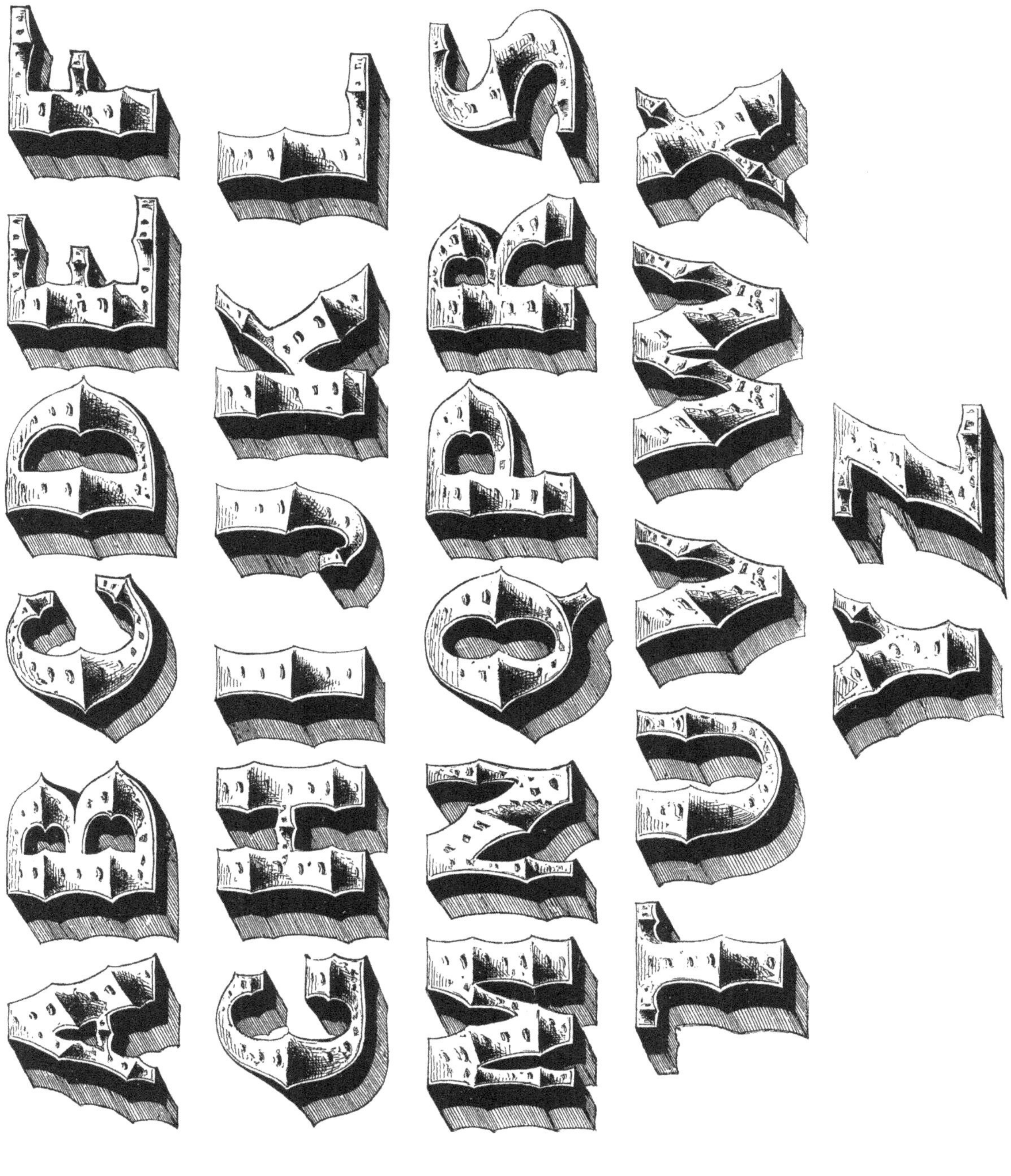

A HIGH RESOLUTION FILE OF THIS
SPECIMEN SHEET CAN BE DOWNLOADED
FROM THE VAULT EDITIONS' WEBSITE.

Vault Editions Ltd

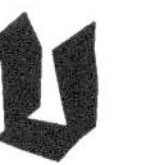

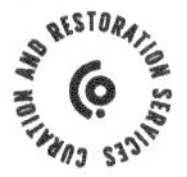

INDUSTRY STD

VAULTEDITIONS.COM

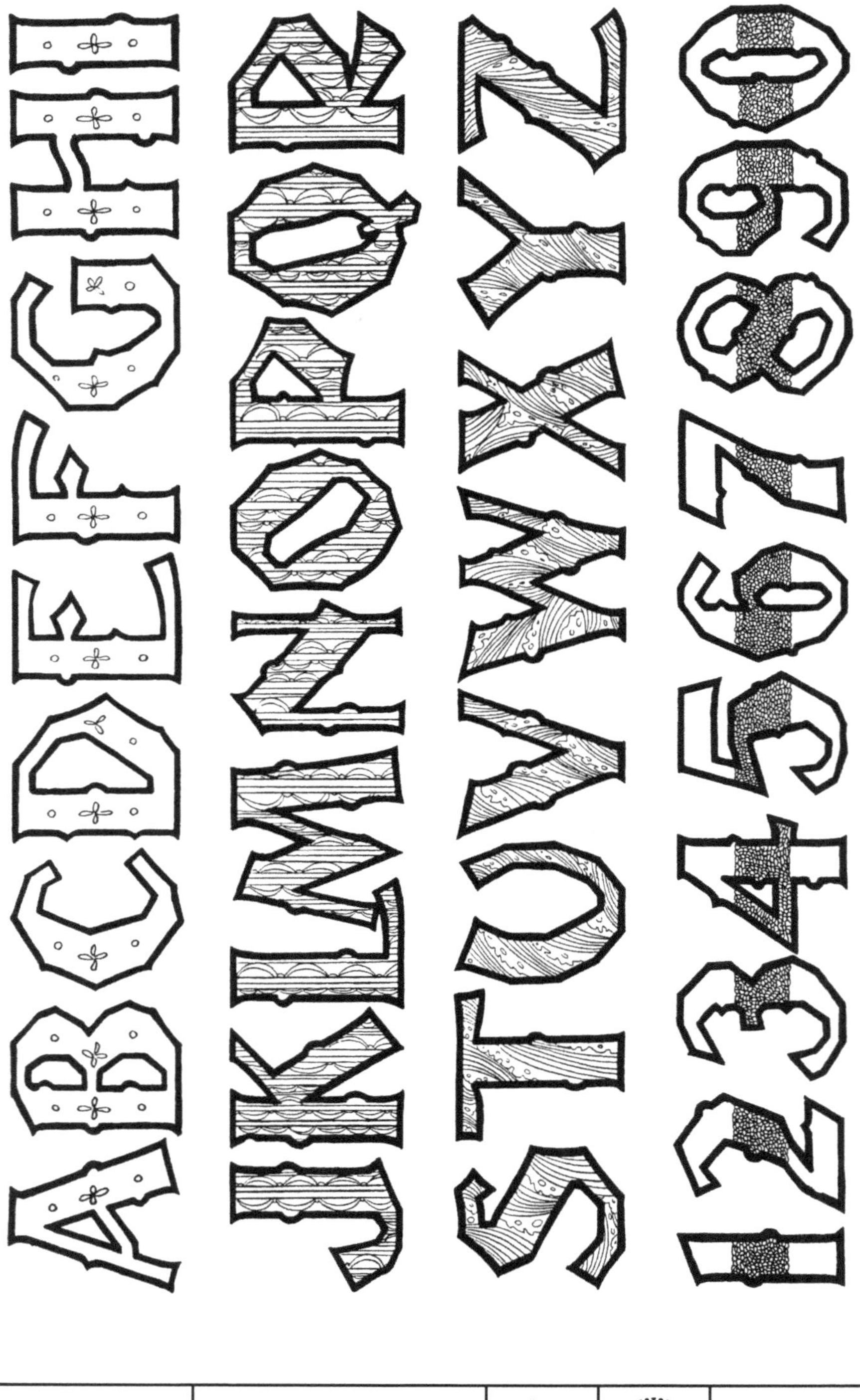

121

ABCDEFGHI
JKLMNOPQR
STUVWXYZ
1234567890

Vault Editions Ltd

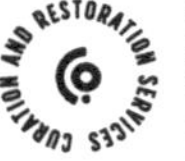

PRACTICE MAKES PERFECT
TRD · MRK

INDUSTRY STD

VAULTEDITIONS.COM

121

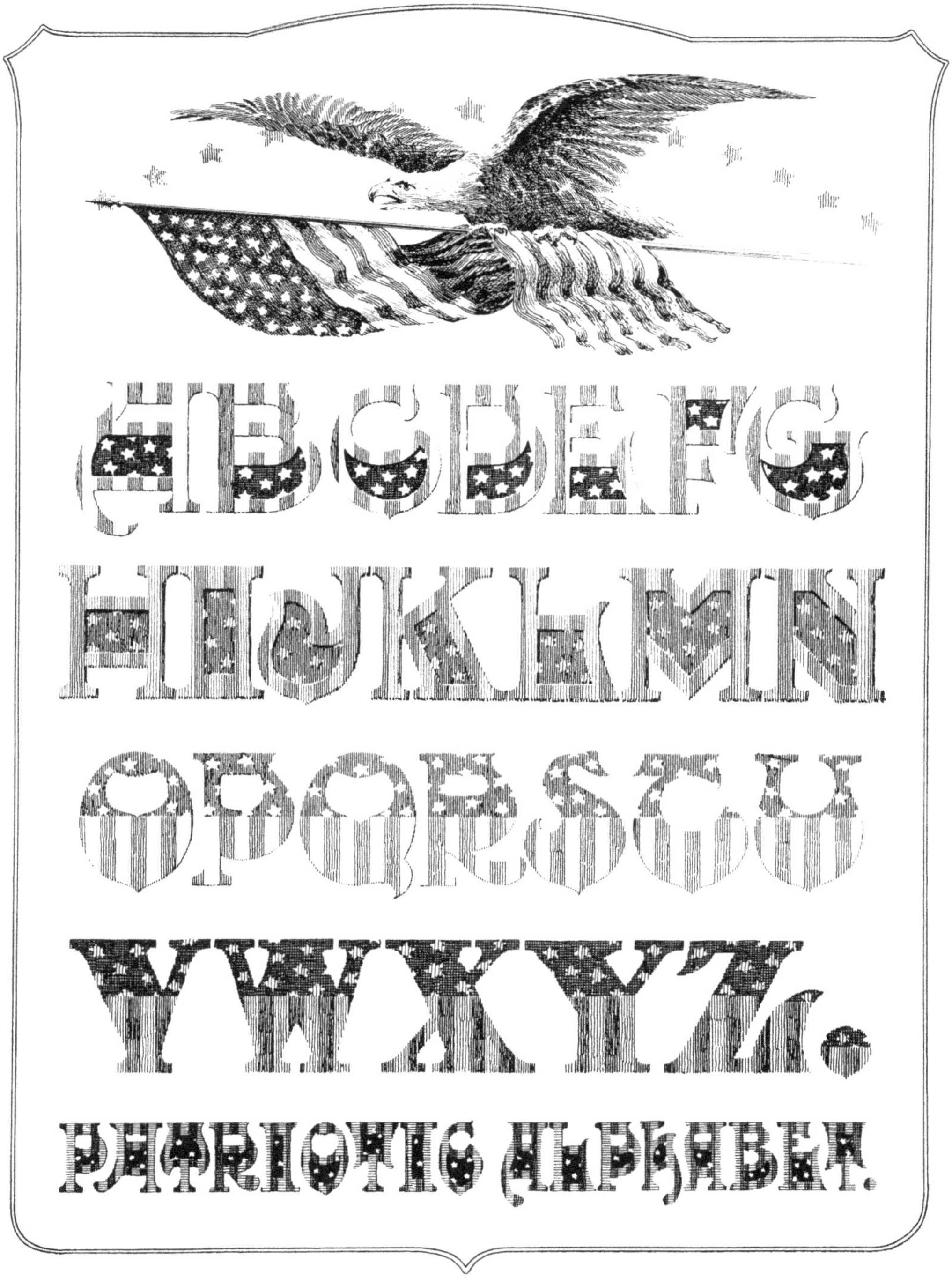

ABCDEFG
HIJKLMN
OPQRSTU
VWXYZ.
PATRIOTIC ALPHABET.

123

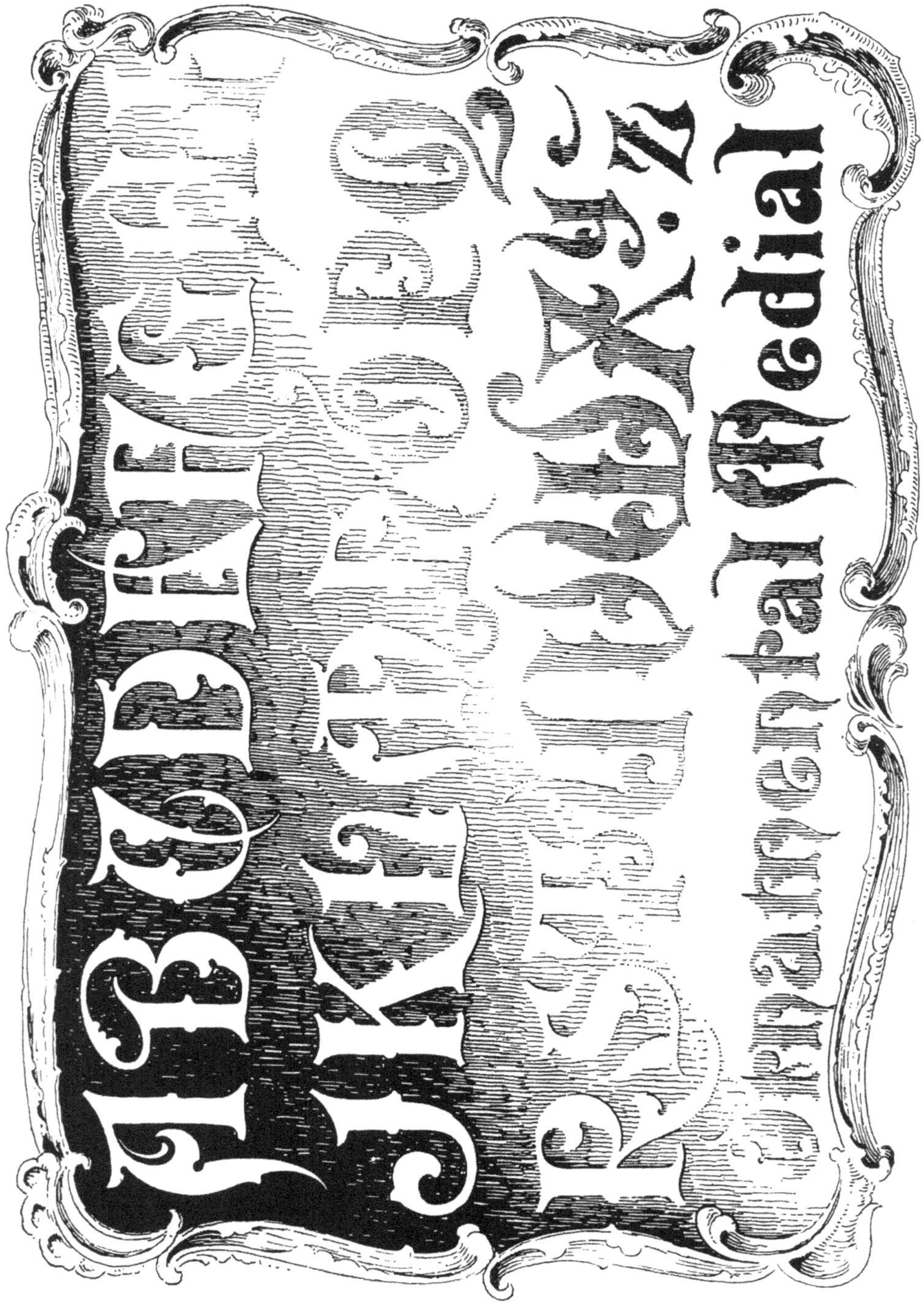

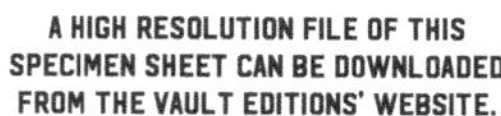

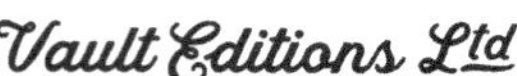
Vault Editions Ltd

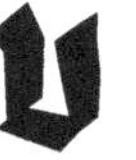

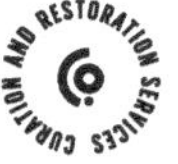
COATING AND RESTORATION SERVICES CO.

PRACTICE MAKES PERFECT
TRD MRK

INDUSTRY STD

VAULTEDITIONS.COM

124

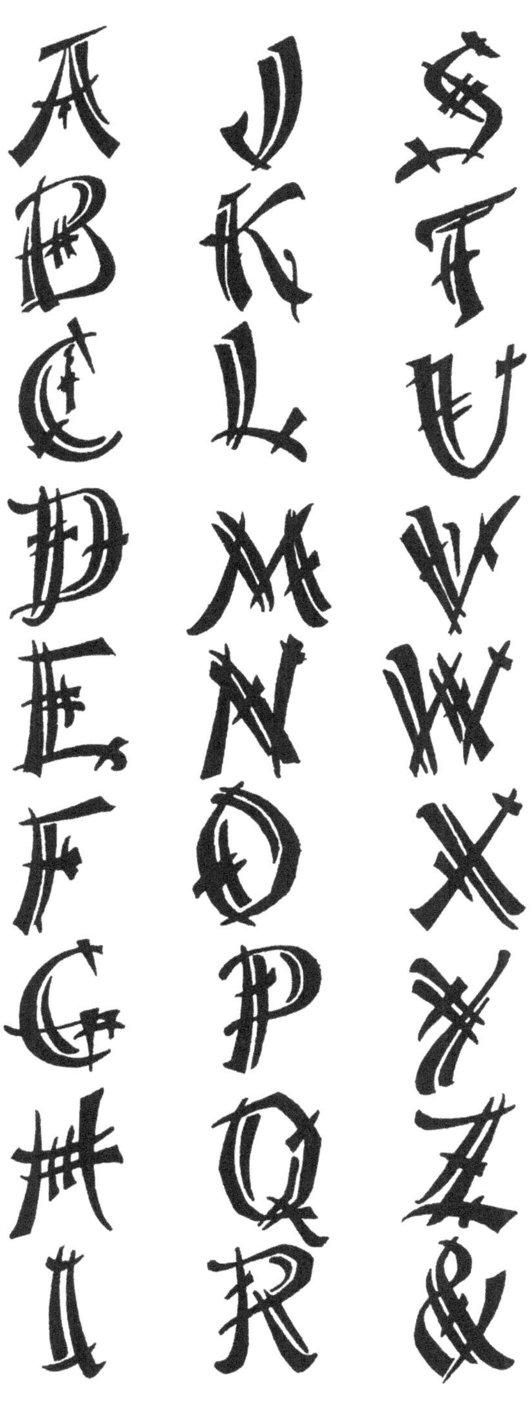

Vault Editions Ltd

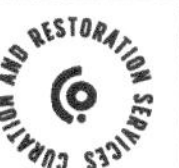

CURATION AND RESTORATION SERVICES

PRACTICE MAKES PERFECT

INDUSTRY STD

VAULTEDITIONS.COM

125

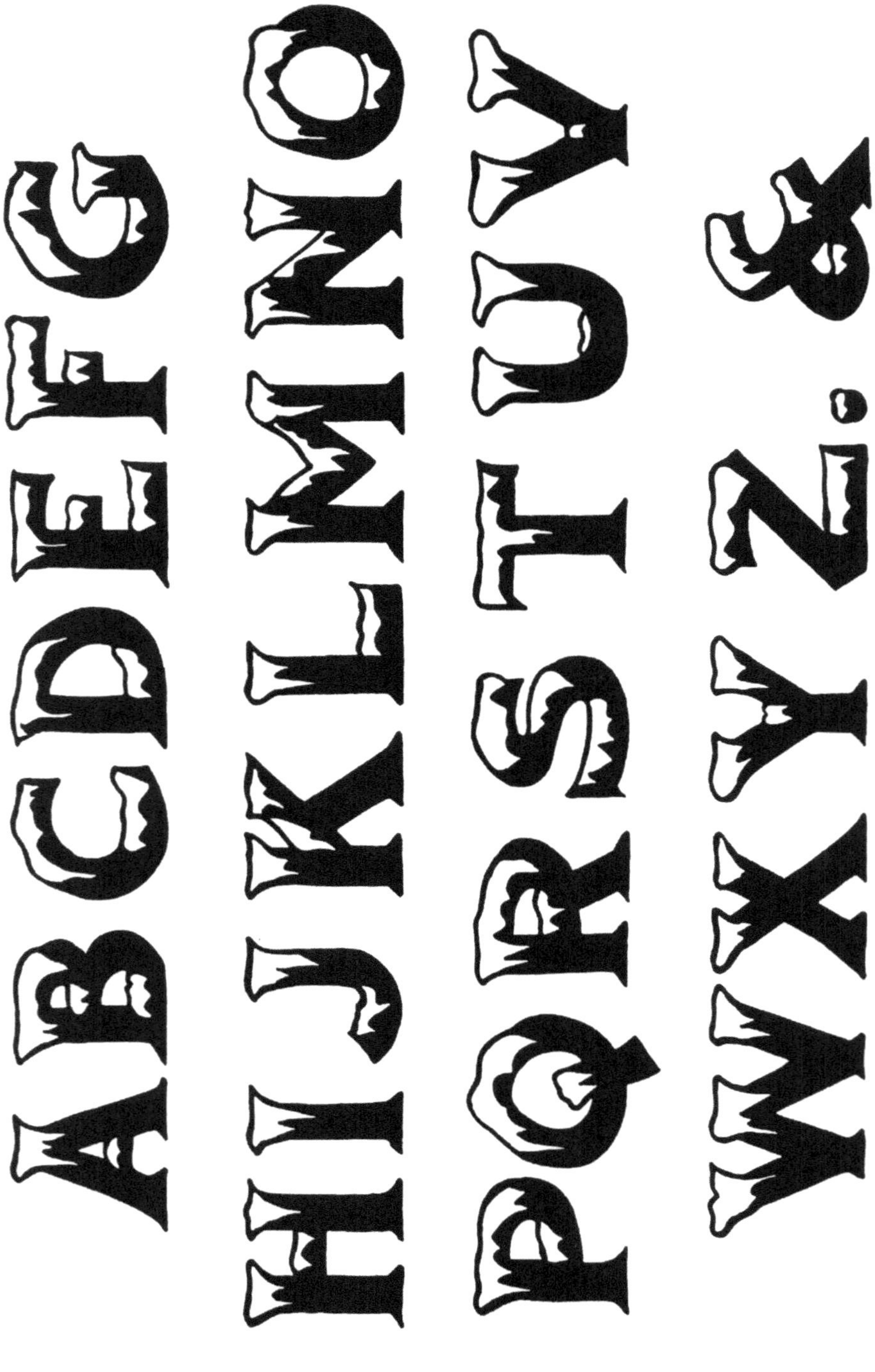

ABCDEFG
HIJKLMNO
PQRSTUV
WXYZ&.

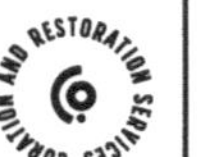

abcdefgh
ijklmn
opqrs
tuvwxyz

Snow-Capped

Vault Editions Ltd

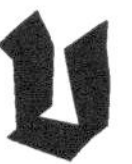

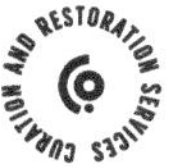

CURATION AND RESTORATION SERVICES

PRACTICE MAKES PERFECT
TRD · MRK

INDUSTRY STD

VAULTEDITIONS.COM

127

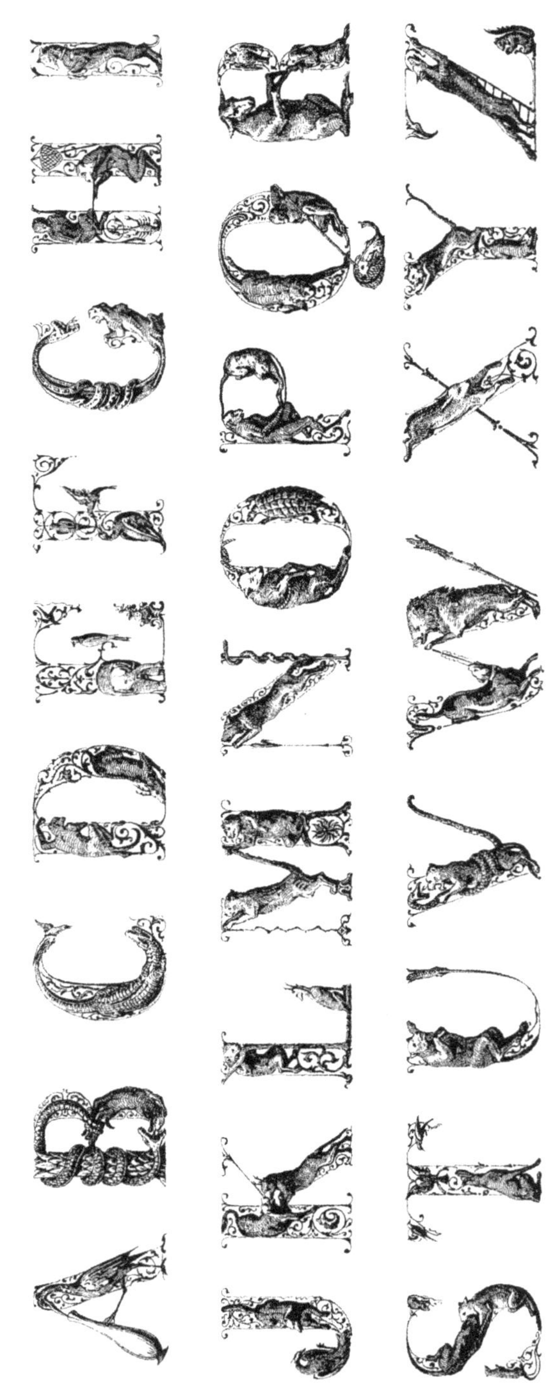

Vault Editions Ltd
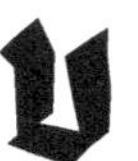
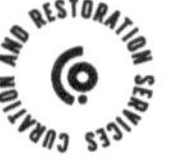
CURATION AND RESTORATION SERVICES

PRACTICE MAKES PERFECT

INDUSTRY STD
VAULTEDITIONS.COM

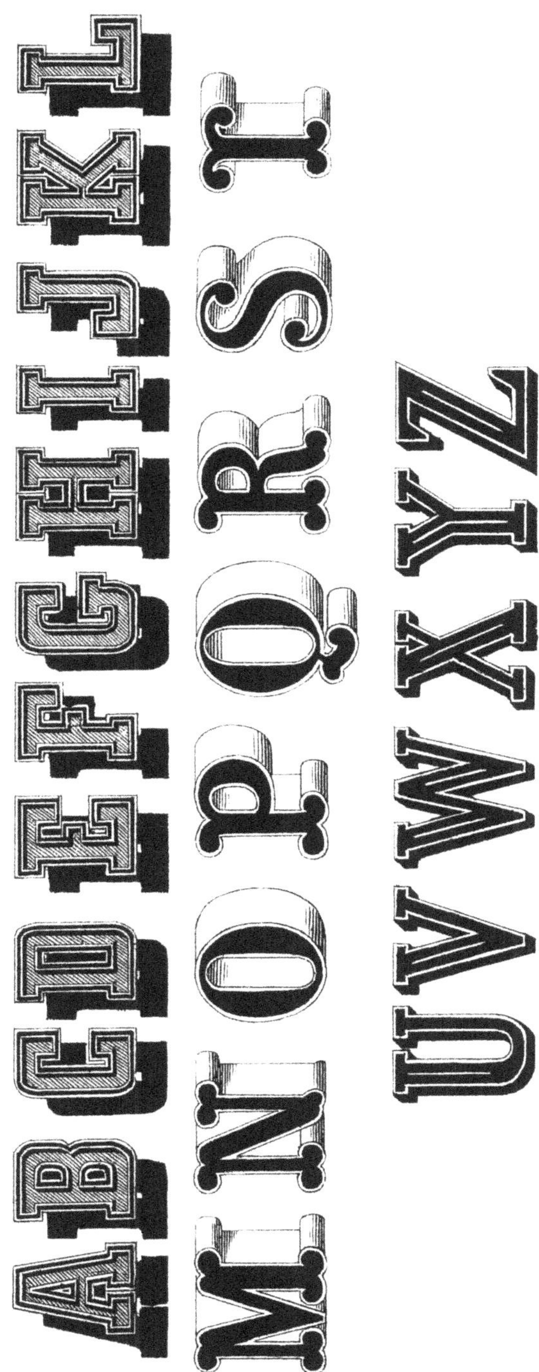

A HIGH RESOLUTION FILE OF THIS
SPECIMEN SHEET CAN BE DOWNLOADED
FROM THE VAULT EDITIONS' WEBSITE.

Vault Editions Ltd

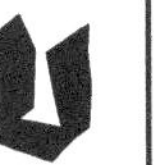
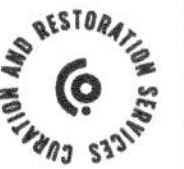

PRACTICE
MAKES
PERFECT

INDUSTRY STD

VAULTEDITIONS.COM

129

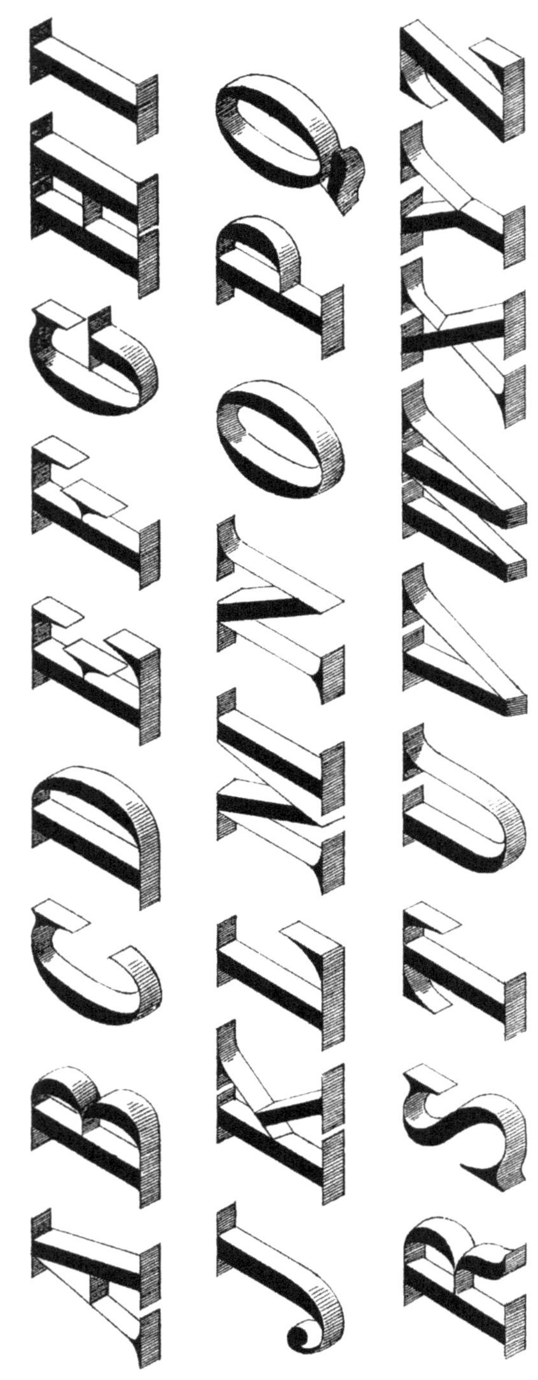

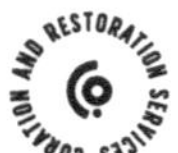

130

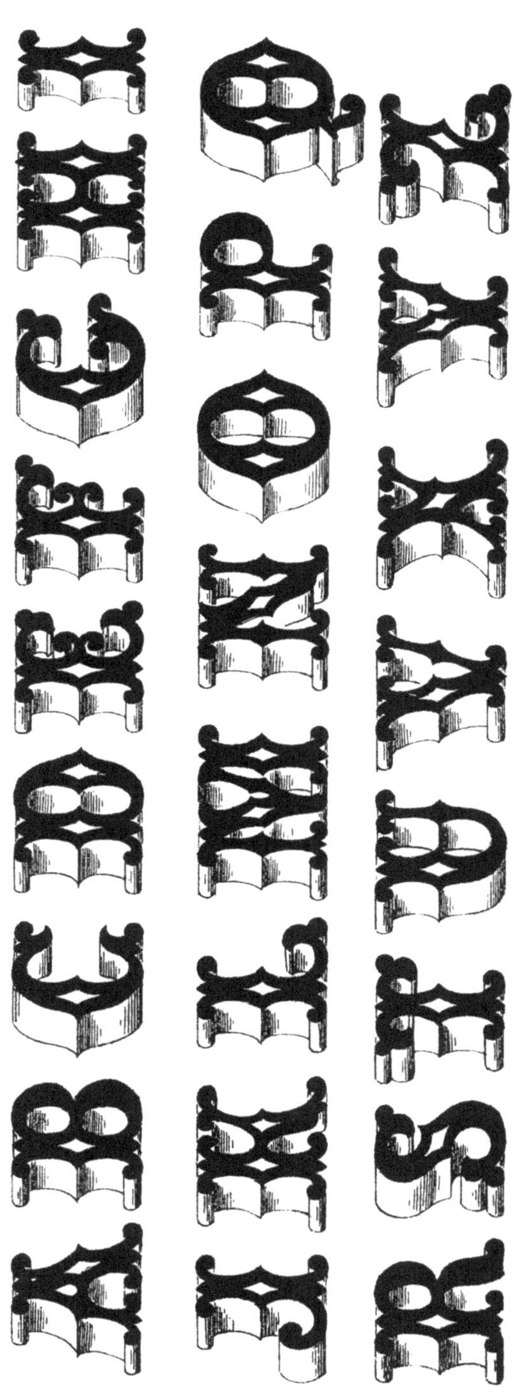

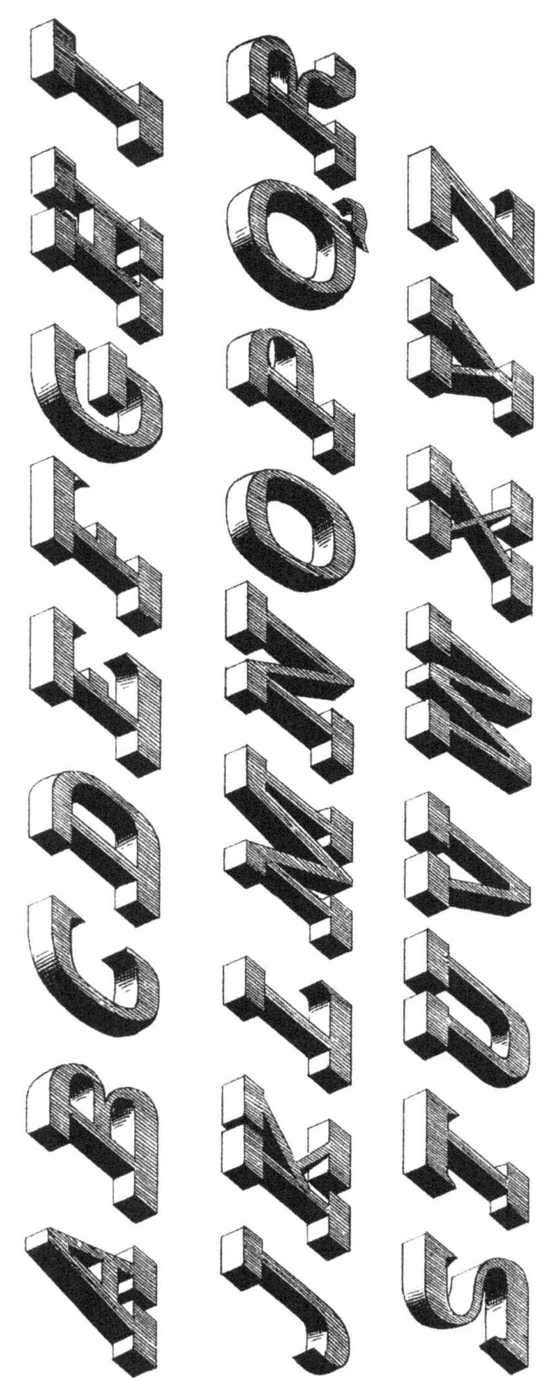

Vault Editions Ltd

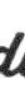

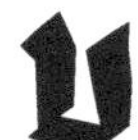

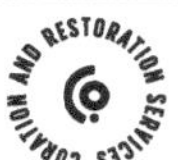
PRACTICE MAKES PERFECT

INDUSTRY STD

VAULTEDITIONS.COM

.DESIGNER.
L. TURGIS

SIGN PAINTER
LETTERING ARTISTS
REFERENCE BOOK

.TYPEFACE.
ALPHABET №4

LOWER CASE ← → WEIGHT: REGULAR ← → PUBLISHED: 1845

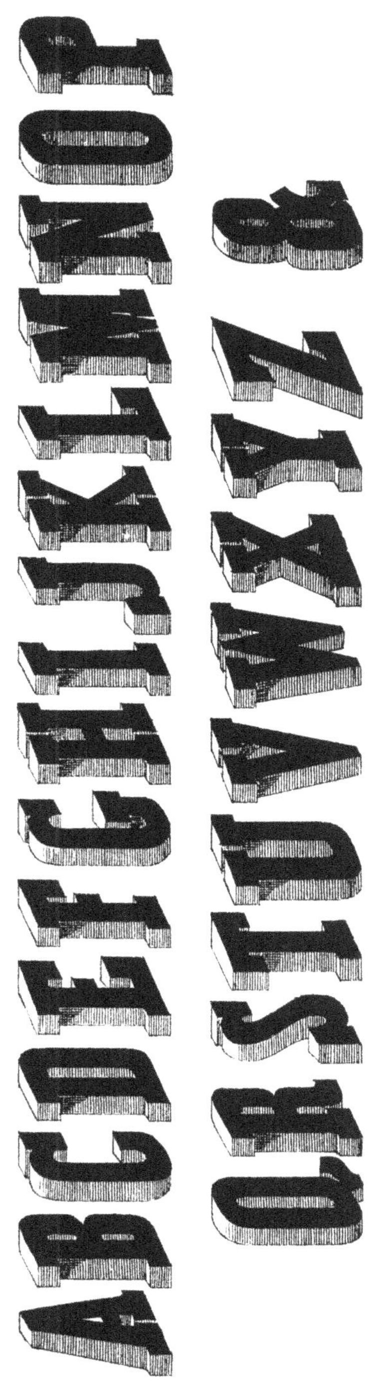

133

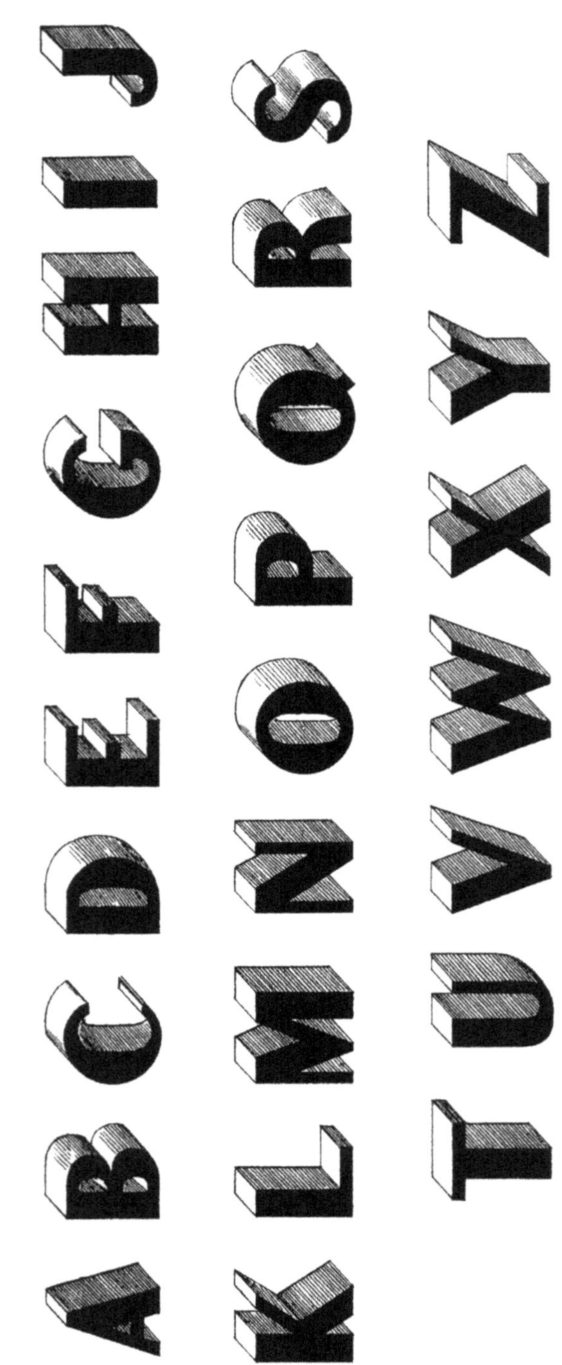

Vault Editions Ltd

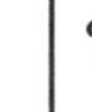
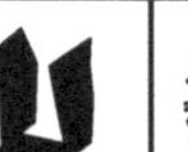

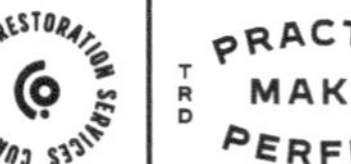

INDUSTRY STD
VAULTEDITIONS.COM

134

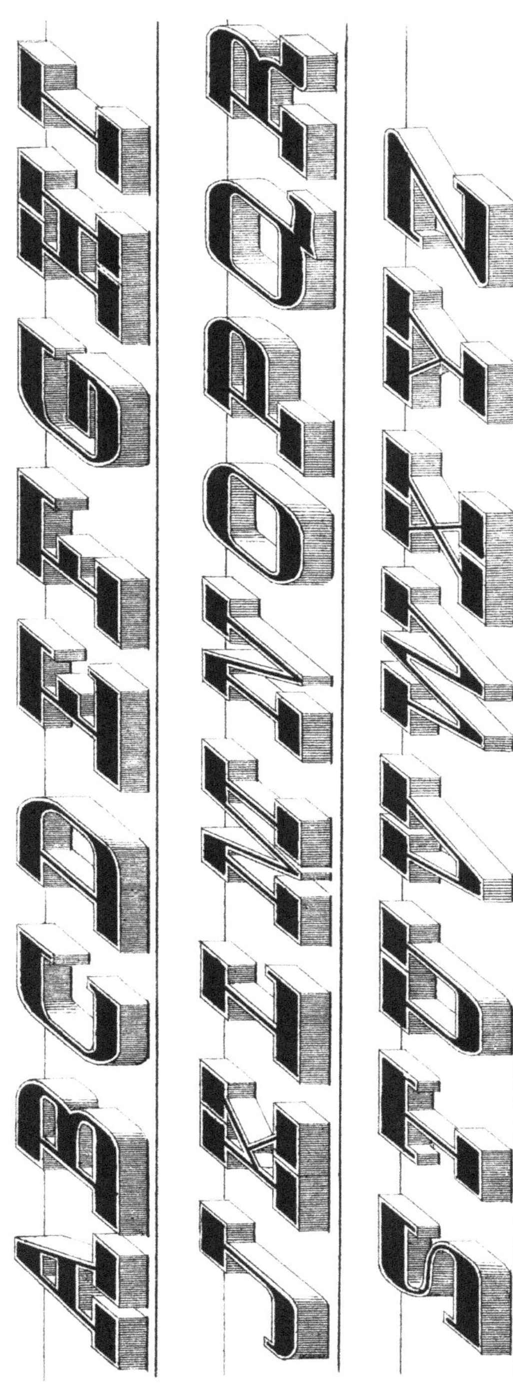

135

136

A HIGH RESOLUTION FILE OF THIS
SPECIMEN SHEET CAN BE DOWNLOADED
FROM THE VAULT EDITIONS' WEBSITE.

Vault Editions Ltd

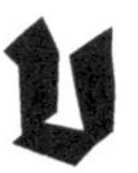
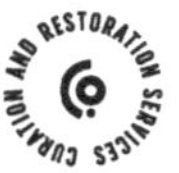

CURATION AND RESTORATION SERVICES

PRACTICE
MAKES
PERFECT
TRD   MRK

INDUSTRY STD

VAULTEDITIONS.COM

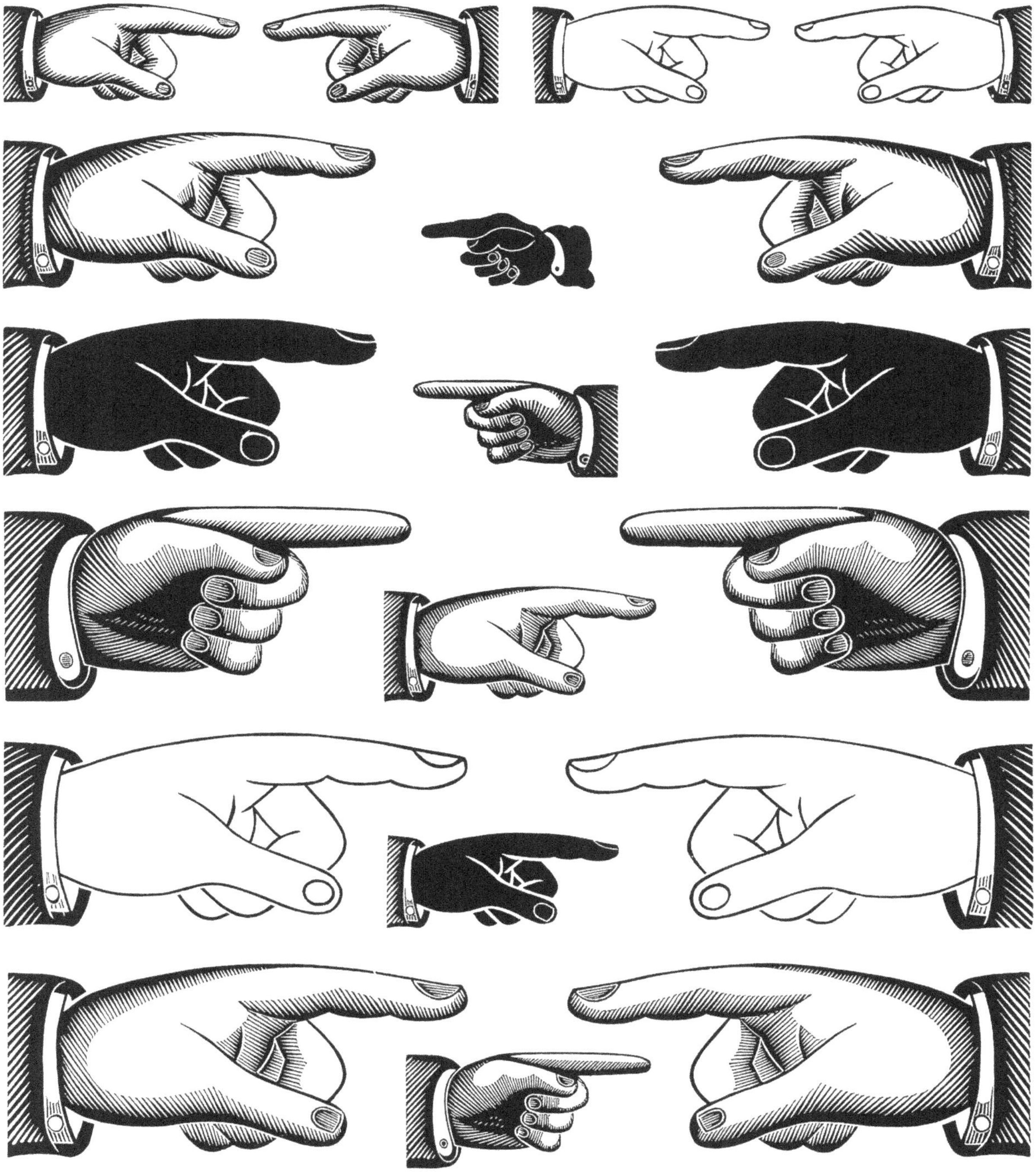

Vault Editions Ltd

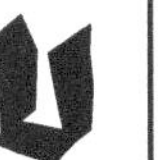

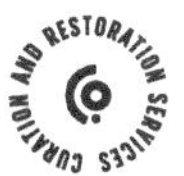

CURATION AND RESTORATION SERVICES

PRACTICE MAKES PERFECT
TRD MRK

INDUSTRY STD

VAULTEDITIONS.COM

138

Vault Editions Ltd

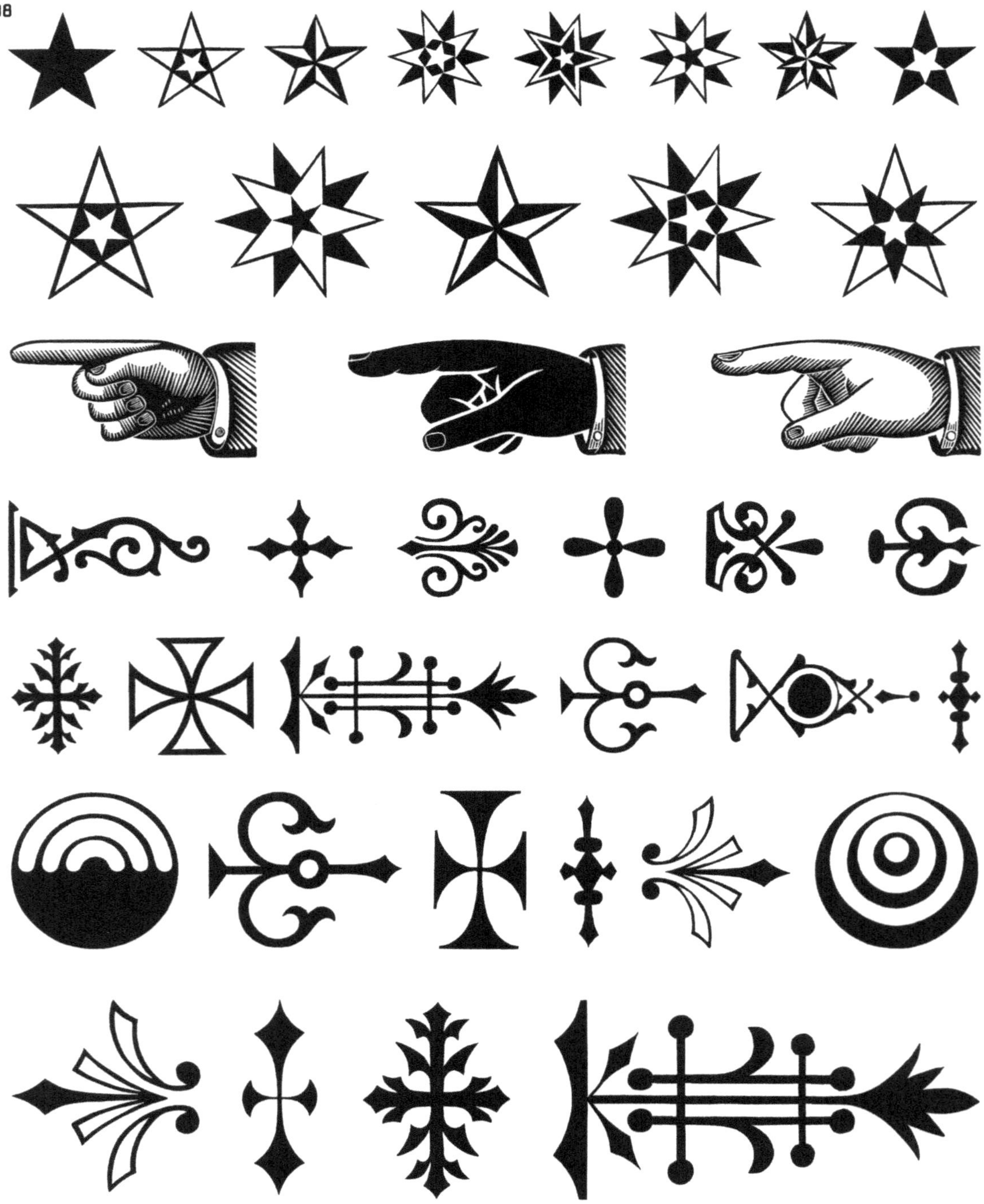

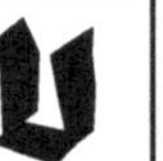

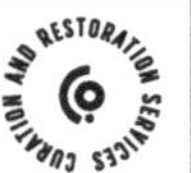

PRACTICE MAKES PERFECT

INDUSTRY STD

VAULTEDITIONS.COM

139

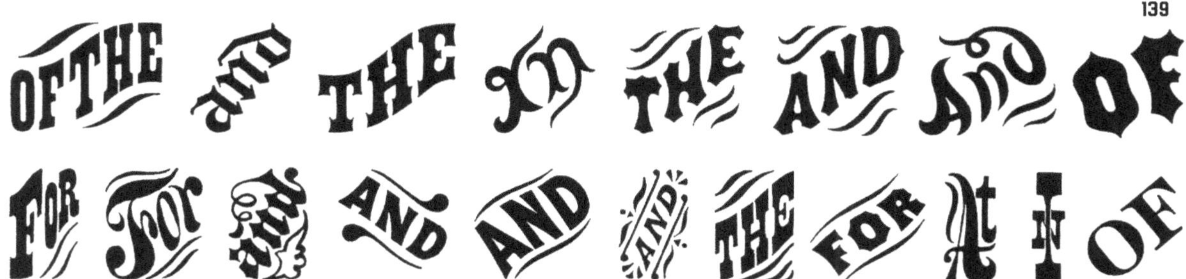

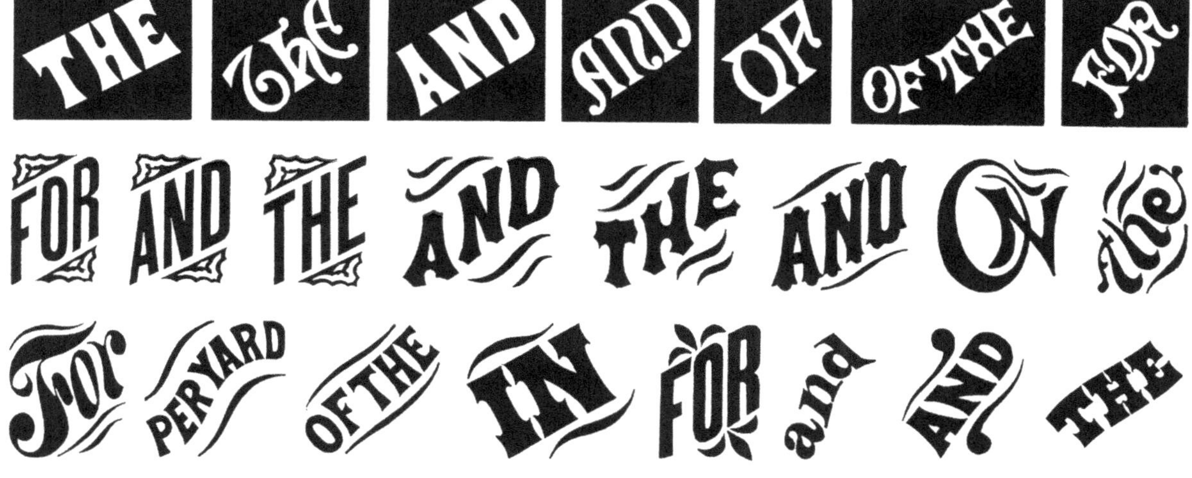

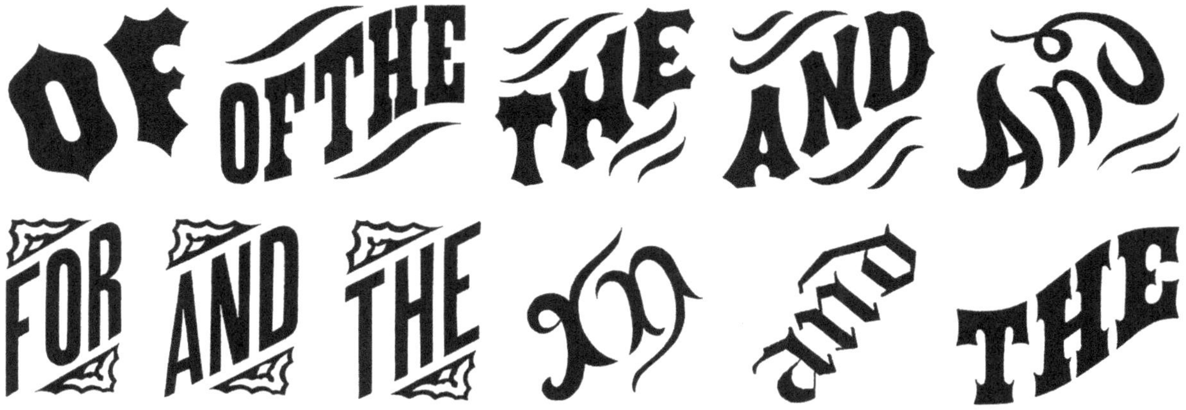

140

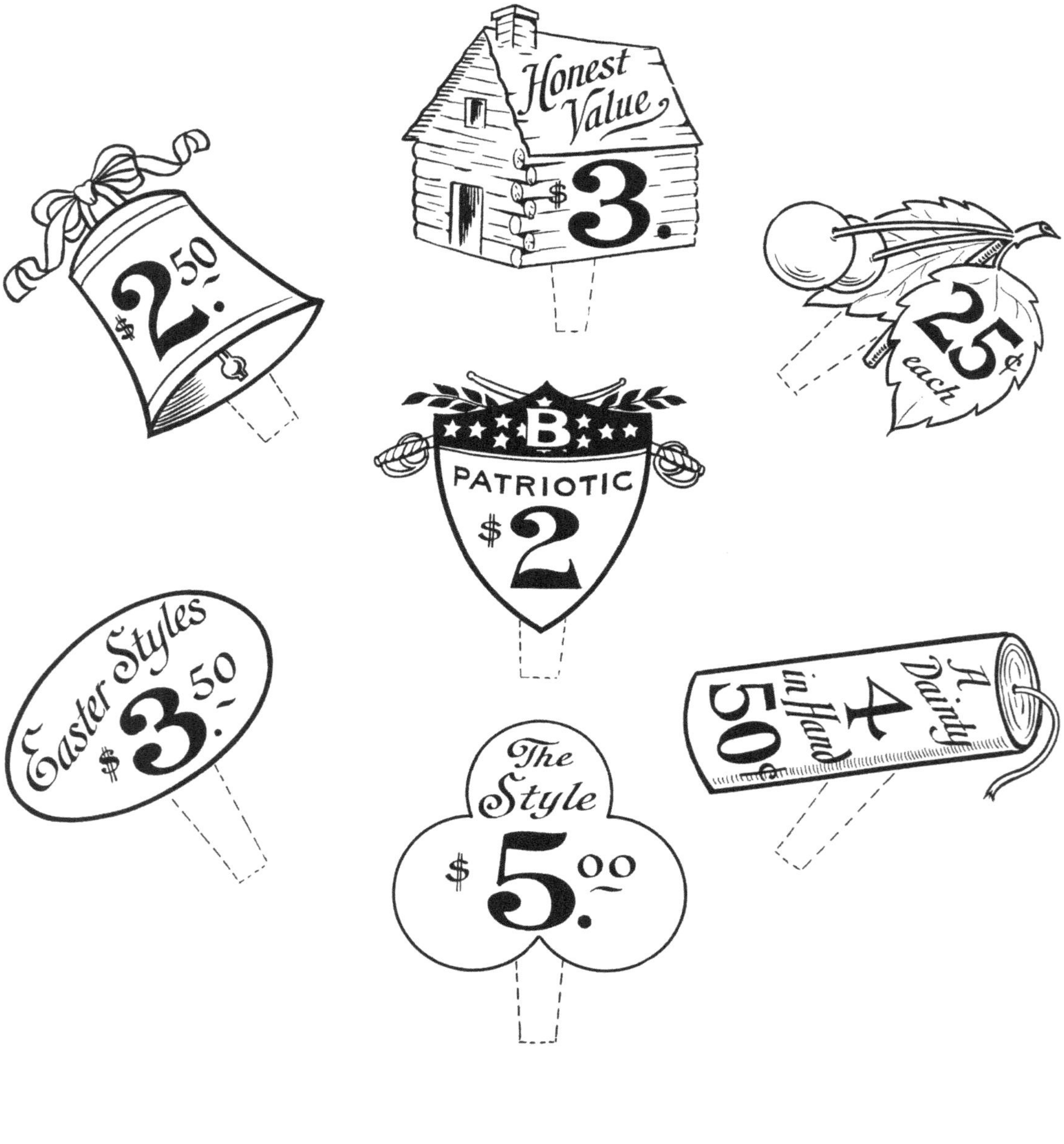

Vault Editions Ltd 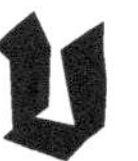 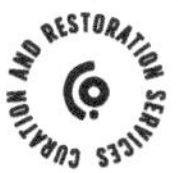

PRACTICE MAKES PERFECT

INDUSTRY STD

VAULTEDITIONS.COM

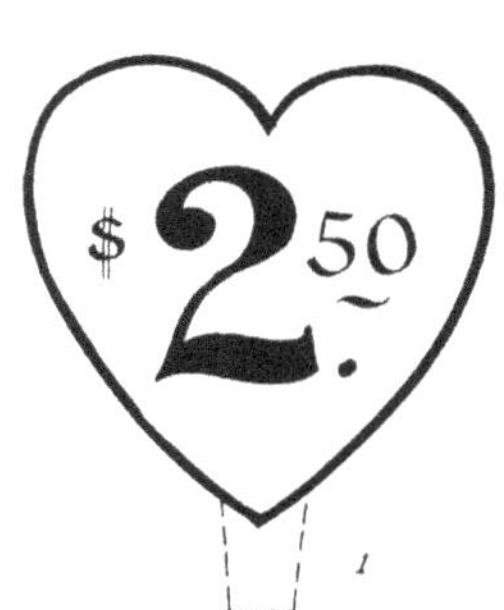

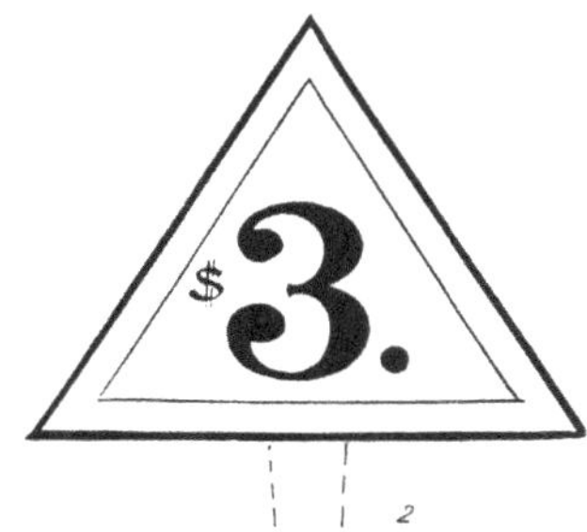

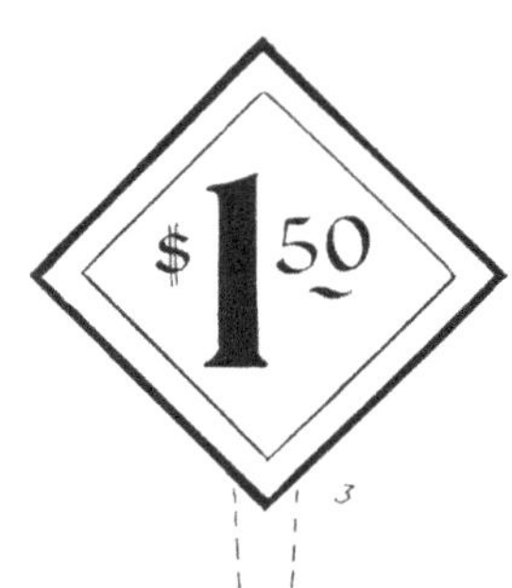

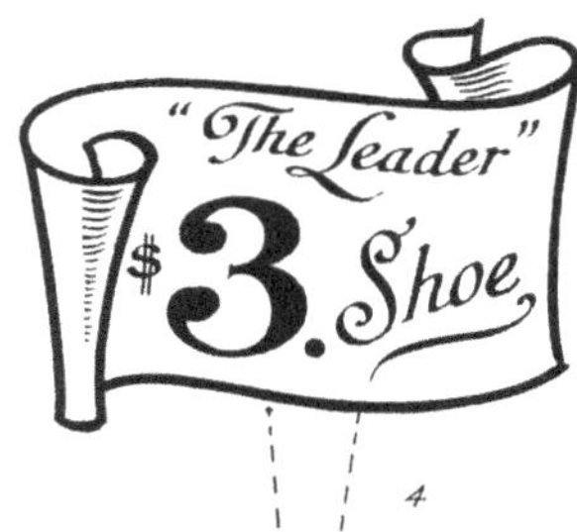

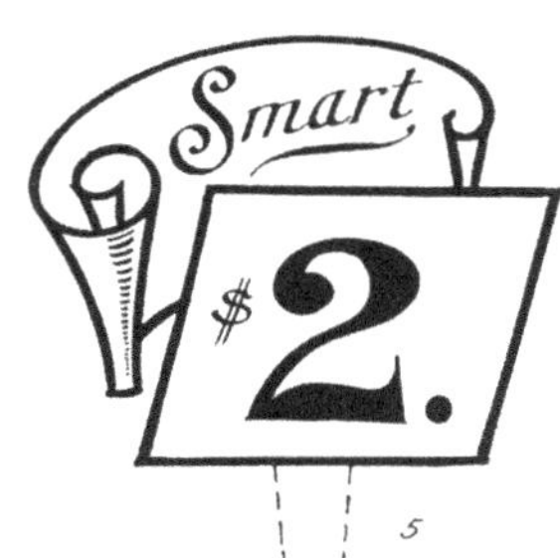

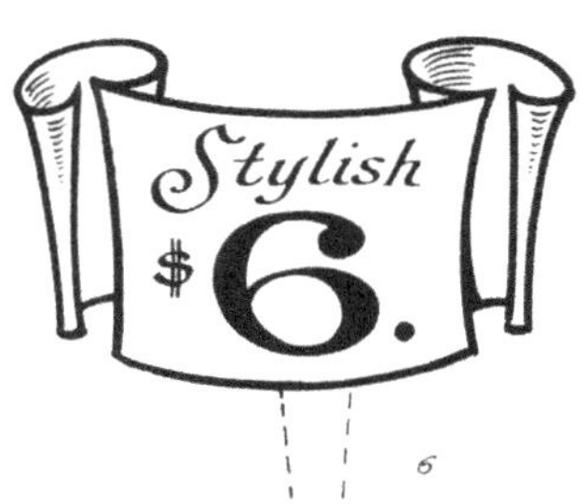

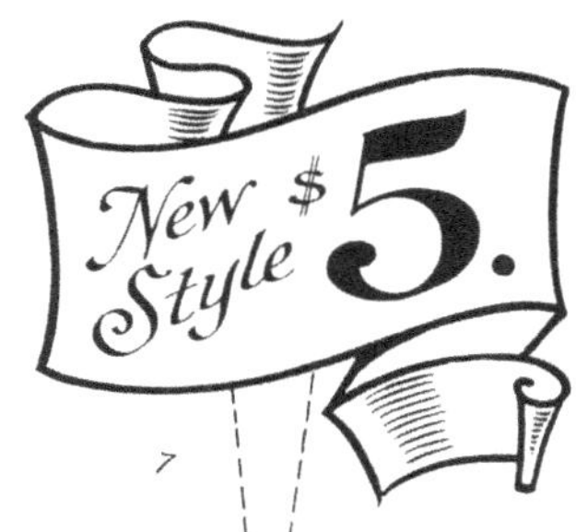

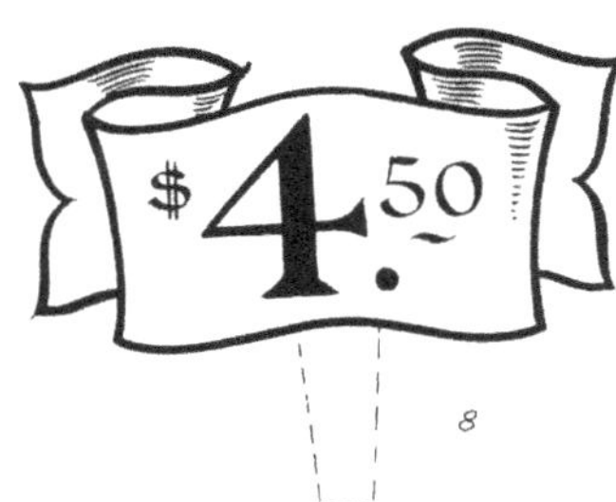

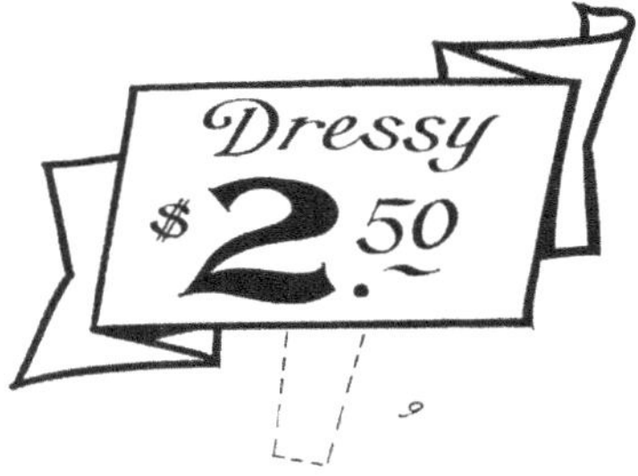

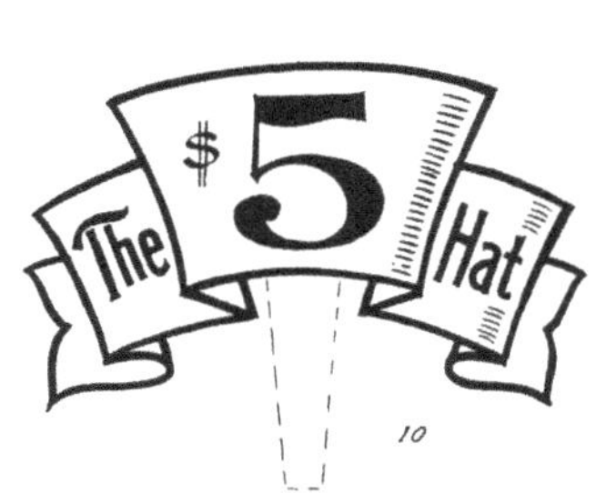

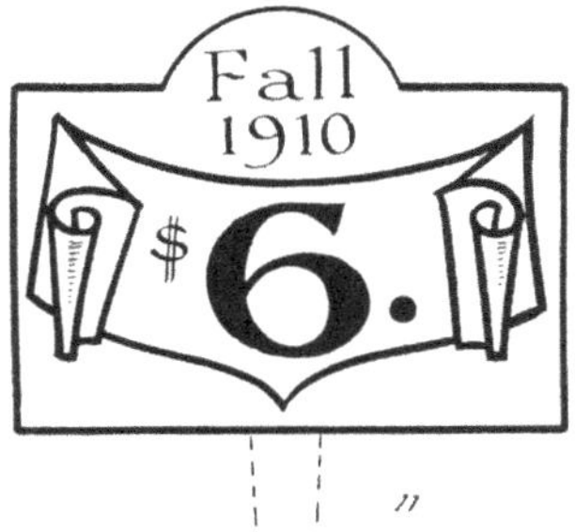

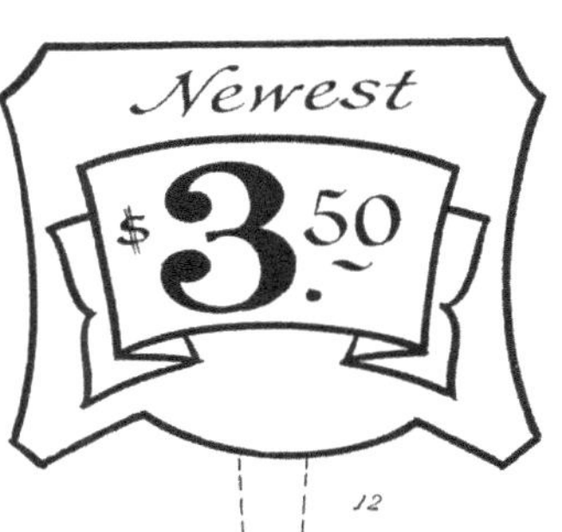

Vault Editions Ltd

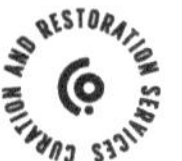

CURATION AND RESTORATION SERVICES

PRACTICE MAKES PERFECT
TRD MRK

INDUSTRY STD

VAULTEDITIONS.COM

142

8¢
17¢
$1.00 1.
80¢
$10.00 10.
Extra Value $6.00
$2.95
25¢
$3.00 3.
$2.00 2.
$1.00 1.
To-Day's SPECIAL 19¢
25¢
Regular 50¢ Value
Special 38¢
While they Last 15¢
$1.50 1.
69¢
75¢
9¢
50¢
Bargain 10¢
$1.00 1.
$3.25 3.

Vault Editions Ltd

CURATION AND RESTORATION SERVICES

TRD PRACTICE MAKES PERFECT MRK

INDUSTRY STD
VAULTEDITIONS.COM

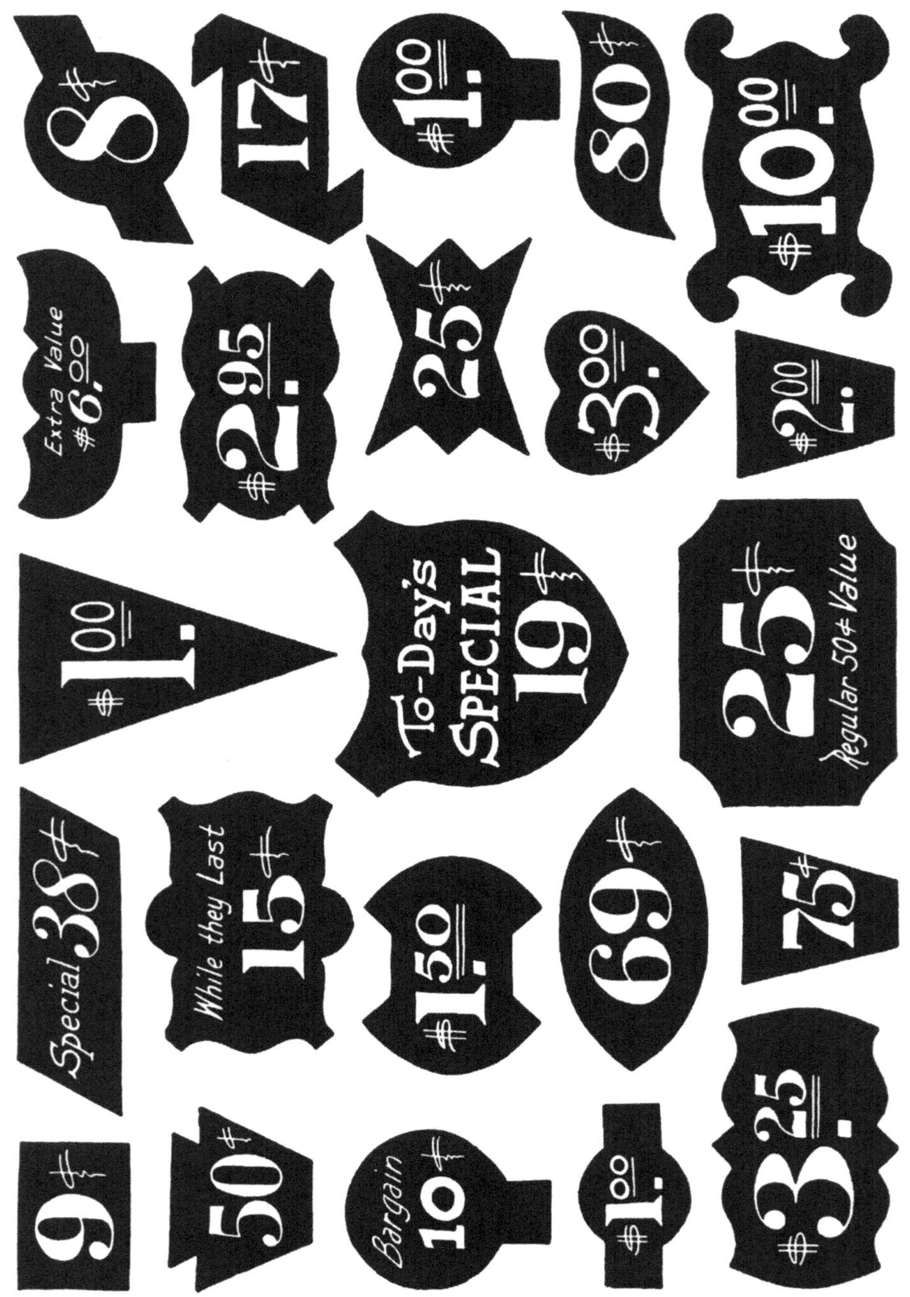

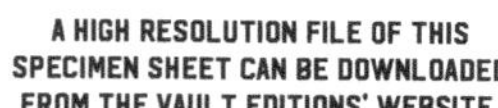

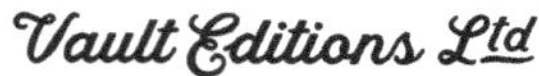

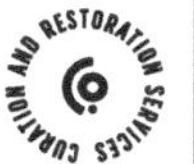

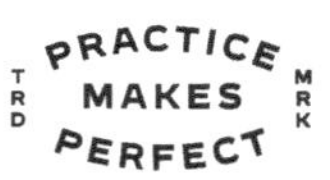

143

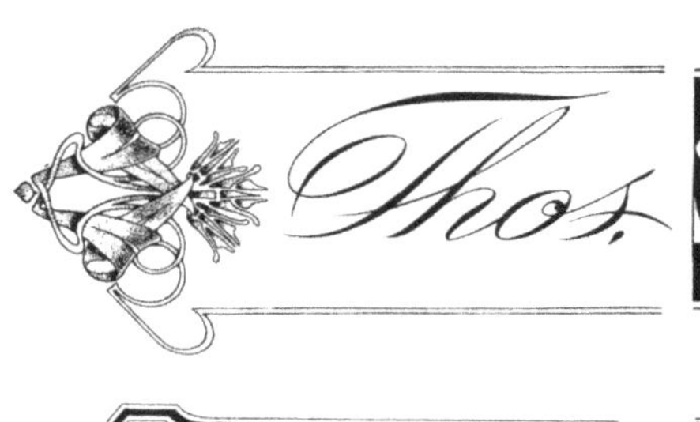

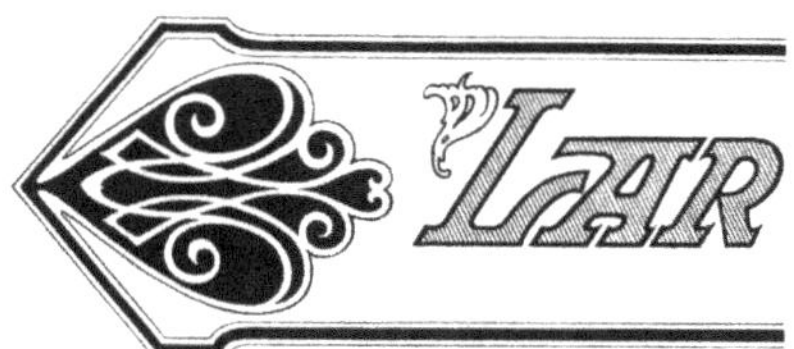

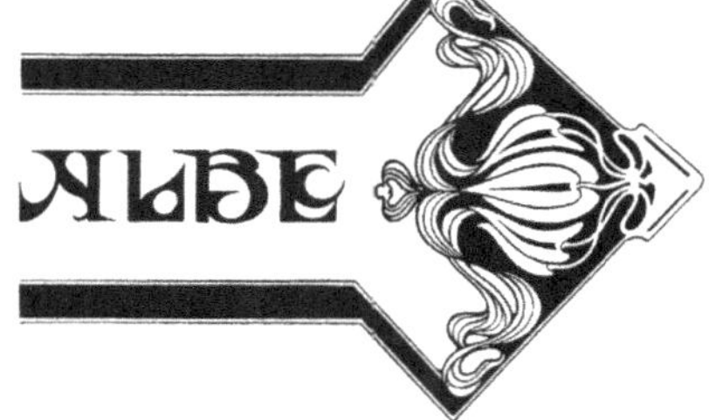

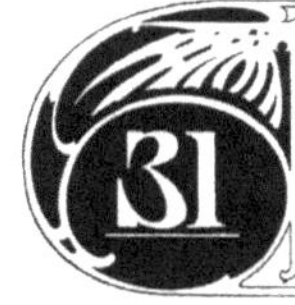

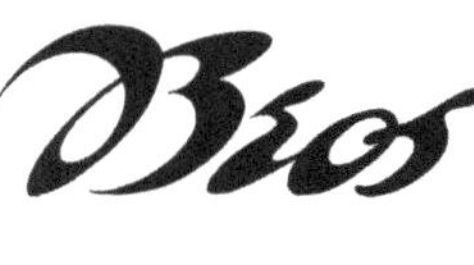

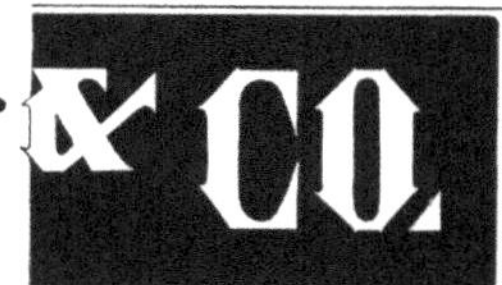

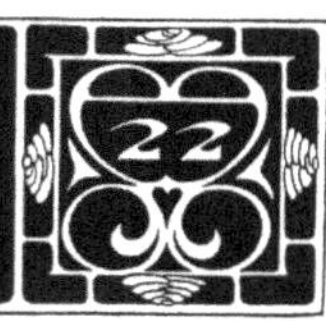

144

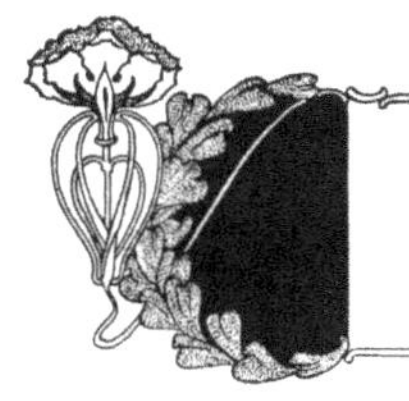

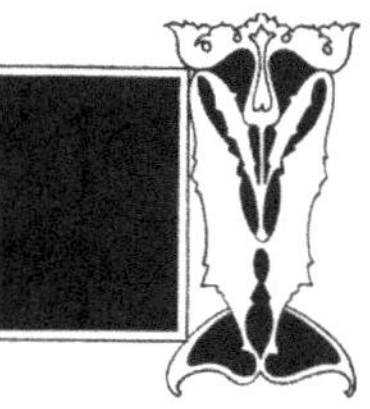

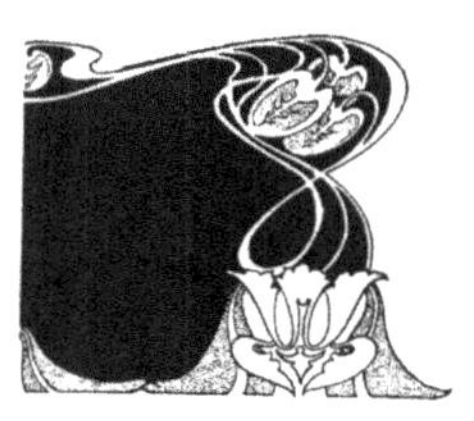

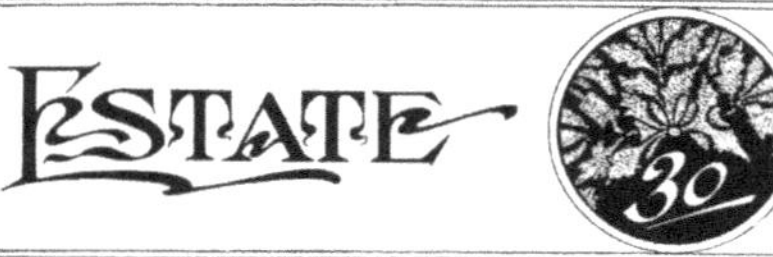

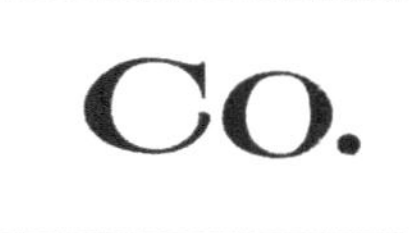

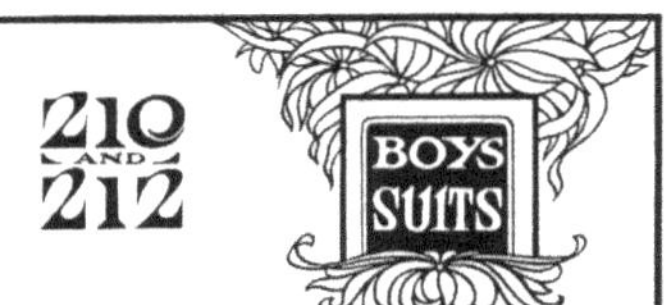

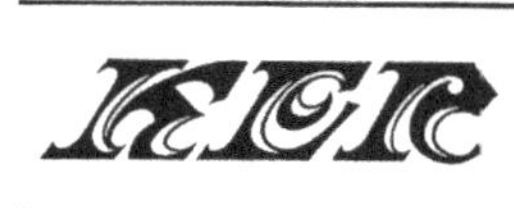

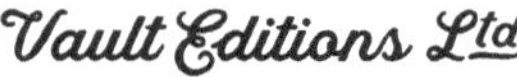

Vault Editions Ltd

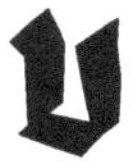

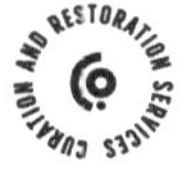

PRACTICE MAKES PERFECT
TRD · MRK

INDUSTRY STD

VAULTEDITIONS.COM

145

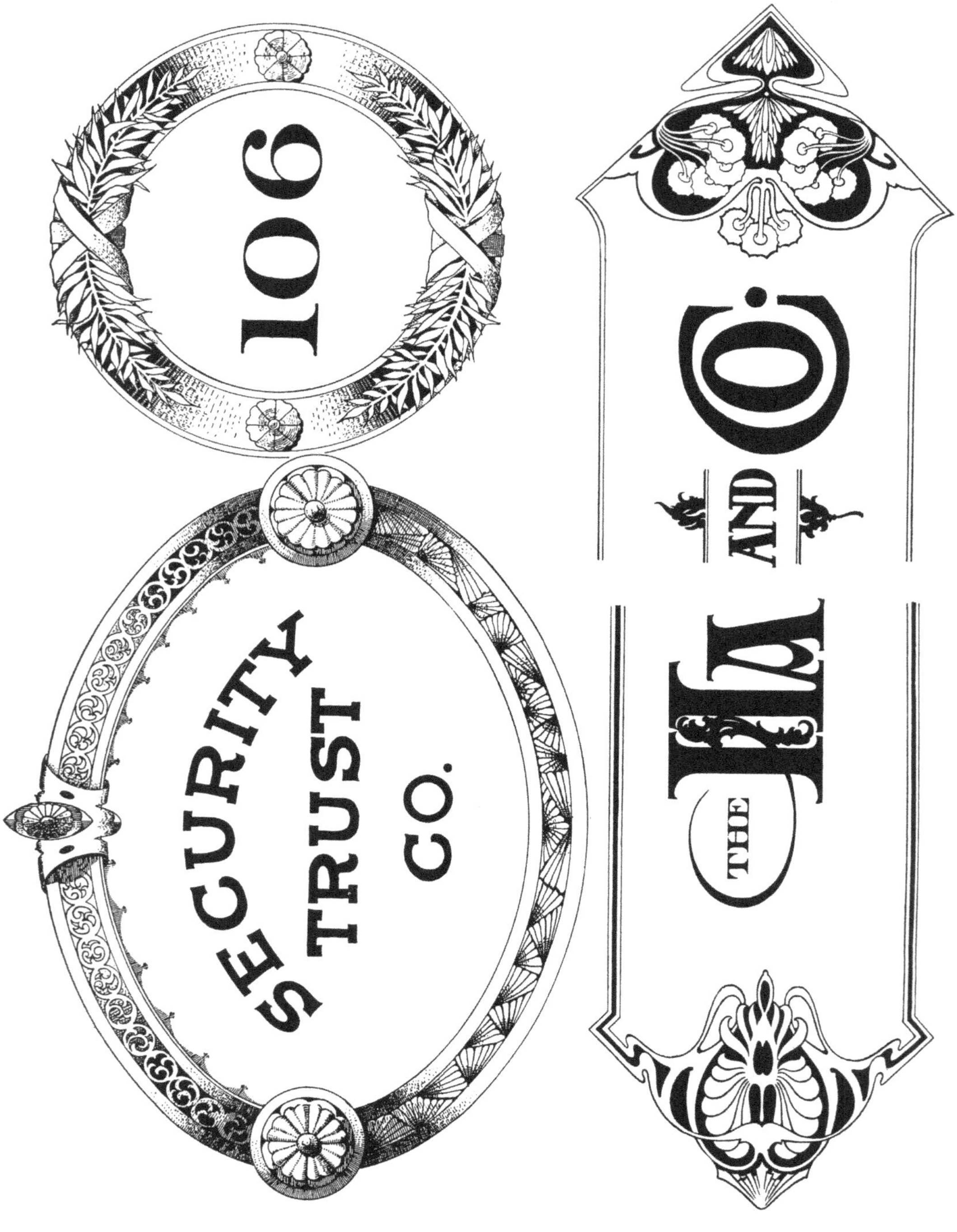

Vault Editions Ltd

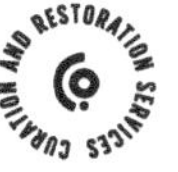

CURATION AND RESTORATION SERVICES

PRACTICE
MAKES
PERFECT

INDUSTRY STD

VAULTEDITIONS.COM

146

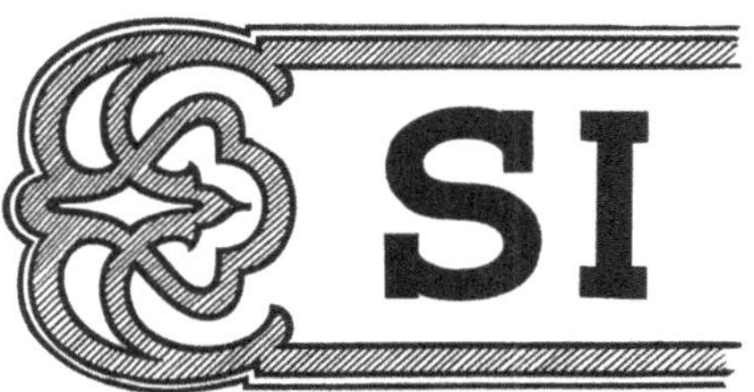

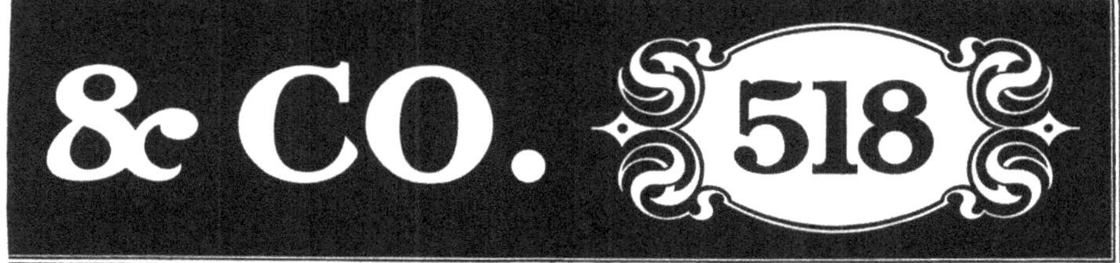

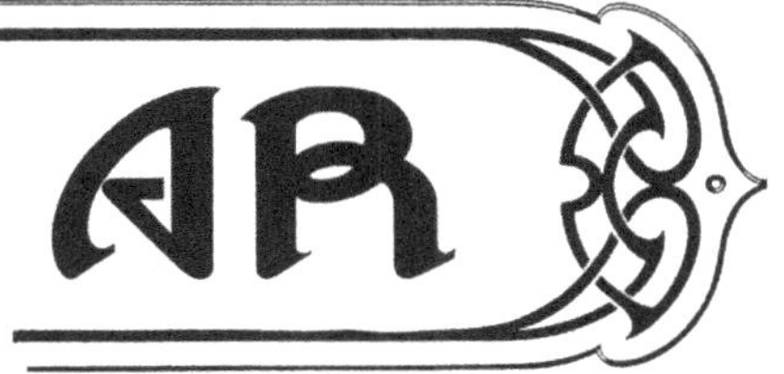

147

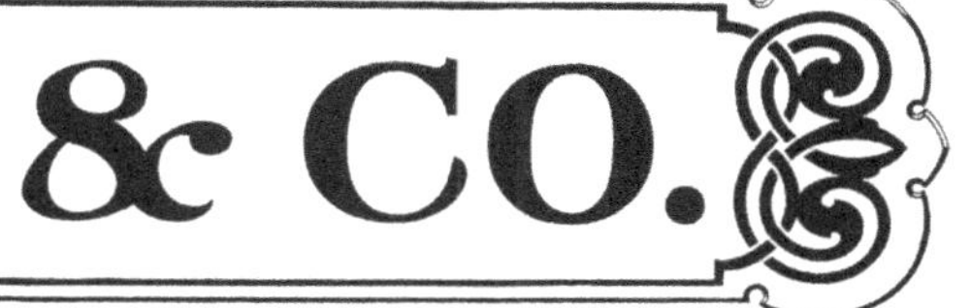

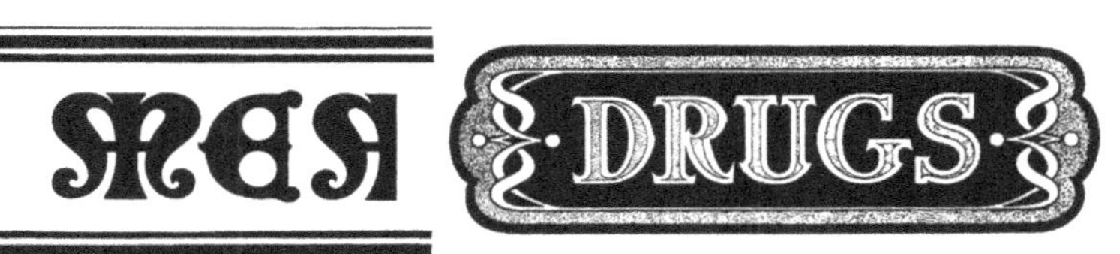

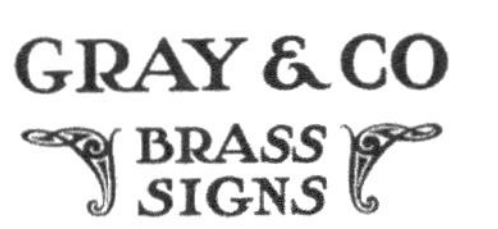

Vault Editions Ltd

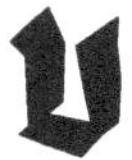
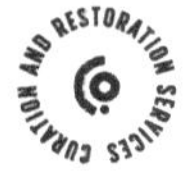

CURATION AND RESTORATION SERVICES

PRACTICE MAKES PERFECT
T R D — M R K

INDUSTRY STD

VAULTEDITIONS.COM

148

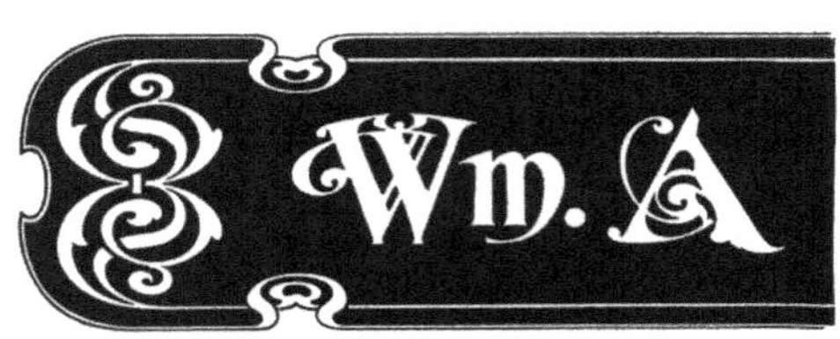

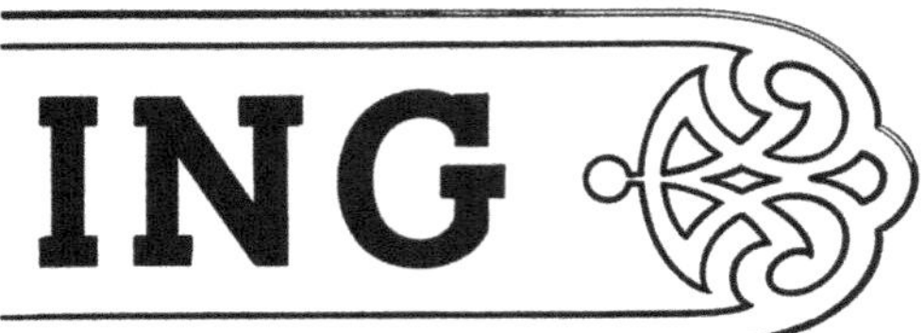

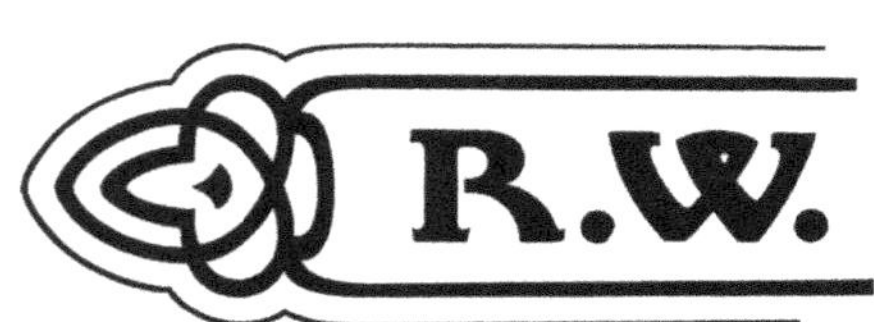

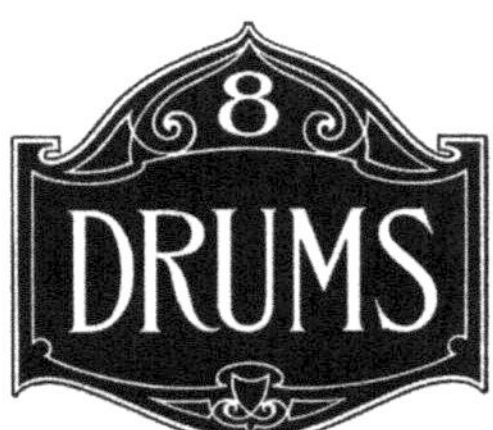

149

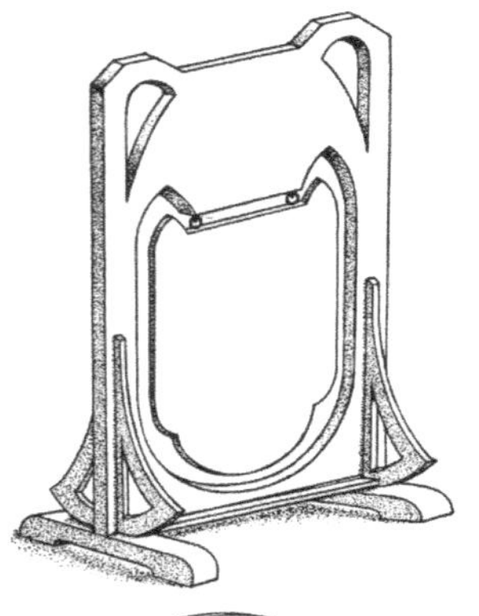
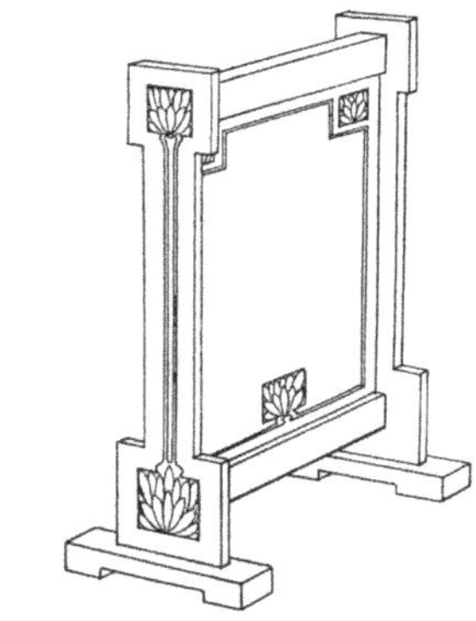
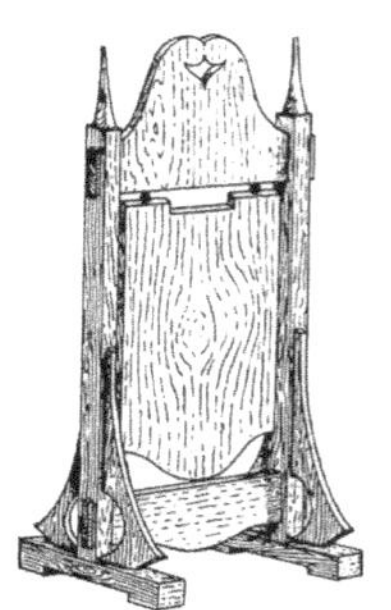
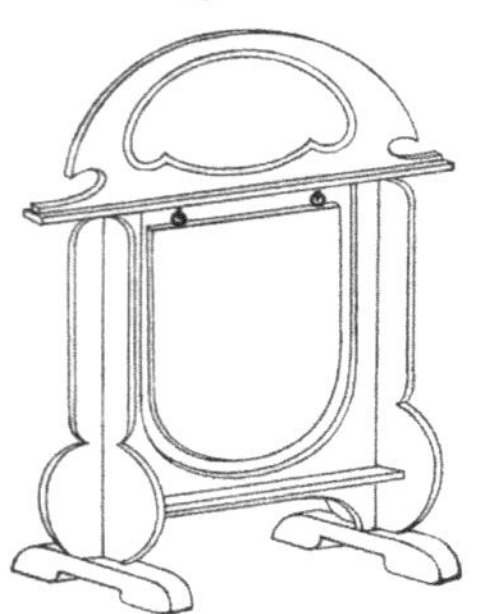
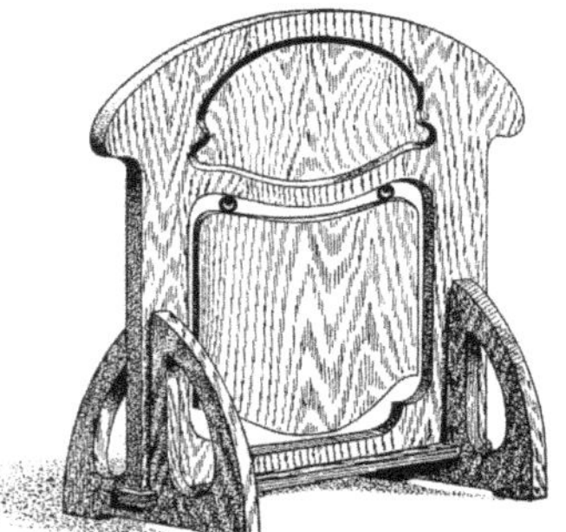
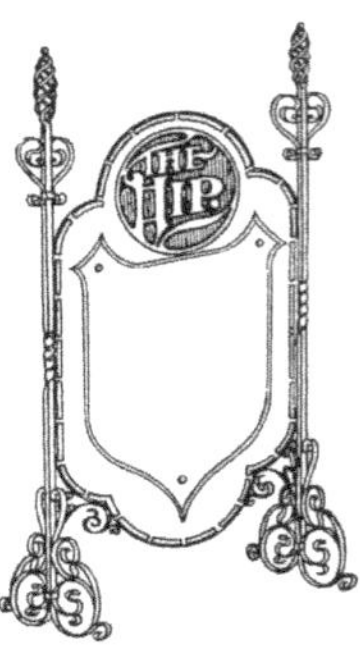

Vault Editions Ltd

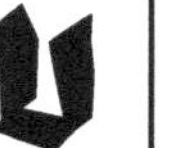
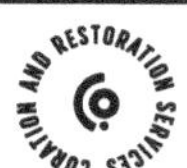

150

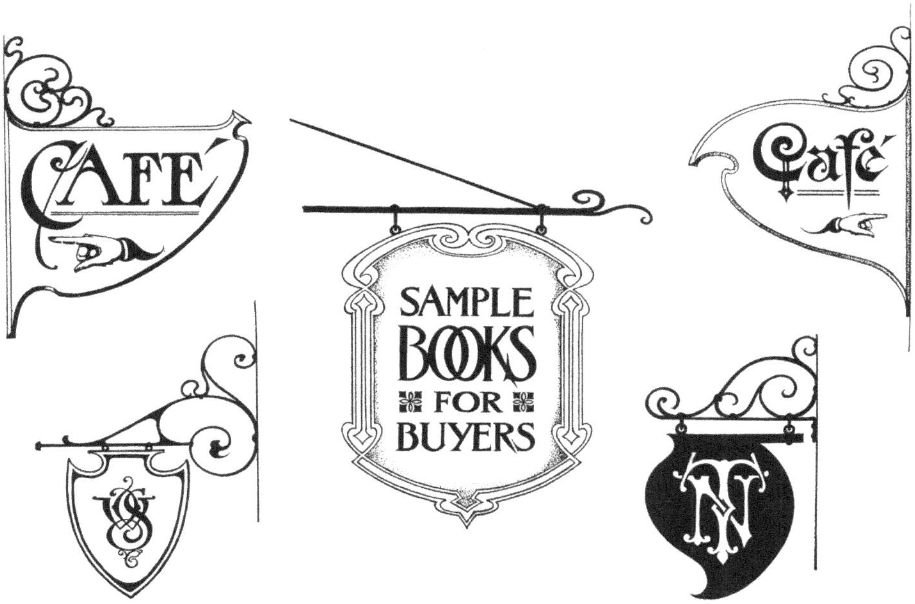

151

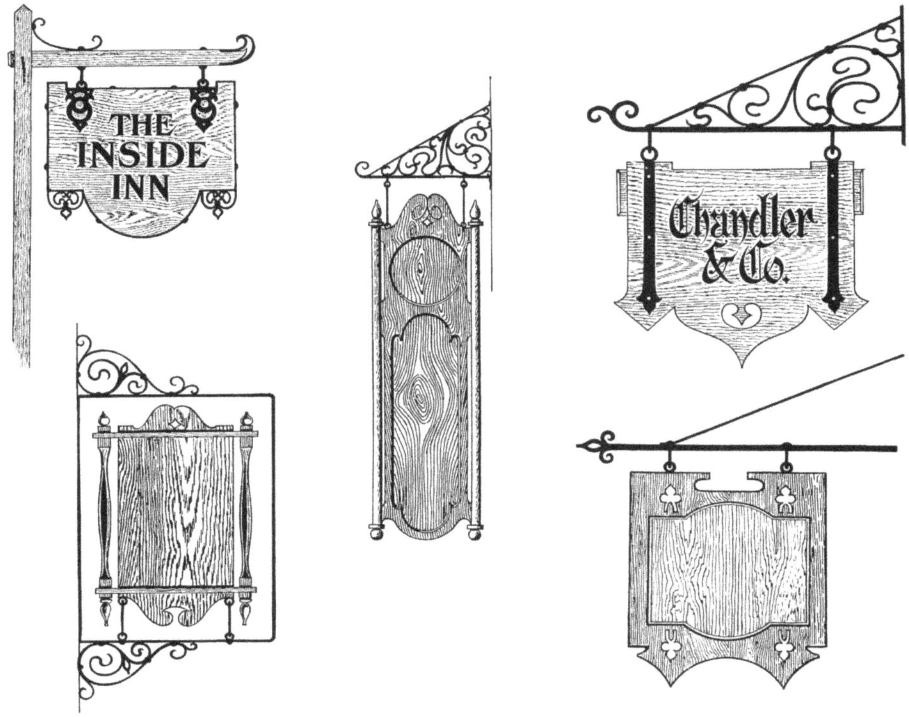

Vault Editions Ltd

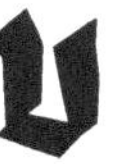
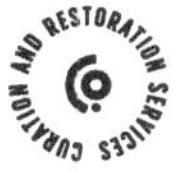

CURATION AND RESTORATION SERVICES

PRACTICE MAKES PERFECT

INDUSTRY STD

VAULTEDITIONS.COM

152

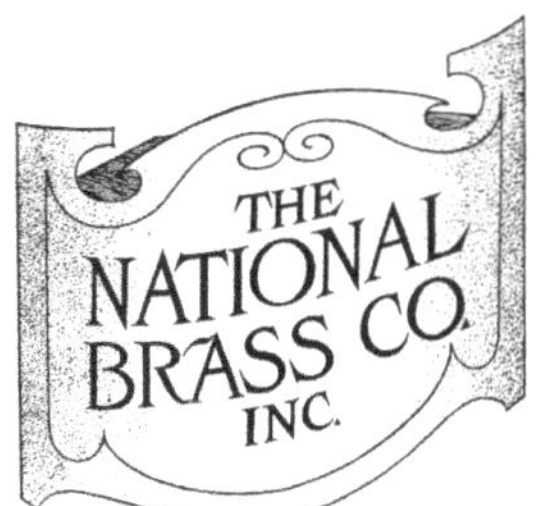

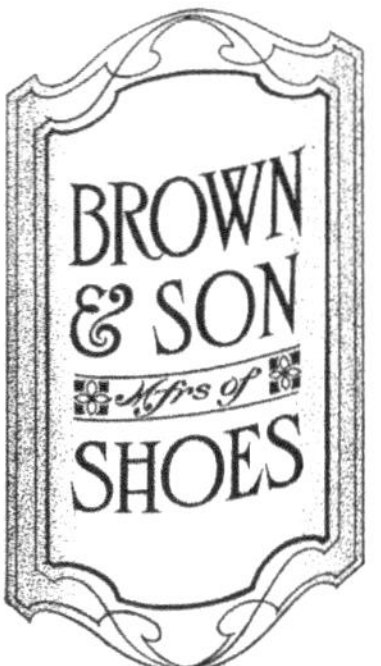

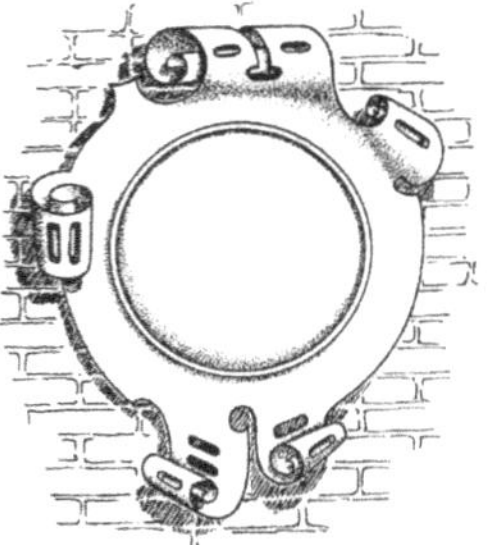

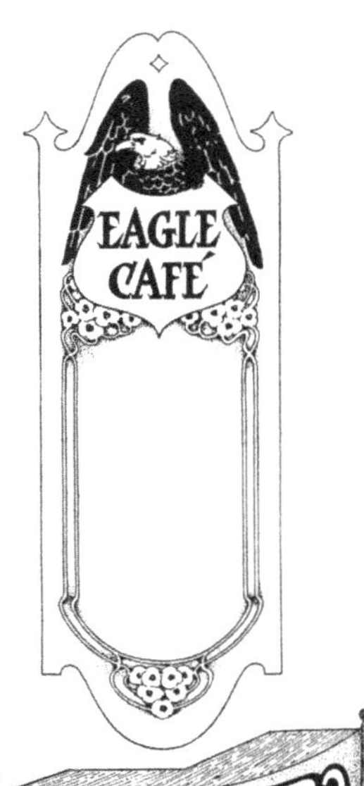

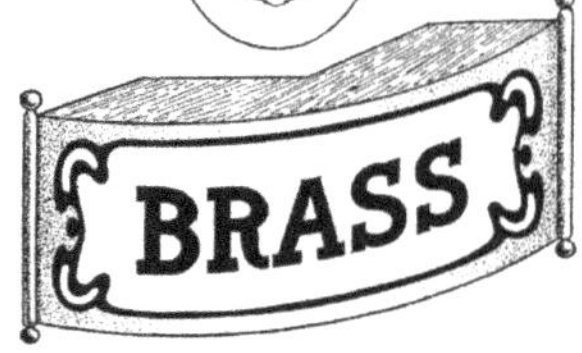

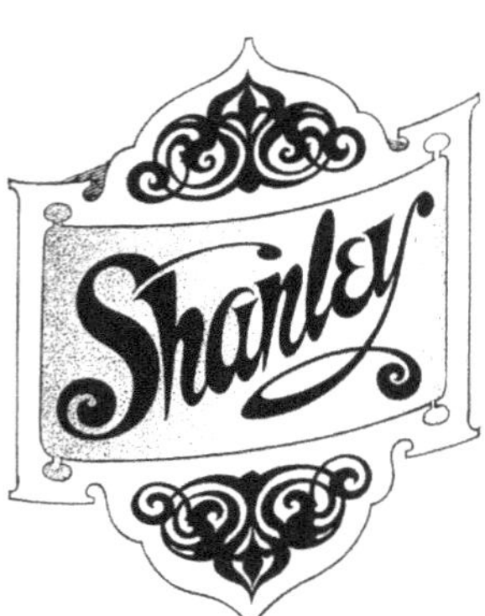

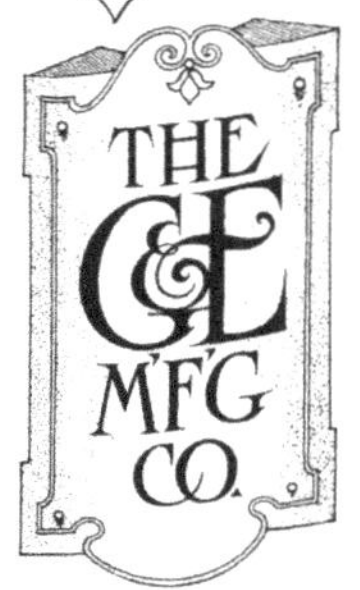

153

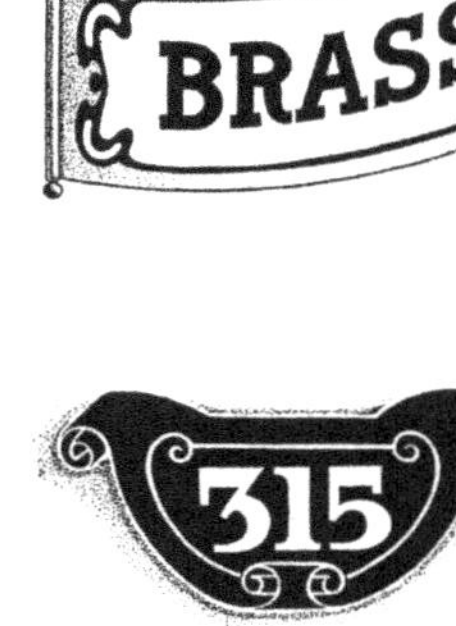

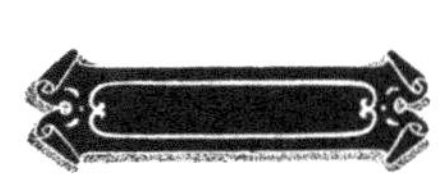

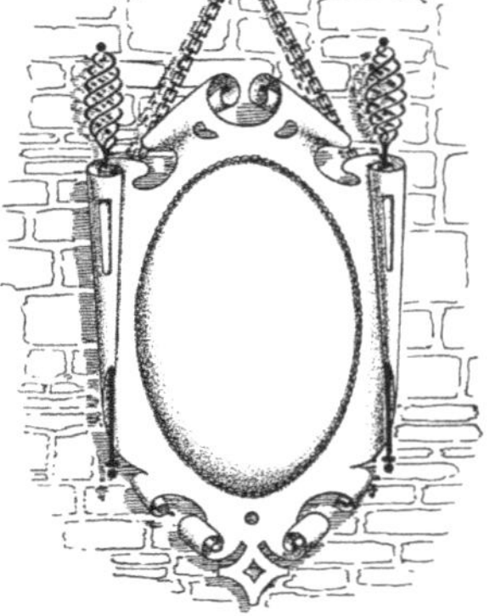

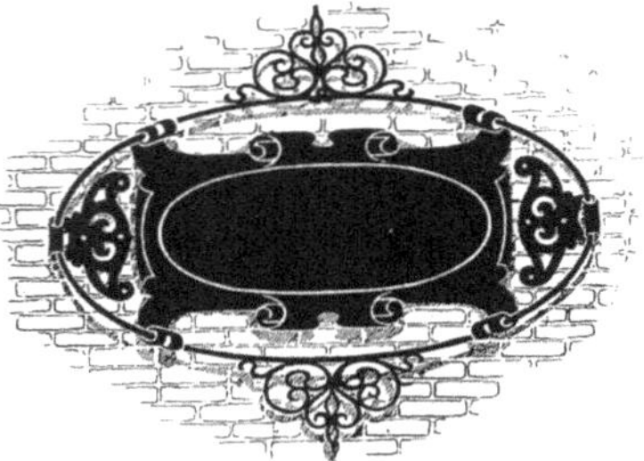

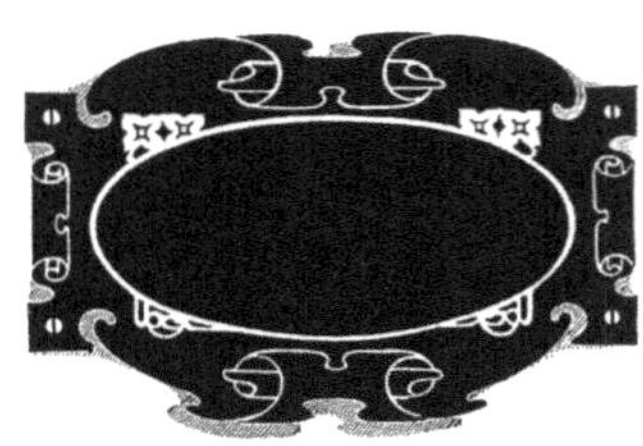

Vault Editions Ltd

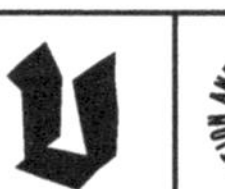
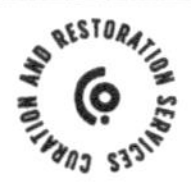

CURATION AND RESTORATION SERVICES

PRACTICE
MAKES
PERFECT
TRD MRK

INDUSTRY STD

VAULTEDITIONS.COM

154

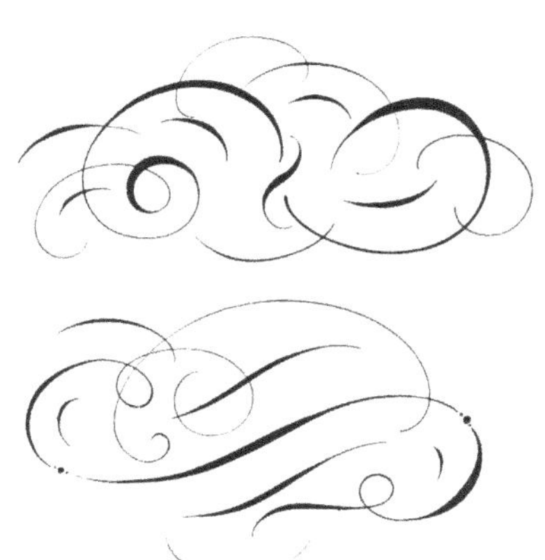

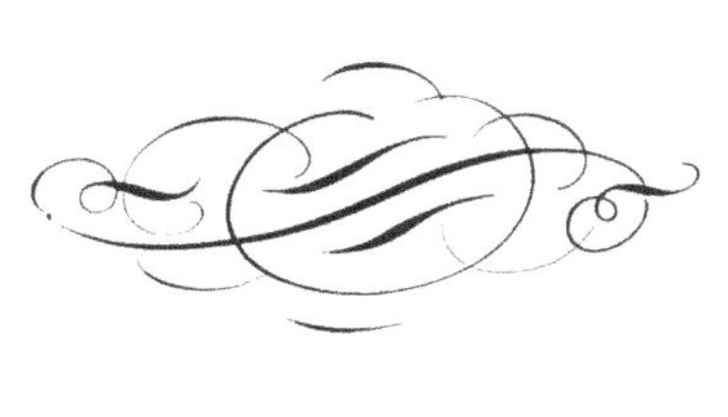

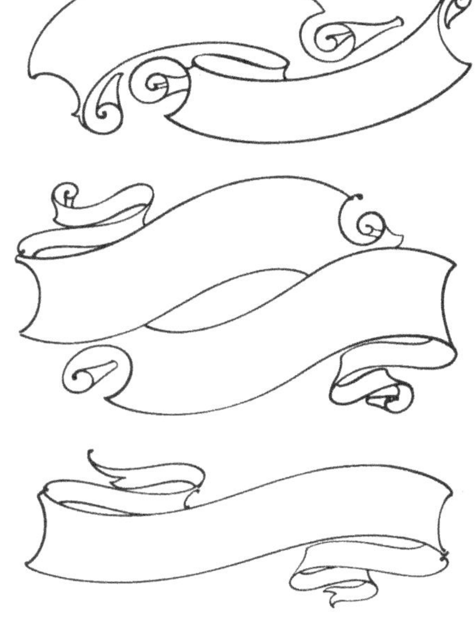

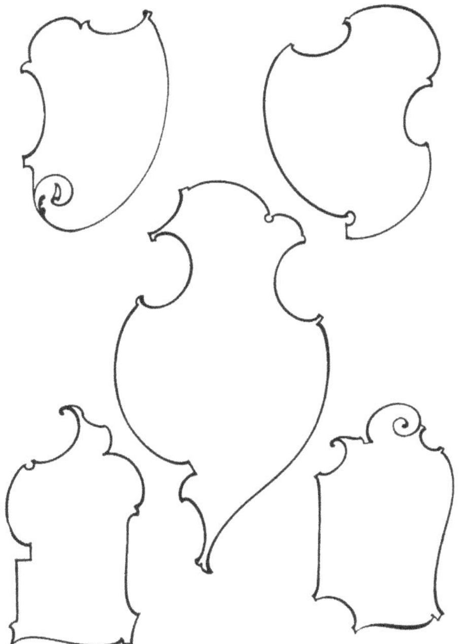

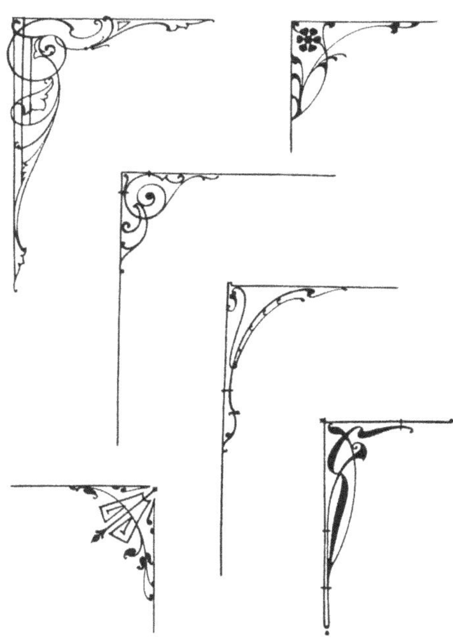

Vault Editions Ltd

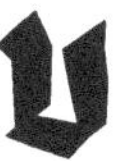
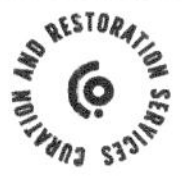

PRACTICE
MAKES
PERFECT

INDUSTRY STD

VAULTEDITIONS.COM

155

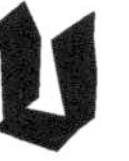
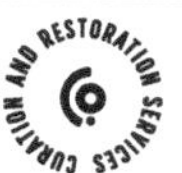

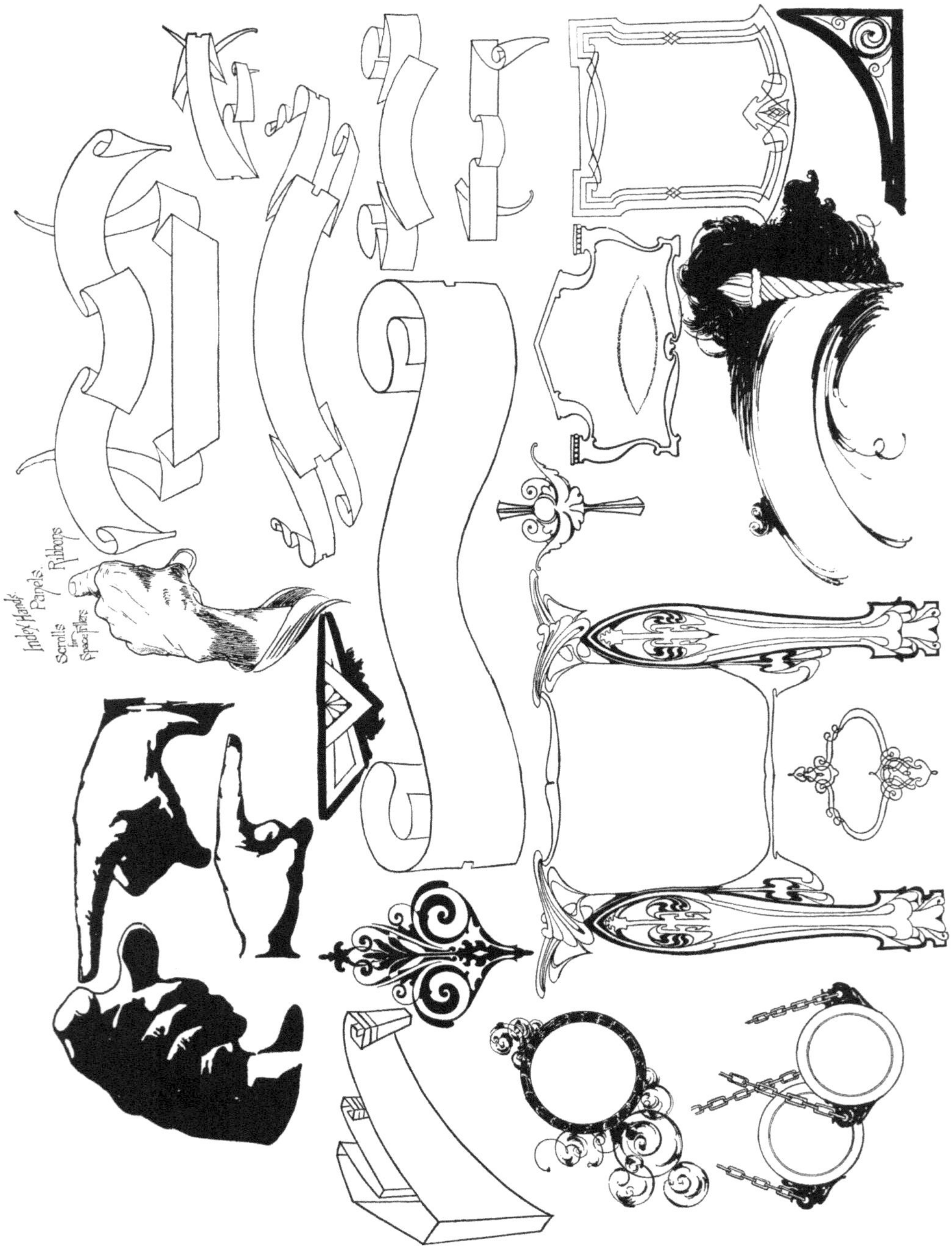

CURATION AND RESTORATION SERVICES

T R D PRACTICE MAKES PERFECT M R K

INDUSTRY STD

VAULTEDITIONS.COM

156

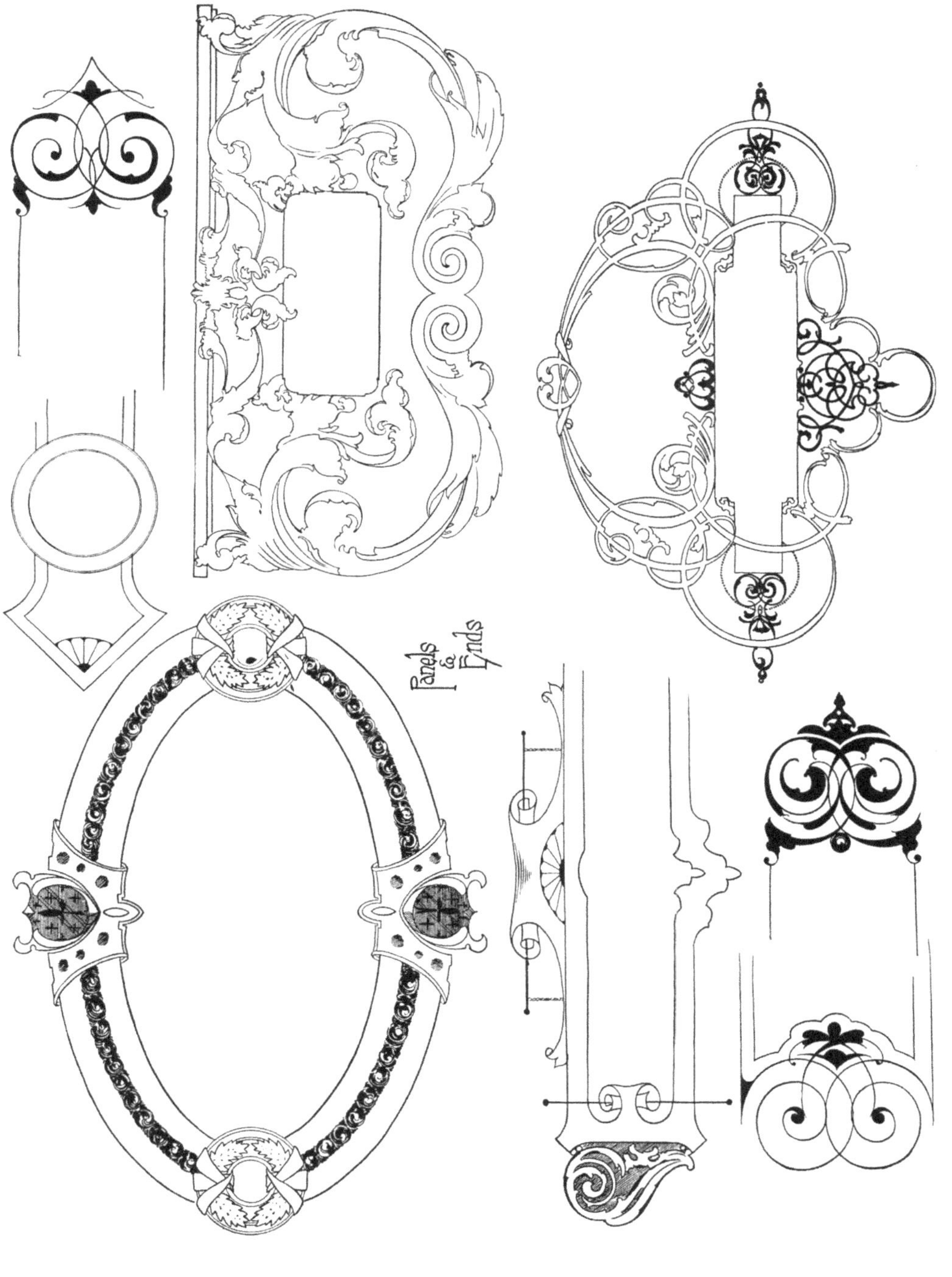

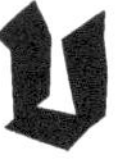
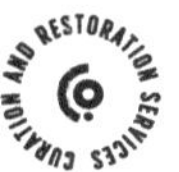

157

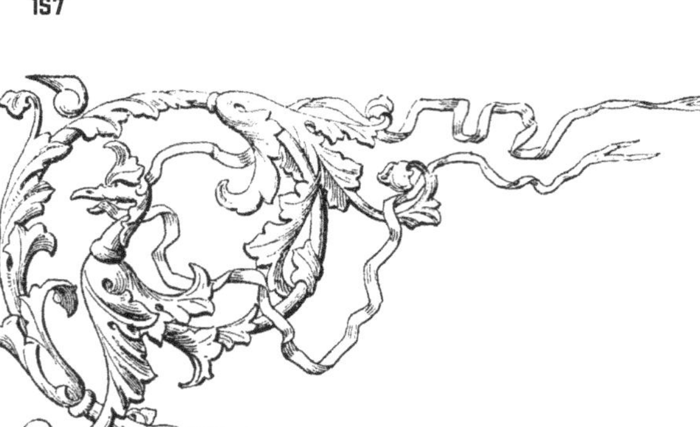

158

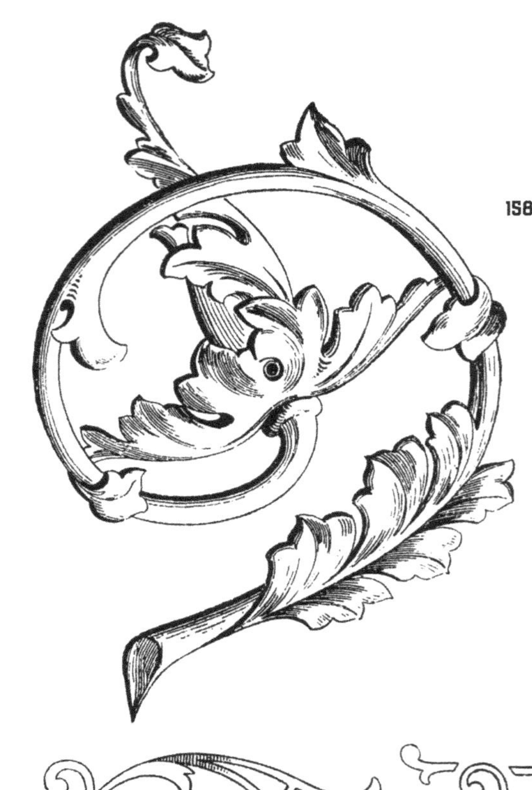

159

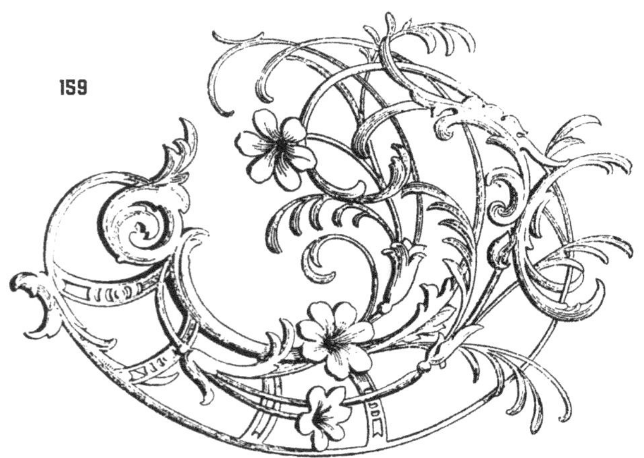

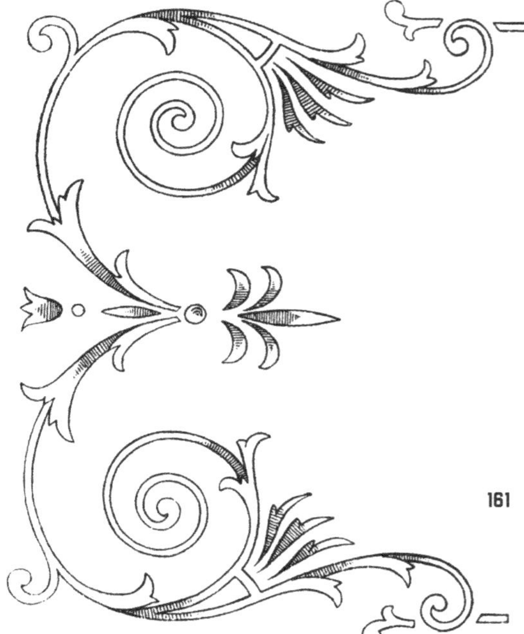

160

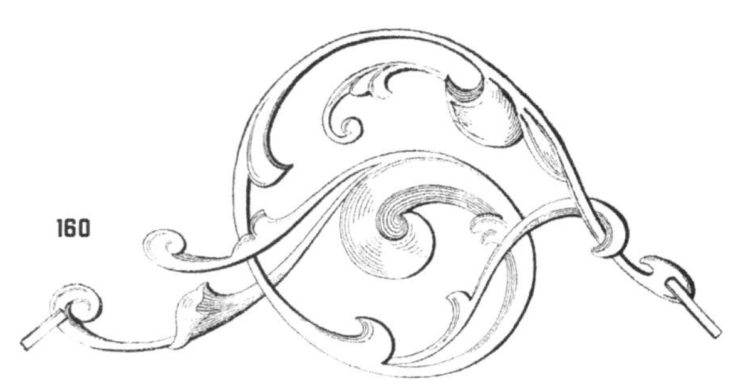

161

Vault Editions Ltd

CURATION AND RESTORATION SERVICES

PRACTICE MAKES PERFECT

INDUSTRY STD
VAULTEDITIONS.COM

162

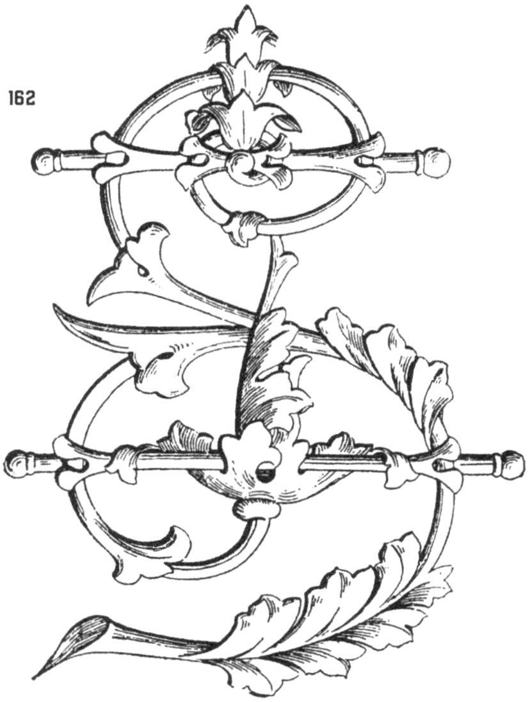

163

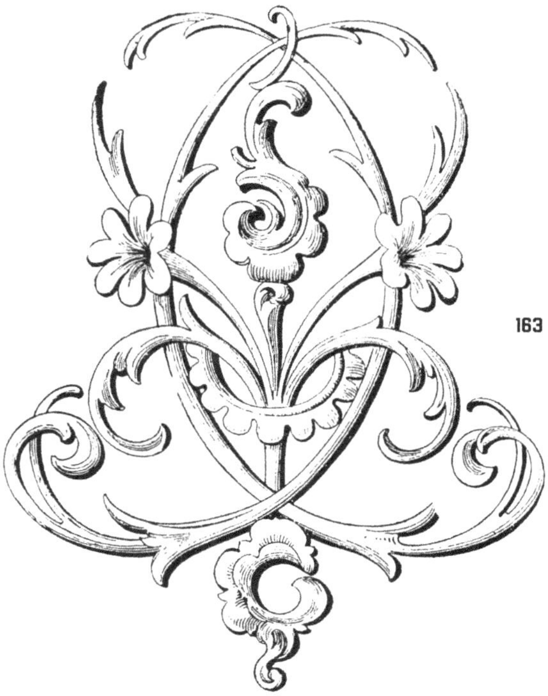

164

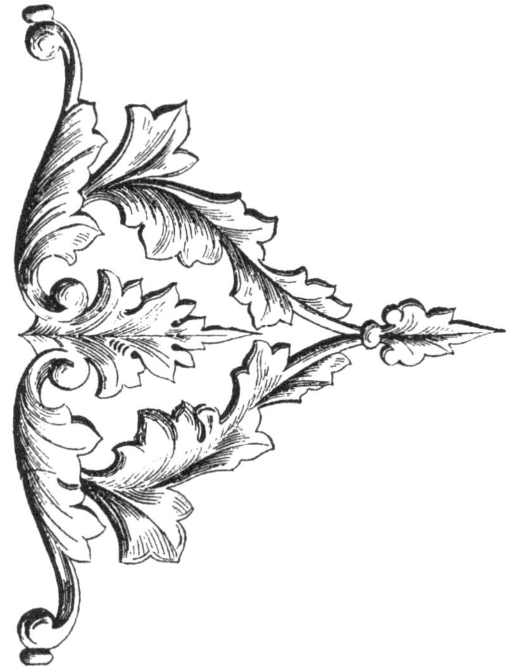

165

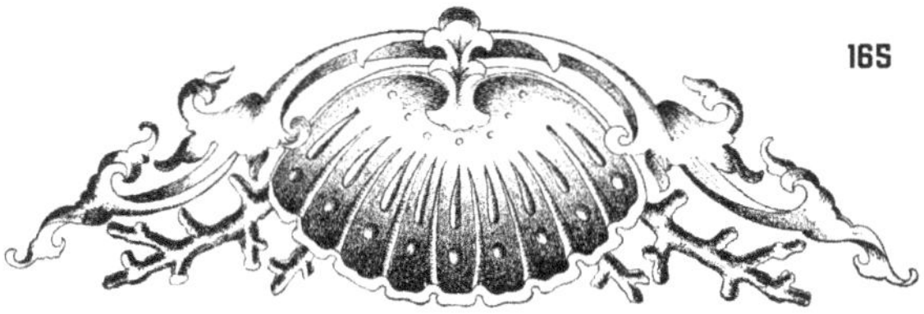

166

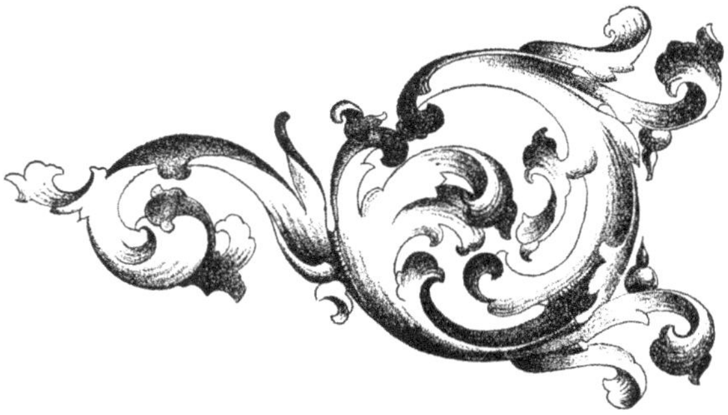

Vault Editions Ltd

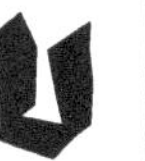

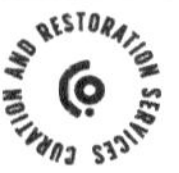

PRACTICE MAKES PERFECT

INDUSTRY STD

VAULTEDITIONS.COM

167

168

169

170
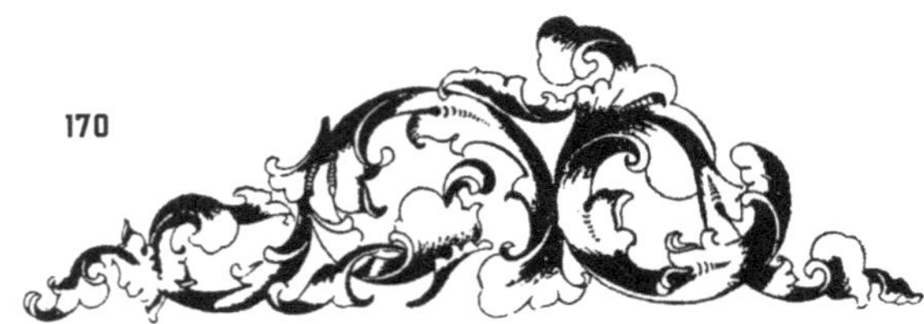

171

172
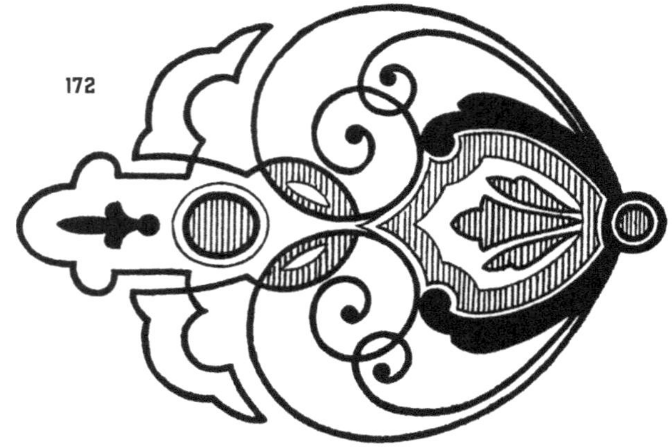

173

174

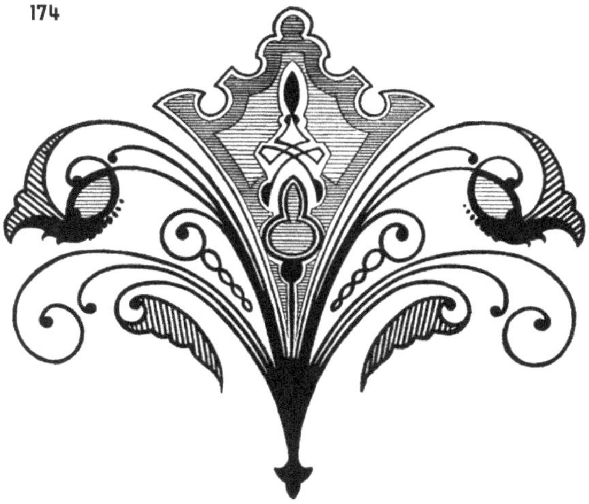

175

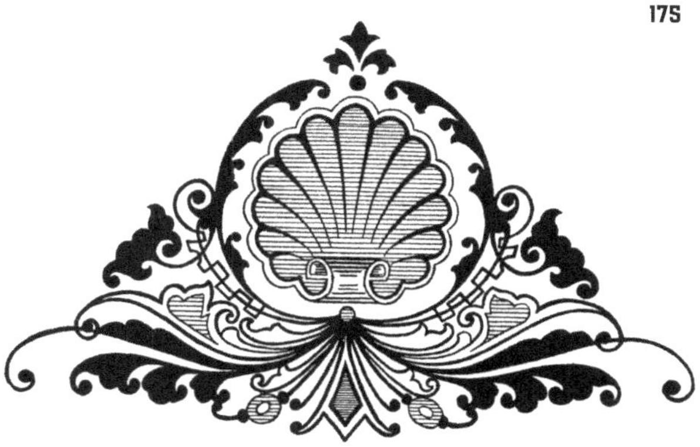

176

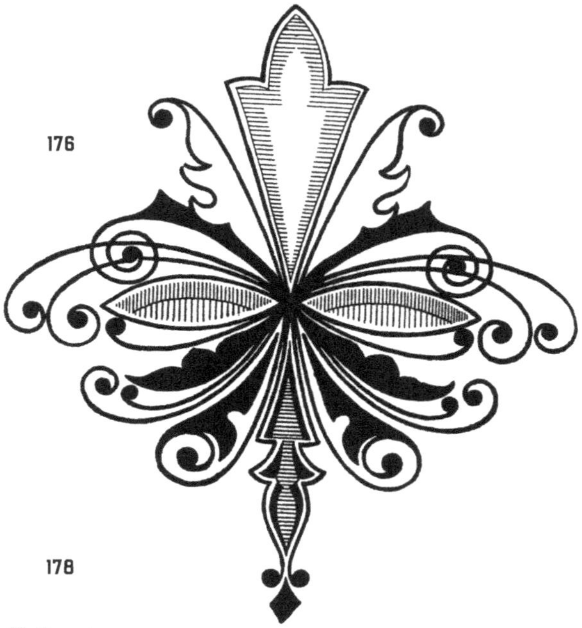

177

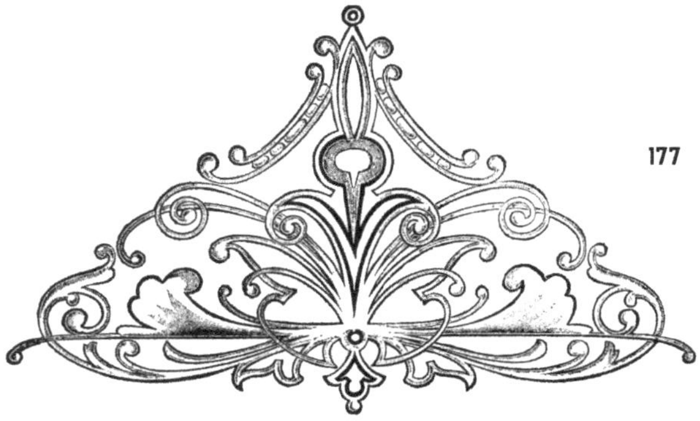

178

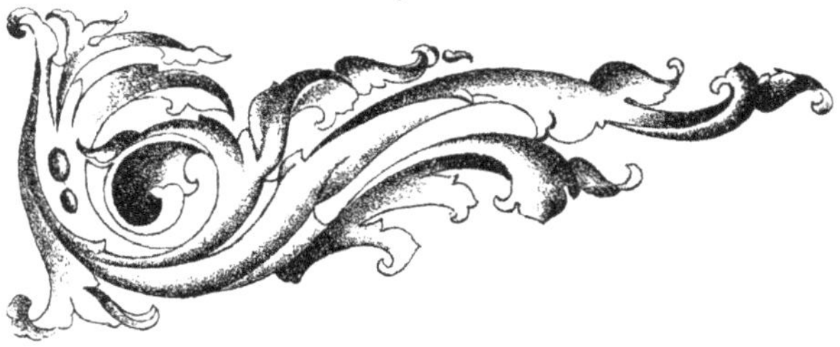

179

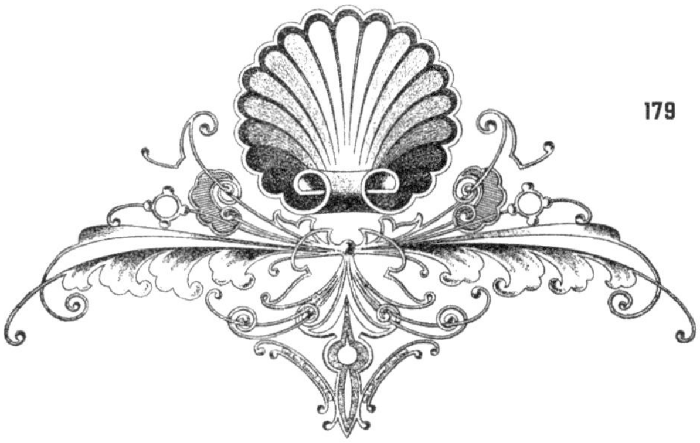

Vault Editions Ltd

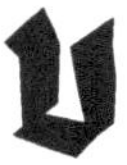

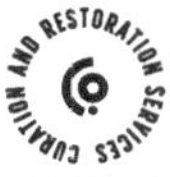

PRACTICE
MAKES
PERFECT
T R D — M R K

INDUSTRY STD

VAULTEDITIONS.COM

180

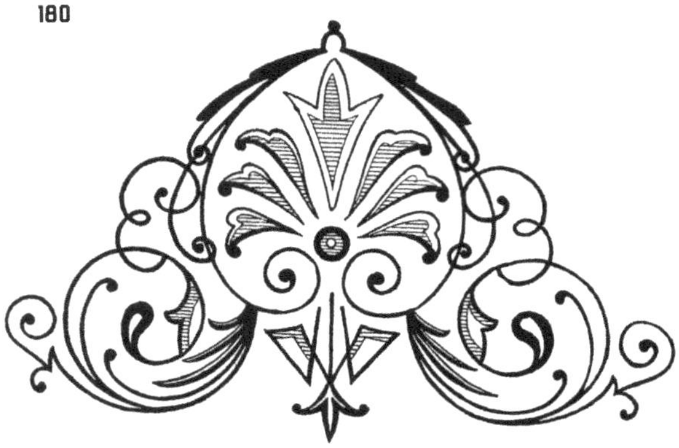

181

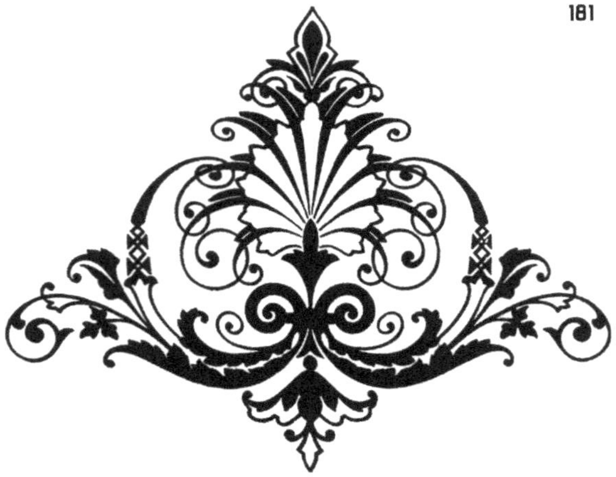

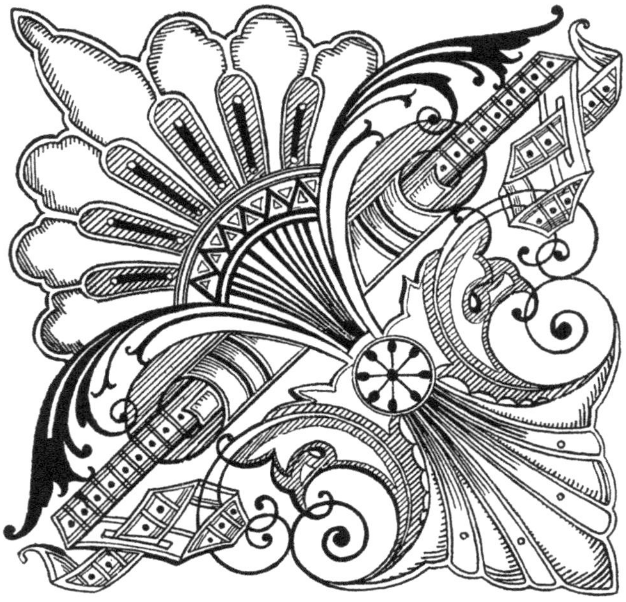

182

183

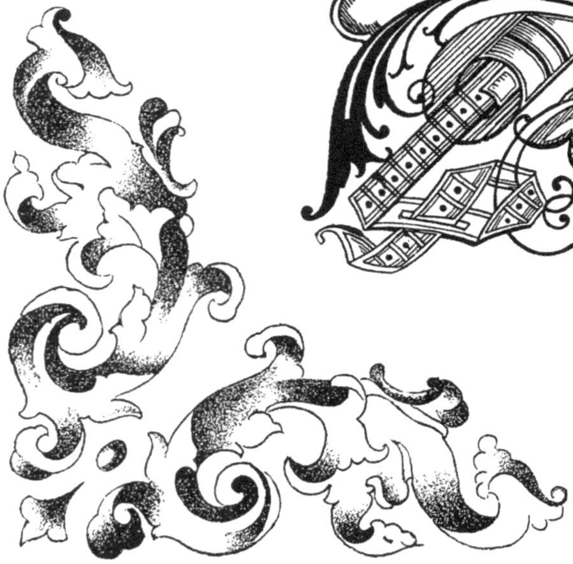

184

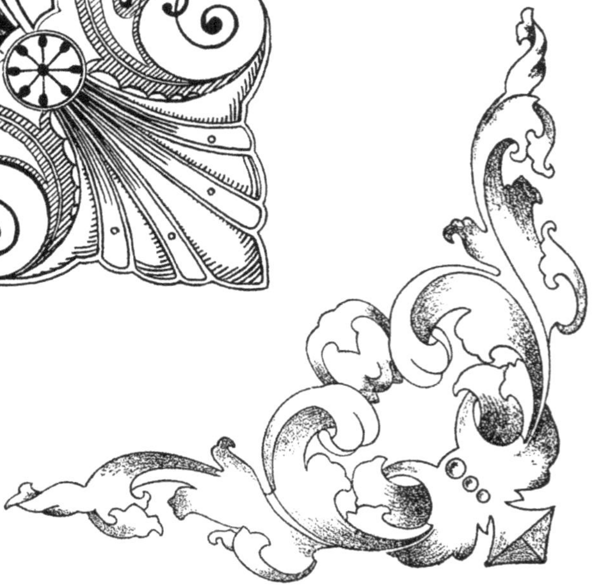

Vault Editions Ltd

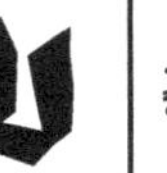

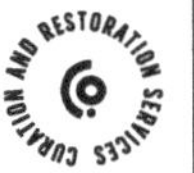

PRACTICE
MAKES
PERFECT

INDUSTRY STD

VAULTEDITIONS.COM

185

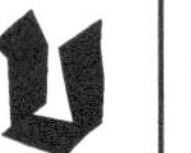
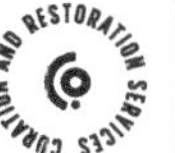

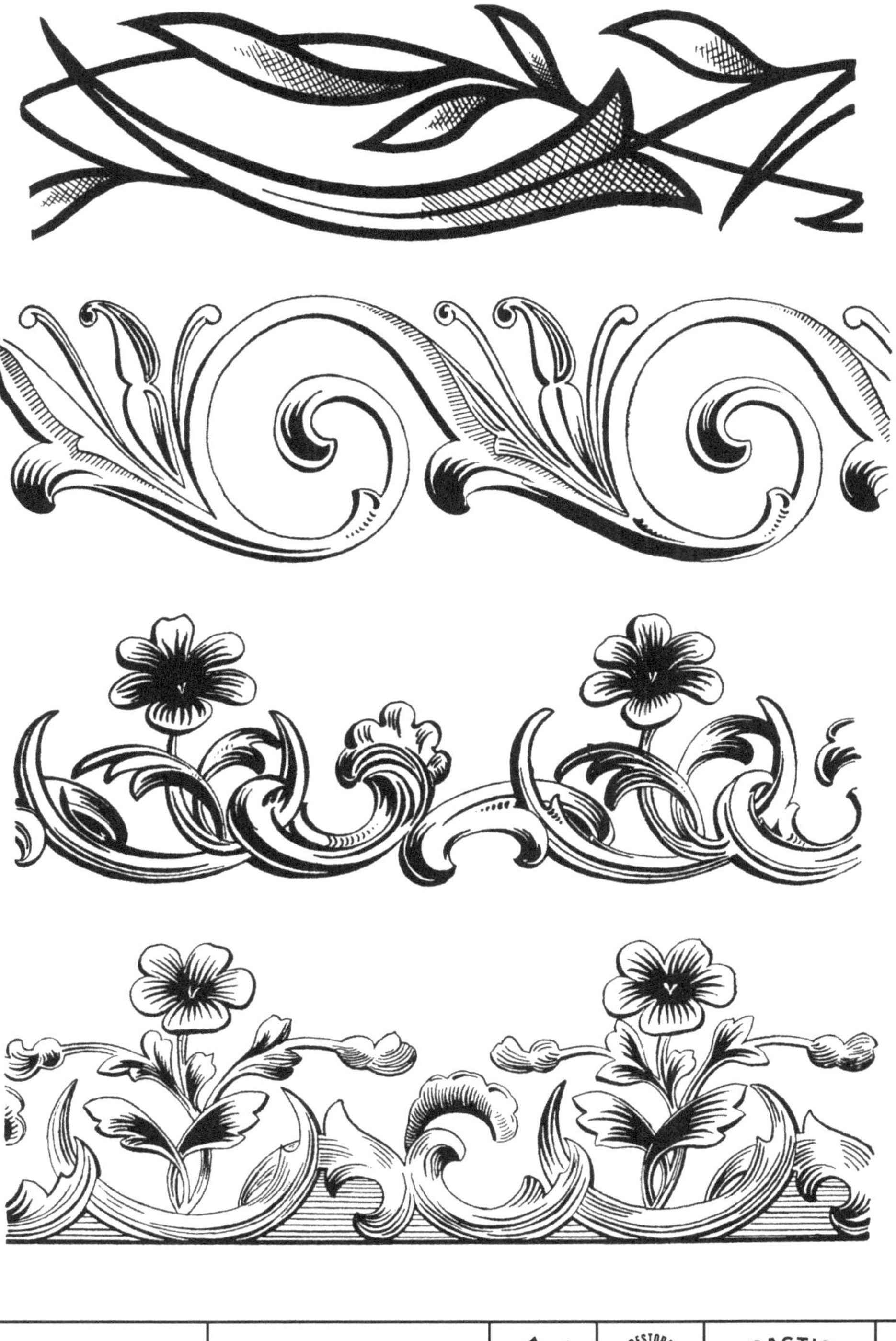

Vault Editions Ltd

CURATION AND RESTORATION SERVICES

PRACTICE MAKES PERFECT

INDUSTRY STD

VAULTEDITIONS.COM

VAULT EDITIONS

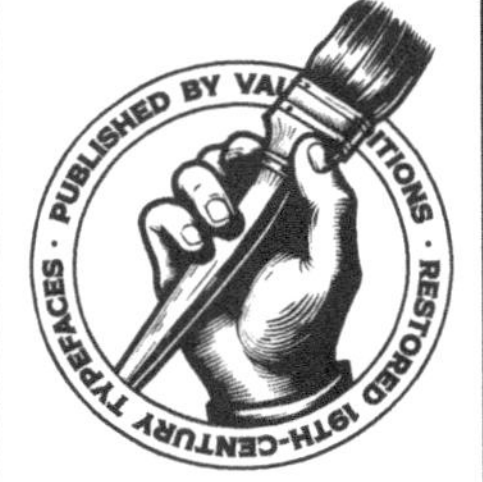

VAULT EDITIONS

This publication is a new work created by Vault Editions Ltd

DOWNLOAD YOUR FILES

Follow the instructions below to access your downloadable files

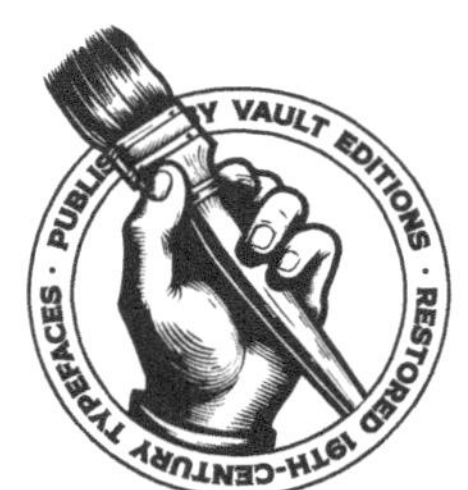

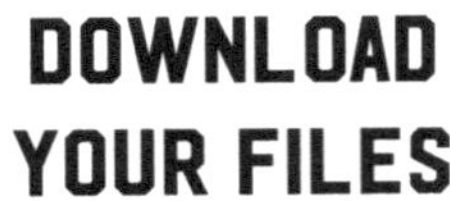

LEARN MORE

At Vault Editions, our mission is to create the world's most comprehensive collection of image archives for the practical use of artists and designers. If you have enjoyed this book, you can discover more of our titles at vaulteditions.com

REVIEW THIS BOOK

As a family-owned and operated independent publisher, reviews are essential to the success of our business. Please leave an honest review of this book wherever you purchased it.

JOIN OUR COMMUNITY

Are you the creative and curious type? If so, you will love our community on Instagram. Every day, we share bizarre and beautiful artwork ranging from 17th and 18th-century natural history and scientific illustrations to mythical beasts, ornamental designs, anatomical drawings and more; join our community of 280K+ people today by searching @vault_editions on Instagram.

STEP ONE

Enter the following web address on a desktop or laptop computer in your web browser.

vaulteditions.com/pages/sal

STEP TWO

Enter the following password to access the download page:

sala23364838sxda

STEP THREE

Follow the prompts to access your high-resolution files.

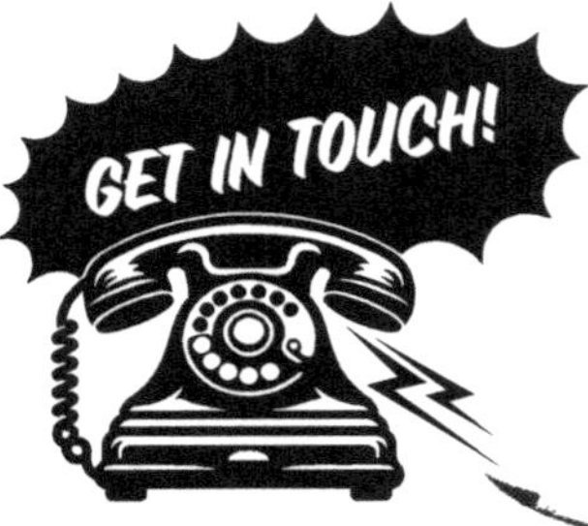

TECHNICAL SUPPORT

For technical support, please email: info@vaulteditions.com

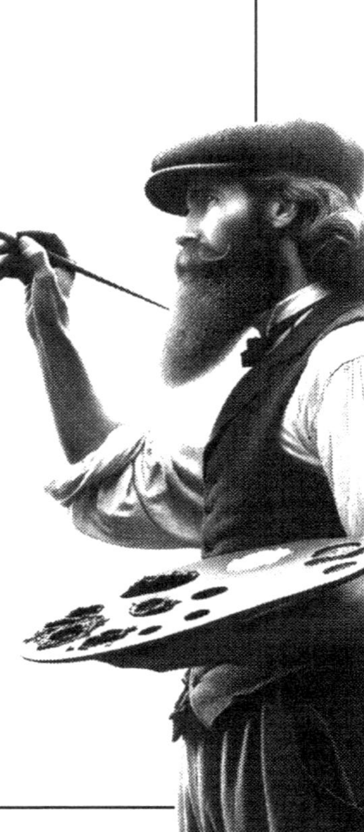